MY BLOODY
VALENTINE

MY BLOODY VALENTINE

Couples Whose Sick Crimes Shocked the World

Edited by Patrick Blackden

First published in Great Britain in 2002 by

Virgin Books Ltd
Thames Wharf Studios
Rainville Road
London W6 9HA

Introduction; Beyond Good and Evil; Numbered for the Bottom; Love
Will Tear Us Apart © Patrick Blackden
The Lonely Hearts Killers © Antonio Mendoza
Oh, Manchester, So Much to Answer For; The Ken and Barbie Killers;
The Banality of Evil © Russell Gould
Heads and Tail; Killing in Company © Simon Whitechapel
Dead Man's Curve; Ghost of a Girl © Martin Jones
Trailer Park Terror © Kerri Sharp

A catalogue record for this book is available from the British Library

ISBN 0 7535 0647 5

Typeset by TW Typesetting, Plymouth, Devon
Printed and bound in Great Britain by
Mackays of Chatham PLC

CONTENTS

INTRODUCTION

Murder and sex crime are characteristically solitary pursuits. A previously trusted partner might become witness rather than accomplice, as Ian Brady and Myra Hindley found to their dismay when David Smith, a friend of Brady's who appeared to have subscribed to his mentor's misanthropy, called the police after witnessing the murder of Edward Evans. If you're going to indulge in serial murder or rape and don't want to get caught, it's best to do it alone. And yet there *are* killer couples – sometimes husband and wife – who slay without remorse until they are caught.

These crimes seem especially horrific – Brady and Hindley and Fred and Rose West are generally reviled in Britain, even more than solo serial killers such as Dennis Nilsen. The principal reason for this is that the vast bulk of serial murder is committed by men, with female victims; the same can be said of sex crime. In aiding and abetting such crimes, the female partner in a killer couple can be thought to be betraying her sex, joining in with the worst outrages that men can inflict upon women. While the degree of complicity in the actual rapes and murders varies, the fact that the men would find it far more difficult to attract victims without a female accomplice is certain.

Simon Whitechapel, in his essay on Gerald and Charlene Gallego, mentions a comic published by Christian evangelists in California in 1974:

It opens with a fourteen-year-old girl called Donna hitchhiking alone to Los Angeles. By the fourth frame a van has stopped for her. There is a man at the wheel with a woman by his side. The two of them invite Donna aboard. She thinks, 'It looks safe! There's a girl with him!' So she accepts their invitation and gets aboard, and within a few hours she is dead . . .

This assumption of safety – that if a man is already accompanied by a woman he is unlikely to be intent on rape-murder – leads perhaps to the cruellest betrayal. Many of the couples in this book travelled together to pick up hitchhikers and passers-by – the Gallegos, the Birnies, Paul Bernardo and Karla Homolka and Ian Brady and Myra Hindley; the Wests would have seemed a trustworthy, happy family unit until the home-made sex toys and restraint devices were brought out.

It is here that arguments about whether or not one partner would have been able to carry out the crimes alone fall down; even when one partner is clearly dominant over the other, such as David Birnie and his common-law wife, Catherine; the very fact of her presence meant that he could easily procure victims. Even if he'd wanted to rape and kill without her, he might not have been nearly so successful in doing so.

The infatuation that some women have for dangerous criminal men has been somewhat patronisingly described as 'Bonnie-and-Clyde syndrome', or hybristophilia, from the Greek root *hybridzein*, meaning to commit an outrageous offence. It has been defined by the sexologist Dr John Money as 'being sexuoerotically turned on only by a partner who has a predatory history of outrages perpetuated on others'. Power is an aphrodisiac, it is said, and what power greater than that of life or death? That the female player in such a relationship is considered to be suffering from a syndrome, abdicating her own responsibility for her actions, is revealing of a strain of implicit sexism in the ideas of some criminologists – and some traditional feminists, who seek to exonerate women for their actions, however horrific, in precisely this way. The implication is that the female partner in a killer couple is a victim; and, indeed, some are, having come from extremely abusive backgrounds into equally abusive relationships with their boyfriends. But this does not apply in all cases.

An FBI survey on the girlfriends of criminal sadists characterised them as 'sexually naïve . . . compliant victims'. This may apply to some, but certainly doesn't work for Charlene Gallego, Karla Homolka or Rose West. Some of the women in this book actively sought out high-dominance men possessed by enormous sexual appetites; some merely acquiesced in their partners' demands for sex slaves, while others did far more.

Janice Erlbaum, in a piece entitled 'Sick Chicks' on the Popsmear website (www.popsmear.com), has identified differing degrees of complicity in killer couple relationships, which appear to depend to an extent on the dominance relationship between the partners. The American psychologist Abraham Maslow, researching sexual behaviour among women during the 1930s, found that his subjects fell into three broad groups: high-dominance, medium-dominance and low-dominance, with levels of sexual experimentation and promiscuity growing with the level of dominance. His subjects appeared to prefer men from their own dominance group, but slightly more dominant than themselves. High-dominance men were unlikely to be sexually or emotionally satisfied by relationships with medium- or low-dominance women, although medium-dominance women could be in thrall to high-dominance men to a startling degree of emotional dependency. Such groupings are too conveniently neat to account for the whole range of potential human relationships, but they can be useful in giving us a rough estimate of the kinds of relationship enjoyed by each killer couple.

Erlbaum, listing the degrees of complicity in hybristophiliacs, has termed the first 'women who think criminals are sexy'; this seems to be an extension of normal – or socially acceptable – characteristics of attraction. Bad boys and outlaws have always been attractive to the opposite sex; self-confident, assertive and dominant, the appeal of the macho rebel is what links the perennial appeal of James Dean to the thousands of fan letters received by convicts in Western countries.

Some women marry the criminals they write to: Doreen Lioy married 'Night Stalker' Richard Ramirez after a fifteen-year courtship. Some go still further: Veronica Lynn Compton wrote to the jailed Kenneth Bianchi, one of the 'Hillside Stranglers', and eventually agreed to murder a woman and inject her with sperm provided by Bianchi to show that the killer was still on the loose. Her would-be victim, Kim Breed, was, however, something of an athlete, and managed to fend off Compton's efforts to strangle her; Compton was tracked down and received life imprisonment for attempted murder. While incarcerated, she began another correspondence with a serial killer, this time Douglas Clark. Her wish to take an active role in the killings takes her out of this category of hybristophiliacs and into the fifth – high-dominance women who seek even higher-dominance men.

The second level of complicity has been dubbed by Erlbaum, somewhat flippantly, 'pissed-off teenage girls'. Caril Fugate falls into this category, as does another teenager, Wendy Gardner, whose case is not profiled in this book, but deserves a mention here. The appeal of the bad-boy mystique when paired with raging hormones and teenage resentment can lead to a sticky end. When Gardner's grandmother refused to let the precocious thirteen-year-old spend the night at her fifteen-year-old boyfriend James Evans's house, Gardner went anyway and together they plotted the grandmother's demise. They discussed the relative merits of various methods of murder, and even planned to involve Gardner's eleven-year-old sister; Gardner is reported to have told Evans, 'When we tie her up you can fuck her instead of me 'cause I'm sick of you doing it to me all the time.'

It eventually fell to Evans to strangle the grandmother, although Gardner appears to have masterminded the event; the couple stayed at their victim's house for days afterwards – in a scene of bizarre teen domesticity similar to that of Starkweather and Fugate following the slaying of Fugate's family – until Gardner's younger sister managed to escape and call the police.

Both teenagers were found guilty of murder in the second degree, despite Gardner's efforts to portray herself as an innocent teen by taking her teddy bear to court; the taped confession she'd already given to police was damning enough:

> I got up and talked to James some more and I said, 'I want to kill her so bad.' She was making me so angry and then James goes, 'She's making me angry, too' . . . I said, 'I just want to kill her.' And then (James said) 'If I kill her, will you love me?'

Erlbaum defines a third level as the 'compliant victim'; this is the category into which most of the women in this book have attempted to place themselves, whatever their level of actual complicity.

Their responsibility is limited, it is argued, because they were beaten into submission, or at the very least afraid of being beaten. It's interesting to note that this defence has worked more often for women than for men: Karla Homolka received an extraordinarily light sentence for her involvement in her partner's murders, compared with that meted out to James Miller, who was arguably less complicit in the murders committed by James Worrell.

One of the most infamous cases of a compliant victim began in California during the spring of 1977, when Cameron Hooker kidnapped a twenty-year-old hitch-hiker, Colleen Stan, and kept her in the house he shared with his wife, Janice, for the next seven years. She spent most of the time in a series of boxes; when out, she was obliged to fulfil the duties of a sex slave to Hooker. For the first eight months she was taken out only to be raped or beaten, before Cameron Hooker made her sign a contract of servitude with him on behalf of 'The Company'.

The idea of 'The Company' had come from a pornographic magazine – the fiction of a ring of rich, omnipotent sex-slave traders who kidnap women and sell them on the black market, a fiction not unlike many others circulating in the SM underground. Janice, whose body had been brutalised by Cameron throughout their marriage, was held up as the example of a girl who'd run off and been found again, her hips and knees mangled by Company agents – there was no escape for Colleen. Colleen, disoriented from having been kept for so long in sensory deprivation broken only by rapes and beatings, accepted this story and signed the contract.

After seven years, Janice was worried that Colleen and Cameron were growing too close. Colleen was no longer kept in a box at all times but was now able to run errands for the Hookers – she wouldn't escape, as she believed she was being watched by The Company.

Janice had refused to speak to her husband's slave for the first few years, but had by now grown closer to her, and finally admitted to Colleen that she was free to go. There was no Company – Cameron had made it all up.

Despite the fact that Cameron would have been unable to realise his fantasy of having a sex slave without Janice, the latter received immunity from prosecution for her testimony against him. The full story of the 'girl in the box' is published in *Perfect Victim*, also available from Virgin Books.

Myra Hindley has attempted to portray herself as a compliant victim in recent years, claiming that Ian Brady beat her often and that she was so far in thrall to him that she had no responsibility for her own actions:

> Within months he had convinced me there was no God at all: he could have told me that the earth was flat, the moon was made of green cheese and the sun rose in the west, I would have believed him, such was his power of persuasion.

Hindley appears, however, to fit into a category not listed by Erlbaum, a midway point between the compliant victim and the high-dominance woman seeking an even more dominant man: a medium-dominance, emotionally dependent woman infatuated with a high-dominance, sexually potent man.

The relationship between Brady and Hindley, or David and Catherine Birnie, characterises this domination imbalance: Brady had little sexual use for Hindley except when he could cause her pain or humiliate her; similarly, David Birnie's sexual needs were not satisfied by Catherine, prompting him to seek out a series of sex slaves. At the trial of Catherine Birnie a psychologist asserted that her relationship with David Birnie was the worst case of personality dependence she'd ever seen. Worrell and Miller, and Leopold and Loeb can be seen as demonstrating similar relationships.

In this dominance relationship the man is not necessarily the dominant partner: the murders committed by the 'Honeymoon Killers' were initiated by Martha Beck. That a high-dominance woman should settle for a medium-dominance man is rare: most high-dominance women, as we have seen, are attracted to men even more dominant than themselves, which takes us to the fifth stage of complicity.

In the case of Karla Homolka or Charlene Gallego the women were intelligent – the FBI study quoted by Simon Whitechapel in his piece on the Gallegos records an FBI survey that asserts that the girlfriends of sexual sadists are 'uniformly better educated and [more] intelligent than their men' – and actively sought out criminally minded, high-dominance men. These women not only helped their partners to kill, they often initiated a new stage in the atrocities, ever keen to up the ante, translating their partners' fantasies into grisly reality. Russell Gould reports, in his piece on Bernardo and Homolka, that 'Paul asked [Homolka] what she would think of him if he was a rapist, and her reply was that she would like that.'

But Homolka and Gallego both claimed to have been compliant victims, and, while they may have been beaten, there is ample evidence of their part in rape-murder, including video evidence of Homolka fellating Bernardo following the latter's rape-murder of Homolka's younger sister, telling her lover how far she'd go for him:

> We raped a little girl. Down here in my room. You went out and you found her, brought her back to

the house. Brought her downstairs. I was shocked.
You fucked her . . . I let you do that. Because I love
you. Because you're the king . . . If you want to do
it fifty times more we can do it fifty times . . .
'Cause you deserve it.

If Homolka's tale of reduced responsibility was believed by the authorities, the actions of the women
exhibiting the highest degree of complicity in rape-
murder put them beyond the pale. Carol Bundy's
putting make-up on the severed head of a prostitute to
facilitate her boyfriend's taste for necrophile fellatio, or
Judith Neeley's injection of one of the women she and
her husband killed with liquid drain cleaner – no level
of victimisation can be held to account for such gleefully
deranged acts.

Space has not permitted the inclusion of all known
killer couples in this book: missing, among others, are
Judith and Alvin Neeley, Frederick and Maria Manning,
and Bonnie and Clyde. Also missing are a number of
women who are known to have helped their husbands
to procure victims for rape-murder, among them Lloyd
Higdon's first wife and later his girlfriend, Lucille
Brumit, in Michigan during the 1960s, and Mrs Joyce
Ballard of Chatham, Kent, who in 1968 lured a
twelve-year-old girl into the flat she shared with her
husband Robert to her death. But the most interesting
cases can be found in the following pages – cautionary
tales for any who have experienced the folly of mad
love.

BIBLIOGRAPHY
Erlbaum, Janice, *Sick Chicks*, www.popsmear.com.
McGuire, Christine & Norton, Carla, *Perfect Victim*,
    Virgin Books, London, 1992.

Wilson, Colin, *The Mammoth Book of True Crime*, Robinson, London, 1998.

Wilson, Colin & Seaman, Donald, *The Serial Killers*, Virgin Books, London, 1997.

1. BEYOND GOOD AND EVIL – NATHAN LEOPOLD AND RICHARD LOEB

INTRODUCTION
Chicago, 1924. The Jazz Age – an era of bootleggers, speakeasies and gangsters; of dope fiends, perverts and an urban licentiousness that shocked Middle America; of youthful rebellion and the sexual possibilities provided by the mass-produced automobile. High-profile court cases filled the papers – from gangster trials to prosecutions against liberated women involved in 'sex harems' – but one case in particular was to obsess America for decades. The tale of two precocious students who murdered a boy for no apparent motive, with suggestions of perversions too dark to be openly discussed – the case of Leopold and Loeb.

NATHAN LEOPOLD
The Leopolds were a respectable, wealthy family of German Jews who had emigrated to the USA in the mid-1800s. The family had amassed their fortune transporting freight on the Great Lakes, and had settled in the Kenwood area of Chicago.

Nathan Leopold Jr was the youngest of four sons, a sickly child who wasn't expected to live out a full lifespan. His glandular problems, involving a calcified pineal gland and hyperthyroidism, led to a level of physical weakness that he never outgrew – this, and his position as the youngest child in the family, led to the nickname 'Babe'.

Nathan's birth was difficult and his mother was never to recover her health in the subsequent years, a fact for which the boy held himself largely responsible. She died of nephritis, an inflammatory condition of the kidneys, when Nathan was seventeen. Her death was a huge blow to the young man, and led him to renounce his Christian faith – a benevolent god could never allow the suffering he'd seen his mother go through – and become an atheist.

As was typical of wealthier US families at the time, the care of the four boys was left to a series of governesses. When Nathan was five his care fell to Mathilda Wantz, newly arrived from Germany. Nathan, a precocious infant who is reputed to have spoken his first words at four months and was later found to have an IQ of 210, taught the non-English-speaking 'Sweetie' Wantz a few useful English phrases – for a brief period Wantz would greet members of the household with the phrase 'Go to hell', believing herself to be wishing them a good morning.

Wantz had curious ideas about care and intimacy, sharing baths with Nathan and his older brothers. She encouraged a mutual physical familiarity, inviting the brothers to examine her fully and showing them her sanitary towel. While it isn't known how the governess rewarded and chastised the older brothers, Nathan's special treat for good behaviour was being allowed to put his penis between her legs while she lay on his face.

With Nathan's mother ill and his father busy at work, the governess was able to run the household in her unique way with impunity. But all this changed one day, as Mrs Leopold came upon 'Sweetie' roughly pulling a twelve-year-old Nathan, home sick from school, out of bed. She was sacked.

Nathan wasn't popular with his peers, at Harvard School or in his neighbourhood. His advanced intelligence and physical weakness were an isolating combination, and he had trouble making friends. His habit of repeatedly impressing his superior intelligence upon acquaintances didn't endear him to anyone, and he was considered grossly conceited. His relations with the opposite sex were especially disastrous. Socially, he didn't want to mix with women – intellectually, he considered them inferior – and the only heterosexual sex he had during his teens was with prostitutes. He devoted himself instead to learning, becoming proficient in a number of languages and spending much of his spare time bird-watching.

Perhaps inevitably for a young man with so little fulfilling social contact, Nathan developed a rich fantasy life, which was to be explored by analysts later on:

> He endeavoured to compensate for [his physical inferiority] by a world of fantasy in which his desire for physical perfection could be satisfied. We see him therefore fantasising himself as a slave, who is the strongest man in the world . . . In some way or other [in these fantasies] . . . he saved the life of the king. The king was grateful and wanted to give him his liberty, but the slave refused. [1]

This specific fantasy began when he was five years old and continued into his teenage years.

His desire for physical perfection was matched only by his championing of intellectual supremacy. In a world where God is dead, all morality is relative; if nothing is true, everything is permitted. Nathan was keen to explain his philosophy to analysts later in life:

> In such a philosophy, without any place for emotions or feelings, the intelligence reigns supreme. The only crime that he can commit is a

crime of intelligence, a mistake of intelligence, and for that he is fully responsible.[2]

Nathan had been influenced by the moral relativism of modern thinkers such as Nietszche, and had drawn up his own schematic of the perfect man, similar to Nietszche's *Übermensch* or superman. In this points-based system he awarded himself 63 and various acquaintances marks ranging from 30 to 40. The highest mark, 90, was awarded to his best friend, Richard Loeb, who he was to meet aged sixteen at the University of Chicago.

RICHARD LOEB

Albert Loeb, Richard's father, was a millionaire executive responsible for Sears, Roebuck's phenomenally successful mail-order business. Ann Bohnen Loeb, Albert's wife, came from a large Catholic family whose members disapproved of her marriage to a Jew, his financial and social success notwithstanding. Loeb's family, however, accepted her unreservedly. The couple had four sons, of whom Richard was the second youngest.

The Loebs also employed governesses to look after their sons, and, while the Leopolds' Mathilda Wantz may have been considered too liberal in her treatment of her charges, a similar accusation could not be levelled at Richard's governess, the severe Miss Struthers. The governess was taken on aged 28, when Richard was four years old.

Miss Struthers dedicated herself to Richard's academic success. She spent an enormous amount of time reading to and tutoring him, and employed strict discipline to ensure his undivided attention. He was kept from playing with other children, and soon began to enjoy her company more than that of his peers.

The governess's tactics paid off. Richard was a bright boy, with an IQ of 160, and moved quickly through the education system, finishing grade school at twelve and high school at fourteen, and entering the University of Chicago directly afterwards. But this insistence on academic precocity was also something against which Richard rebelled.

Miss Struthers was an extremely strict disciplinarian and quick to punish him, so Loeb learned early on to lie and avoid being hurt. The governess believed his lies, and soon lying, which came easily to him, became an integral part of his personality. Her insistence that he read nothing but the classics led to his clandestine obsession with detective fiction, and thence to an early fascination with criminality:

> He developed early the tendency to mix with crime, to be a detective; as a little boy shadowing people on the street; as a little child going out with his fantasy of being the head of a band of criminals and directing them on the street . . . This boy early in his life conceived the idea that there could be a perfect crime, one that nobody could ever detect; that there could be one where the detective did not land his game; a perfect crime.[3]

Miss Struthers finally left when Richard was fourteen, following an argument with Mrs Loeb.

As with Nathan Leopold, Richard Loeb led a rich fantasy life (see above), in which he was a master criminal, the leader of a gang. He would plan crimes and be admired by his cronies for the skill with which they were carried out. He insisted that certain of his fantasies predated his experiences of actual criminal behaviour – he stole money and objects with no compunction at age eight or nine, ashamed only when he was caught – and his obsession with detective fiction. One of his fantasies, reported to the analyst Dr Healy, is particularly telling:

> He began, certainly before he was nine years of age, with very curious, abnormal criminalistic ideas, picturing himself as someone in a jailyard, naked, abused, whipped, and all of the comfort he gets out of it is that the people looking through a jailyard fence sympathise with him. Asked who sympathised with him, he says at first it was people in general and then later on it was mostly young girls . . . To use his own expression, 'I was abused.' It was a very pleasant thought. Punishment inflicted in jail was pleasant. 'I enjoyed being looked at through the bars, because I was a famous criminal.'[4]

Sex was a taboo topic with Miss Struthers, but Richard learned the basics by talking to the family chauffeur. He was never highly motivated sexually, however. While his good looks and affable character afforded him a number of advantages with women, he didn't consider relationships, sexual or not, a high priority, believing himself to have a less developed sex drive than that of his friends. Far more important as a motivating force was the desire for criminal glory.

Richard Loeb met Nathan Leopold at the University of Chicago. Both were sixteen years old, and were soon to become fast friends.

THE COMPACT

Loeb was keen to leave Chicago and transfer to the University of Michigan, to get away from home. Leopold followed him, but was shunned by Loeb, who had become involved with his fraternity. Zeta Beta Tau had accepted Loeb on condition that he should not fraternise with Leopold – stories of homosexuality were beginning to circulate, which the fraternity refused to tolerate. Leopold returned to Chicago and graduated, then began law school. Loeb would return to Chicago following his graduation.

The rumours of homosexuality appear to derive from a letter sent to Loeb's fraternity, the author of which is unknown. It describes an evening at the Loeb estate, in which Loeb, Leopold and one of Loeb's fraternity brothers were drinking. During the night, Loeb got up to go to the bathroom and upon his return got into bed with Leopold. Copies of the letter were also sent to the friends' brothers.

The full story didn't come out until Leopold and Loeb were analysed. They both admitted to a 'compact' in which Loeb would participate in Leopold's homosexual fantasies if Leopold would help Loeb commit crimes:

> For Loeb, he says, the association gave him the opportunity of getting someone to carry out his criminalistic imaginings and conscious ideas. In the case of Leopold, the direct cause of his entering into criminalistic acts was this particularly childish compact.[5]

Leopold would be allowed to insert his penis between his friend's legs at special dates; at one time it was three times in two months, then they settled at one insertion per criminal act. They also experimented with oral sex, but this didn't appear to satisfy Leopold in the same way. The particular dynamic of their sexual relationship is explained here:

> Loeb would pretend to be drunk, then [Leopold] would undress him and he would almost rape him

and would be furiously passionate at the time, whereas with women he does not get that same thrill and passion.[6]

That Leopold's homosexuality and Loeb's criminal tendencies became inseparable is pointed to by the fact that the 'compact' began on the day of their first criminal act together – cheating at bridge. But, while Leopold's side of the compact appears to have remained consistent, Loeb's criminal urges grew ever more serious. With each successful crime, the stakes were upped – from card-sharping and stealing small objects to stealing and vandalising cars; from making prank calls to their teachers to false fire alarms and then to arson. One abortive plan involved burgling a friend's house, taking a gun to shoot the nightwatchman if the situation demanded it; but their car broke down and they burgled Loeb's fraternity house instead.

Their fantasies complemented each other perfectly; it seems unlikely that they would individually have followed a path similar to the one they followed together. The analyst Dr Glueck viewed their crimes as explicitly resulting from their meeting of minds:

I think the Franks crime was perhaps the inevitable outcome of this curious coming together of two pathologically disordered personalities, each one of whom brought into the relationship a phase of their personality which made their contemplation and execution of this crime possible.[7]

PLANNING AND PREPARATION

We even rehearsed the kidnapping at least three times, carrying it through in all details, lacking only the boy we were to kidnap and kill . . . It was just an experiment. It is as easy for us to justify as an entomologist in impaling a beetle on a pin.[8]

In November 1923 Leopold and Loeb began to plan the kidnap and murder of a young boy. The motivation appears to have been partly to commit the perfect crime; an intellectual exercise carried out by two bored students who saw themselves as beyond conventional morality. The murder would also become a symbolic marriage between the pair: a public secret that would forever bind them to each other, a hidden truth that they would carry into their adult lives.

The collection of the ransom money was seen to be the most difficult part of the plan, and was thus planned first. They debated for some time over the best method for collection, and finally came to an agreement: they would have the money thrown from a moving train, after the train had passed a given landmark. The next problem was the system of notification to the father. Their elaborate solution was to devise a number of relays: the father would receive a special delivery letter telling him that his son had been kidnapped and was being held for ransom; he would be instructed to secure $8,000 in $50 bills and $2,000 in $20 bills, all old, unmarked and out of sequence, which he should place in a cigar box, securely tied, wrapped in white paper, the ends sealed with sealing wax. The aim of this was to give the impression that the package would be delivered to a messenger employed by the kidnappers themselves.

The father would then receive a phone call instructing him to proceed to a rubbish bin whose location would be given. Here he would find a note advising him to proceed to a drugstore with a public phone booth. He was to be called at this phone booth, the drugstore being close to the railway, and given only enough time to rush out, buy a ticket and board a train, without giving him enough time to instruct detectives as to his whereabouts. In the train he was to proceed to the rear car, where another letter would be left for him, telling him where and when to throw the package.

Happy with their plan, Leopold and Loeb then pondered the problem of whom to kill. They considered killing their fathers or brothers, but concluded that this would leave them under too much scrutiny. They decided then to leave the victim's identity until the day of the kidnapping itself; the sole conditions were that the boy should have a rich father who was able to pay the ransom, and that he should be known to either Leopold or Loeb, so that they could easily lure him into the car. They planned to drive past Harvard School on the day and select the most suitable boy.

The boy was to be knocked unconscious and taken to the dump site, where he would be murdered, to avoid any chance of their being identified. The plan dictated that they each take an end of a rope tied around his neck and pull, to share equally in the crime. The disposal of the body was the next problem, and they hit upon the culvert at Wolf Lake, a spot with which Leopold was familiar through his bird-watching, as the perfect place. The culvert was a drainage tunnel connecting two lakes under a railway. Its location was so obscure that even Leopold had not initially been aware of it, and it saved them having to dig a grave. They didn't expect the body to be found for a long time, and planned to make it difficult to identify in any case by disfiguring the face and genitals – to make it unclear as to whether or not the boy was circumcised – with hydrochloric acid.

As they couldn't use one of their cars, which could easily be traced back to them, they developed another elaborate scheme to hire a car under another name – Morton D Ballard. This involved renting hotel rooms and opening a bank account under this name to build up the skeleton of an identity and thereby avoid suspicion while renting the car. Leopold even rented a car using the name three weeks before the killing.

The preparations were over – the scene was set. Leopold and Loeb were ready to put their plan into action.

KIDNAP AND KILLING

On 21 May 1924 at 11 a.m. Nathan Leopold met Richard Loeb following their classes at Chicago University. They were both nineteen. They drove Nathan's vehicle to a car rental company in Joliet, where they rented a grey Willis Knight under the assumed name. They then had lunch at a local restaurant.

After lunch they had a few last-minute preparations to make: they had to buy some hydrochloric acid, drop off Nathan's car and pick up some supplies from the Leopold house, including a roll of zinc oxide tape.

They then went for a drive, ending up in nearby Lincoln Park, where Loeb wrapped the metal end of the chisel with tape, to use it as a grip. The blunt handle of the chisel was to be a cosh, not a murder weapon. The young men also had guns – Leopold a .38 and Loeb a .45.

Finally, the Harvard School reached the end of the school day, and they lay in wait nearby, hoping to spot a suitable boy. But their hunt was initially unsuccessful as, although they came across several gangs of suitable youths, they failed to follow any of the individuals home. Undaunted, they drove towards the house of Sol Levinson, a local lawyer whose son Loeb knew, hoping to pick him up on the way home. As they headed towards the Levinson house Loeb spotted Robert Franks, a fourteen-year-old boy of his acquaintance.

They pulled up alongside, Loeb asking if Franks wanted a lift home. He declined, but, when Loeb invited him to look at a tennis racket, Franks got in the car. The boy then agreed to go for a drive round the block – while Leopold drove, Loeb hit him with the chisel. The aim had been to knock Franks out directly, but when instead he began to scream and thrash about Loeb hit him again and again on the head until he stopped struggling. Leopold later described the blood as 'rather effusive'.

Loeb then pulled the boy onto the back seat, where, for fear of Franks regaining consciousness and alerting a passer-by, he forced a cloth into the boy's mouth. Franks died of suffocation shortly afterwards. Leopold's composure was shaken by the violence – he hadn't expected there to be so much blood – but Loeb managed to calm him down.

They then wrapped the body in a car robe brought specifically for this purpose, and drove to a quiet street in Indiana, where they bought sandwiches and drinks. Here they remained until dark, whereupon they headed to the dump site. They'd already partially undressed the boy, leaving his shoes and belt by the side of the road, hidden in the grass. The plan had dictated burning all the clothes, but this proved difficult in the case of the boy's shoes and impossible for his belt buckle.

When they reached Wolf Lake they completed the undressing, and poured hydrochloric acid over the face, genitals and an identifying scar. The body was then pushed as far up the culvert as possible. All the clothes were wrapped in the car robe and carried back to the car, one of the socks dropping from the bundle en route.

Leopold called his parents to let them know he'd be a little late arriving home. He then called the Franks home and spoke to Mrs Franks, telling her that his name was George Johnson and that her boy had been kidnapped but was safe; further instructions would follow. The pair then posted a special-delivery letter containing their initial instructions for the ransom collection to the Frankses.

They then drove to Leopold's house, where Leopold picked up his own car and his aunt and uncle, whom he'd previously agreed to drive home. Loeb waited at Leopold's house until Nathan's return, whereupon they had some drinks with Nathan Leopold Sr and played a few hands of cards.

They waited for Nathan's father to go to sleep, then drove the rented car to the Loeb mansion, throwing the chisel out of the window on the way. The Loebs had an incinerator in the basement, and they intended to burn all of the remaining blood-stained clothes there. But the robe wouldn't fit in, and in any case would have smelled terrible, so they hid it in some nearby undergrowth. They also found some cleaning products in the Leopold basement, and set about making a preliminary clean-up of the car. But it was already very late, so they arranged to meet the following day at the university to finish the job.

The next day they drove the rented car to the Leopold garage, where they cleaned it thoroughly using soap, water, petrol and a brush. The family chauffeur, Sven Englund, offered to help, but they told him not to worry. Loeb was concerned that Englund had seen the bloodstains in the car, and assured him that they'd spilled some red wine. Later that day they returned the rented car to the rental firm.

In the early afternoon they went to the Illinois Central railway station, where Loeb bought a ticket to Michigan

City on the 3 p.m. train, got on the train and deposited the final letter of instructions as arranged. Meanwhile, Leopold called the Franks home and told Mr Franks to go to a specified drugstore and wait at a public phone booth for a call. A yellow cab would arrive at his house to take him there. Franks asked for more time, which was not given.

As they drove to a public phone to call Franks, they happened to see a local newspaper with the headline UNIDENTIFIED BOY FOUND IN SWAMP. When they called the drugstore for Franks, he was nowhere to be found. Their plan was starting to unravel – the perfect crime to show its flaws.

THE FRANKSES

Even before receiving the first ransom call, Jacob and Flora Franks, who lived near the Loebs, were alarmed by Bobby's disappearance. When he hadn't come home for dinner, the tension mounted. Flora called Bobby's classmates, and Jacob called the headmaster of Bobby's school to find out if he could be locked in the building. He then called a friend, a lawyer named Samuel Ettelson, and the pair went to the school to search it.

While they were away, Flora received the ransom call and fainted, remaining unconscious until her husband's return. Upon learning of the kidnap, Jacob and Ettelson immediately went to the police station, but, as none of Ettelson's officer friends were then on duty, they decided to return the next day.

The next morning the ransom letter arrived by special delivery; as well as the details given above, it also asked the Frankses not to contact the police, and to be at home during the afternoon to expect a phone call. Jacob began to arrange collecting the money, while Ettelson contacted the chief of detectives at the Chicago police department.

Word had already got out about the kidnapping, and a boy's body had been found at the Wolf Lake culvert by railway workers working on the overhead track. A journalist thought there might be a link, and called the Franks house to describe the dead boy. Jacob didn't think it matched Bobby's description, but sent his brother-in-law to investigate in any case.

The phone rang, and was picked up by Ettelson. He was instructed to wait for a yellow cab that the kidnappers would send, and take it to the drugstore at 1465 East 63rd Street. Ettelson passed the phone to Jacob, and the message was repeated. In the heat of the moment, neither man wrote down the drugstore address, and following the phone call neither could remember where they were meant to go. A yellow cab duly arrived, but the driver had been given no instructions on where to go.

Another phone call followed shortly afterwards. It was Flora's brother. He'd seen the body – it belonged to Bobby Franks.

THE INVESTIGATION
The case instantly made the headlines, and a number of rewards were publicised: Jacob Franks offered $5,000, Police Chief Morgan Collins $1,000 and two Chicago newspapers, the *Tribune* and the *Herald and Examiner* $5,000 each.

State's Attorney Robert E Crowe was assigned the investigation, the successful resolution of which would stand him in extremely good stead for the realisation of his Republican political ambitions. While the failure to remember the drugstore address was a setback, there were a number of other clues to go on.

The first was that a pair of glasses, not belonging to the boy, had been found near the body; unfortunately the prescription was very common. Local newspapers displayed photos of the glasses and the police began contacting eyewear companies in the area.

The second clue was the ransom note itself, which police scientists determined had been typed on a portable Underwood typewriter. The impeccable English used in the note was cause for some alarm, as it pointed to an above-average intelligence on the part of the writer, described by the coroner as 'a dangerous attribute in a criminal'.

The police, acting on the assumption that the kidnappers were well educated, first questioned three bachelor teachers at the Harvard School and searched their apartments. One was quickly released but the other two were held while the investigation continued.

The following Friday, Loeb was at his fraternity house with a friend, and suggested that they try to locate the drugstore whose location had been forgotten by Franks and Ettelson. Just as they set off, two journalists from the *Daily News*, one of whom was also a fraternity member, arrived and decided to go along for the story.

After a number of false starts they eventually happened upon the Van de Bogert & Ross drugstore, where they were told that there had been two calls the previous day for a Mr Jacob Franks. Loeb was jubilant, telling his companions, 'This is what comes from reading detective stories.'[9] One of the journalists asked Loeb if he knew Bobby Franks. Loeb answered that he did, and that, 'If I were going to murder anybody, I would murder just such a cocky son of a bitch as Bobby Franks.'[10]

In the course of the investigation the police had questioned the game warden for the Wolf Lake area, and had been told that one of the most frequent visitors to the area was Nathan Leopold, a keen ornithologist. Police questioned Leopold, but his answers were convincing and he was not considered a serious suspect. But eight days after the murder police discovered that the hinges on the glasses they'd found were very rare, and could be found on only three pairs of glasses sold in the Chicago area; one of these belonged to Nathan Leopold.

THE ARREST

Crowe, concerned that an influential family like the Leopolds could ground his political career if he didn't proceed with caution, arranged for Nathan to be interviewed in a hotel room on 29 May. When the police arrived to pick him up, they asked if he'd lost his glasses. He denied that he had, but during a later search of the house investigators were unable to find them.

Leopold finally admitted that the glasses were his, and that they'd probably fallen out of the breast pocket of his jacket during a bird-watching trip on the weekend before the murder. He was asked to recreate the fall, but the glasses stayed in his jacket.

Leopold was initially vague about the events of 21 May, claiming that he couldn't remember what he'd done. He finally told investigators that he'd spent most of the day with Richard Loeb, bird-watching in Lincoln Park. In the evening they'd picked up two girls and gone for a drive before returning to Leopold's house to pick up Nathan's uncle and aunt.

Leopold owned a Hammond Multiplex typewriter, which the police confiscated, although the typing didn't match that on the ransom note. He agreed that he was sufficiently well educated to have written the ransom note.

Unbeknown to Leopold, Loeb was being questioned in another room at the same hotel. He too said that they'd spent 21 May together, but that they'd parted company in the evening. When pressed, he said that he couldn't remember what he'd done on the night of the murder.

Not suspecting that he was helping to cover up a killing, a friend of the young men delivered a crucial message from Leopold to Loeb, telling the latter to tell the truth about what they'd done with the two girls.

After this Leopold's and Loeb's stories grew more similar: they'd taken the girls to a secluded spot and had sex with them. They hadn't admitted to it until now for fear of getting themselves – and the girls – in trouble. The minor differences between their accounts could be put down to the fact that Loeb had been drinking heavily on the night in question. The investigating team believed them, and Crowe apologised to the young men by taking them out for dinner.

But others still had their suspicions. Two enterprising journalists had discovered that Leopold belonged to a law-student study group. They quizzed the members of the group and found that, while Leopold usually typed up his reports on his Hammond, he'd been known to use a portable, too. They compared documents he'd prepared for his study group with the ransom note – the typing on some of the documents matched the ransom note perfectly. Leopold and Loeb were back in the hot seat.

Leopold admitted that he'd used a portable typewriter a few times, but denied actually owning one. But, when investigators quizzed the maid, she remembered seeing one in the house a few weeks earlier.

When they then interviewed the chauffeur, he stated that on 21 May he'd been working on Leopold's car all day, directly contradicting the statements of the young men, who maintained that they'd had the car that day. When Loeb was confronted with this during an intense interrogation, the truth finally began to emerge.

Faced with Loeb's confession, Leopold could only confess himself. The confessions were very similar, except that each maintained that the other had killed Franks. The press at first sided with Loeb, painting Leopold as the leader of the two, the evil genius who'd used his superior intellect to persuade his weak-willed friend to commit murder. But, as far as Crowe was concerned, both would hang.

Shortly after the confessions were printed in local newspapers, the involvement of the public with the judicial process began to manifest itself in strange ways: a Chicago woman sent each of the boys a bouquet of flowers with a note wishing them well on their imminent executions, and a Milwaukee man volunteered to take the place of one of the defendants on the gallows if paid $1 million by one of the families.

TRIAL AND SENTENCE

With their confessions, the guilt of the two young men was beyond question. They did further harm to their case by helping police to locate the evidence and boasting of their crimes to assorted journalists. The public face they presented was less one of penitence than of unrelenting sassiness. No protestations of innocence; no signs of remorse. The only question was – would they hang?

On the evening of the confessions, Jacob Loeb, Richard's uncle, approached Clarence Darrow, a 67-year-old lawyer famous for his stance against capital punishment, and begged him to save the lives of the pair. Darrow decided to take the case, principally for the opportunity of using it as a forum for a debate on capital punishment itself, and started work the next day.

Crowe assumed that Darrow would plead not guilty by reason of insanity, an assumption reinforced by

Darrow's immediate employment of three Freudian psychoanalysts to analyse the pair.

But as the case opened, presided over by one Judge Caverly, Darrow shocked Crowe and the public by pleading guilty on both counts. He had explained to Leopold and Loeb that this was their best chance of escaping the noose – he would avoid a jury trial, in which a death sentence seemed most likely, and hoped to convince the judge that their relative youth and abnormal psychology worked as mitigating factors in their guilt.

Crowe's objection that the reports of the analysts were irrelevant was overturned, and the court and press were treated to a microscopic examination of the psyches of Leopold and Loeb, in which the true nature of their relationship was revealed.

Or was it? On realising that they stood to gain immeasurably from being found to have abnormal psychologies, Leopold and Loeb may well have lied to analysts throughout. The stigma of homosexuality in their social circle was so great, however, that it is unlikely this would have been their preferred 'abnormality' had it not had some basis in truth. They were, moreover, analysed separately but concurred in the most important details of their relationship, leading one to suspect that, although the pair may have exaggerated certain issues for effect, the psychiatric reports of Leopold and Loeb are largely accurate.

Darrow's ploy was successful, and a number of the speeches he made during the trial, particularly his closing address, which took over two days, have gone down in American legal history as being among the most effective on record. He rubbished the prosecution's claim that the murder was principally carried out for financial gain, and made the judge all too aware that the fate of the young men rested entirely in his hands:

> The easy thing and the popular thing to do is to hang my clients. I know it. Men and women who do not think will applaud. The cruel and thoughtless will approve. It will be easy today; but in Chicago, and reaching out over the length and breadth of the land, more and more fathers and mothers . . . will join in no acclaim at the death of my clients. They would ask that the shedding of blood be stopped, and that the normal feelings of man resume their sway . . . I am pleading that we overcome cruelty with kindness, and hatred with love. I know the future is on my side . . .[11]

On 19 September 1924 Judge Caverly, principally 'in consideration of the age of the defendants', sentenced Leopold and Loeb to life imprisonment at Joliet for the murder charge, and for the charge of kidnapping a further 99 years. He had ignored the bomb threats phoned in, at least two of which threatened to destroy the jail holding Leopold and Loeb if Caverly failed to impose the death penalty; he had ignored the hundreds of letters from clergymen hoping to impress upon him the need to take a firm stance against modern immorality by imposing the ultimate sanction.

AFTERMATH

The families of the principals involved in the case never recovered from its horror. Albert Loeb had suffered from a severe heart attack before the murder in any case, and died a month after his son had been sentenced – he never saw him following the arrest. The Leopold family left Kenwood, with two of the sons changing their names to avoid the shame of the association with Nathan; Nathan Leopold Sr died of heart failure five years after Judge Caverly passed sentence.

Flora Franks became delusional after Bobby Franks' death, but eventually recovered and remarried after the death of her husband, who'd never got over the grief of losing his youngest son.

Judge Caverly, who went to hospital immediately after the trial to recover from exhaustion, subsequently dealt only with divorce cases. Darrow fared better, going on to one last high-profile case, the Scopes 'Monkey' trial, in which he successfully defended a schoolteacher from Tennessee for teaching evolution rather than fundamentalist Christian doctrine.

As for Leopold and Loeb, although the state initially attempted to keep them apart, they eventually ended up together. They opened a school for other inmates, and Leopold continued to learn languages and a variety of other disciplines at a prodigious rate.

On 28 January 1936 Loeb was attacked in the shower with a straight razor by his cellmate, James Day. He died of blood loss and shock. Day claimed that Loeb had made homosexual advances towards him; it seems more likely, considering that the victim's throat was cut from behind, that Day was simply angry about not receiving more of Loeb's monthly allowance. Whatever the motive, Day was judged to have acted in self-defence.

Leopold, following a failed parole application in 1953, was eventually released on parole in 1958, after having spent 33 years in prison. He settled in Puerto Rico to avoid press harassment, worked in a variety of positions, published a study of the birds of the island, and was awarded a master's degree by the University of Puerto Rico. In 1961 he married the widow of a Puerto Rican physician, and died ten years later of a heart attack. He donated his eyes for use following his death; one cornea was shortly afterwards given to a woman, the other to a man.

At least three films are based on the Leopold and Loeb case: *Rope* (1948, Alfred Hitchcock), *Compulsion* (1959, Richard Fleischer) and *Swoon* (1992, Tom Kalin). *Compulsion* is based on the journalist Meyer Levin's book of the same name, a McCarthy-era novel that played on the myth, widely accepted at the time, of homosexual desire as inherently antisocial and potentially murderous. Leopold attempted unsuccessfully to sue Levin for wilful misrepresentation of character following the publication of the novel.

But Darrow's defence itself is also responsible for the easy equation of homosexuality and pathology which is the hallmark of the mythology surrounding the case, for all of the lawyer's importance as a defender of liberal values through some of the most conservative periods of American history. Perversely, it was probably precisely this equation that allowed Leopold and Loeb to escape a sentence of death. There *are* statistical indications that homosexual men may be overrepresented in various types of violent crime, particularly serial murder (see Simon Whitechapel's excellent *Crossing to Kill*, Chapter 17), but homosexuality can clearly not, as it was then, be taken to stand more or less alone as an explanation of Leopold and Loeb's pathology. As you'll see, other couples in this book didn't need homosexuality to 'justify' their desire to kill . . .

NOTES
1. From the report of 'alienists' Drs White, Healy and Glueck in the case of *The People against Nathan Leopold Jr and Richard Loeb*, trial transcript.
2. Ibid.

3. From Clarence Darrow's closing argument, trial transcript.
4. Testimony of Dr Healy, trial transcript.
5. Ibid.
6. Ibid.
7. Testimony of Dr Glueck, trial transcript.
8. Leopold, quoted in the Chicago *Daily News*, 28 May 1924.
9. Loeb, quoted in the Chicago *Daily News*, 27 May 1924.
10. Ibid.
11. From Clarence Darrow's closing argument, trial transcript.

2. THE LONELY HEARTS KILLERS – RAYMOND FERNANDEZ AND MARTHA BECK

INTRODUCTION

True love is eternal, even for convicted serial killers such as Martha Beck and Raymond Fernandez. Known in the late 1940s as the 'Lonely Hearts Killers' for killing spinsters and widows they met through lonely-heart's clubs, Beck and Fernandez passionately professed their love for each other all they way to the electric chair. Though evidence clearly links them to three murders, they were sentenced to death for only one. Investigators and historians have speculated they may have been responsible for up to nineteen deaths. An unlikely couple, they developed an unbreakable bond stemming from their equal love for crime and kinky sex.

The two killers met when Fernandez, a smooth-talking gigolo, answered a lonely-hearts club listing posted by Beck. Fernandez – who boasted of having intimately known hundreds of women – was instantly smitten by Martha, a 233-pound butterball of love. Together, they cut a path of murder and lust throughout the northeastern United States until they were arrested in Byron Center, Michigan, and executed in New York's Sing Sing Prison.

THE SWINDLING ROMEO

Though he billed himself as a Latin Lover, Fernandez was actually born in Hawaii in 1914 of Spanish parents. When he was three years old, his family relocated to Bridgeport, Connecticut, where his dad, an illiterate labourer, had a successful series of business ventures. As a boy, Ray was undersized and sickly, which was something that did not sit too well with Dad. Raymond Sr was very strict in an old-world fashion. He saw education as a detriment for a growing boy and believed that hard labour was the only way to build character. Ray excelled in school, but his dad would punish him if he brought any books home. Not surprisingly, Ray endured regular beatings by his father over his puniness and lack of mettle. Eventually the old man forced Ray to drop out of school and work in a farm he bought as an investment.

When he was fifteen, Ray, together with other boys, was arrested for stealing chickens. When his father was asked to pay a $28.75 fine, the miserly old man refused and Ray had to spend sixty days in jail. After his release, he worked on a series of jobs, saved money and headed to Spain with his father in search of his roots. There, he married Encarnación Robles, the daughter of an affluent family, and fathered, according to different accounts, between two and four children. Not one to stick around for long, Fernandez abandoned his wife and progeny in Cadiz, but returned when one of his children fell gravely ill.

Upon his return, Spain exploded into civil war. It is unclear what side of the conflict Ray favoured, but his father was a vocal supporter of Franco and the Fascists. During World War Two, Ray remained in Spain and served in Gibraltar with the British Intelligence Service. By all accounts he did an excellent job and even had a 'commendation for courage under conditions of greatest danger'. In 1945, with the end of the war, he abandoned his Spanish family again and boarded a merchant marine ship to Curacao. While at sea a hatch fell on his head, nearly killing him and sending him to the hospital with his skull fractured and a three-inch scar on his brain tissue.

It seems that Fernandez's head injury may have led to his unrepentant, murderous nature. Until the accident, Ray seemed to be a normal, intelligent man leading a normal and productive life. After the accident, he emerged from the hospital with blinding headaches, acute and inexplicable sex drives and a new-found penchant for crime. Criminal pathologists believe that frontal-lobe injuries to the brain cause an individual to lose self-control, which Ray obviously did. From Curacao the 'new Ray' boarded a tanker heading to Mobile, Alabama, where, upon arrival, he was arrested for stealing government property. He was sentenced to a year in a federal penitentiary near Tallahassee, Florida, where he had an IQ test that rated him at 135, which is borderline of genius. But this new, darker Ray put his superior intellect to work studying voodoo and black magic that he learned from Haitian prisoners.

He was released from prison on 3 December 1946, a changed man. Ray went to live in Brooklyn with his sister Lena Cano, who hardly recognised her brother. The 'new Ray' was nearly bald, had lost most of his teeth, and had a gruesome scar on his forehead. He claimed to have developed what he thought were mystical powers over the female sex and said he could make love to a woman from a distance using a picture of her and an article of clothing that she wore next to her skin. In court Lena testified that, when Raymond lived with her, he was constantly typing letters, which he sprinkled with 'magic powders' and sent to more than seventy women at a time. With a newly acquired wig of thick black hair, Ray became a swindling Casanova, claiming to have had relations with about fifteen women simultaneously. Many of his conquests he milked for money and dropped once their bank accounts went dry.

Raymond's first known victim was Jane Thompson, a widow he met in 1947 and with whom he travelled to Spain as her husband. Once she met his family in Cadiz, their love affair went south. On 7 November hotel servants in La Linea heard the couple having a heated argument. Ray then stormed out. The next morning Thompson was found dead in her room. The coroner said she died of 'cardiac collapse during acute gastro-enteritis'. Ray quickly left Spain before authorities thought about questioning him. When he arrived in New York he had a will naming himself as her sole heir. He told Thompson's shocked relatives that she died in a train wreck. Later, he modified the story and claimed she had a heart attack. In the meantime, he pilfered $6,000 from her bank account. Then, in a calculated act of callousness, he moved in with Pearl Wilson, Thompson's invalid mother, and took over her lease.

Two years later, after Martha and Raymond's arrest made headlines worldwide, Spanish police revisited the Thompson death and discovered that Ray had purchased a bottle of digitalis, a deadly poison, two days before she perished. In custody Raymond said that Thompson, 'cost me a lot of money and I got nothing from her . . . So I had to take it.' After considering Ray's statements and the new evidence, Spanish authorities said they would bring Ray to trial if he was not found guilty of murder in the United States.

Around the time Ray returned to the States, Martha Beck – prodded by a friend – posted a lonely-hearts club listing, which was answered by Fernandez. Encouraged by the possibilities presented by his new conquest, Raymond packed his bags, left Brooklyn and headed for Pensacola.

LOVING MARTHA

Born in Milton, Florida, in 1919, Martha Jule Seabrook took the name of Beck from a truck driver she married in 1944. Since childhood, Martha suffered from a pituitary malfunction that caused her to gain weight and mature faster than the other girls. She started menstruating by age nine, and by the time she was twelve she was fully developed as a woman and had an unhinged sexual appetite that she was unable to satisfy. Mentally, however, she never fully developed. While she was on Death Row one of the prison matrons befriended her and said, 'Her emotional growth had stopped when she was eight or nine. That's the way she seemed – immature, undeveloped, voluble – the way a small girl is. She had a tremendously vivacious personality, but again it was a child's personality.'

Martha's childhood was dominated by her mother, Vera Seabrook, who was very critical of her and referred to her as 'unwanted', 'different' and 'queer'. As far as Mommy was concerned, Martha was feeble-minded and would easily give in to the desires of the flesh, so she watched her like a hawk and never allowed her to go out with boys. When she was thirteen, Martha was repeatedly raped by her older brother, who threatened to kill her if she told anyone. Though she complied, when she missed a period and feared that she was pregnant, she told Mommy dearest about the assaults. Her mother proceeded to beat her up and accused her of forcing the boy, who was three years older, to take advantage of her. After the assault, Vera decided it would be best to lock Martha in her room whenever she had to leave the house so the girl wouldn't get into any more trouble.

Pathetically, Beck lived in a world culled together from romance novels that was somewhere between reality and fantasy. In 1942, as she ballooned to gargantuan proportions, she completed her studies to become a nurse. Unable to find nursing work, Martha took a job cleaning corpses at a mortuary. Eight months later, as she grew increasingly sick and tired of the dead, she headed for California, where she heard there was a shortage of nurses. When she arrived at Napa, near San Francisco, she found a job working at the Park Victory Memorial Hospital. She also started hanging around bus depots and train stations, where she met soldiers on leave and enjoyed the occasional sexual bout in a nearby motel. By 1944 Beck found herself pregnant by a bus driver. The poor man, facing the prospect of spending the rest of his life with blubbery Martha, drove his bus to a wharf and jumped into the ocean. Unfortunately, he was rescued. After being released from the hospital, the bus driver disappeared, never to be seen or heard from again.

With her husband gone, Martha resurfaced on 11 October at the Mission Emergency Hospital in San Francisco after she collapsed on the street while posting a letter. Several days later she went to a police station and said she had forgotten her identity while eating breakfast at a waffle shop. She was hospitalised for three more days and was diagnosed with 'hysteria, amnesic type'. When her memory returned, Martha claimed that her bout of amnesia was triggered by a suicide attempt after she discovered that the hospital she was working in was a distribution centre for heroin and pot and she didn't want to participate in illegal drug dealing.

Pregnant and on the verge of a nervous breakdown, Martha returned to Pensacola, Florida, and gave birth to a son. She said the baby was from a navy officer she married before he was shipped off to combat in the South Pacific. She described the mysterious husband, whom she called 'Joe Carmen', as handsome, rich, six-foot tall and with wavy, blond hair. The mystery man swept her off her feet in a whirlwind romance and married her at a naval chapel in Norfolk, Virginia. Then, modifying the story, she told everyone that he was killed in action. Curiously, she never asked for or collected her navy widow's pension. Her tale of woe made it to the local press and Martha became something of a local celebrity. A local bus driver by the name of Alfred Beck was so touched by her misfortune that he felt the need to divorce his wife and take Martha's hand instead. By the time they married on 13 December 1944, Martha was pregnant again. However, six months later, she caught Alfred with another woman, divorced him, and descended into a greater state of depression and despair.

KINKY SEX

In February 1946, Martha took a job as superintendent in the Pensacola Crippled Children's Home, which she still held by the time she met Ray. When Martha and Raymond met, they both lied to each other. Fernandez claimed to be a wealthy Spanish businessman looking for company. Martha lied about her weight and her finances. Nevertheless, they had sex – which they both liked wild and kinky – and Martha fell hopelessly in love with her Latin con man. After a week of bedroom pyrotechnics, the swindling Romeo returned to New York to get back to his con work.

A few weeks later, his monumental Juliet showed up on his doorstep unannounced with her two children in tow. Though surprised, he allowed her to stay. Settled in Pearl Wilson's apartment, they decided to send the old lady packing to her son's home in South Carolina. Clearing the slate, Martha left her kids with the Welfare Department. Then, claiming to be homeless, she called from a telephone booth and said that she had swallowed six tablets of dichloride of mercury and was waiting to 'fall on my face and die'. A county judge charged her with child abandonment, adjudged her to be an unfit mother and sent her two children to Florida to live with Martha's mom.

With the children gone, Martha was hell-bent on keeping her Ray faithful. Recognising the merit of his swindle, she saw no reason to stop working it. A master manipulator, she devised a plan that would keep his unhinged philandering in check while they emptied the bank accounts of their lovelorn victims. Martha convinced Ray that, if she posed as his sister, the women would be more trusting and willing to sign over their savings. In between scams, she promised, the two would enjoy torrid bouts of extreme sex. It is unknown how many women fell for the scam, but a list of names found when they were arrested indicated that there were at least sixteen victims in twelve different states.

The first known widow worked over by the swindling sweethearts was Esther Henne, a 41-year-old teacher from Pennhurst, Pennsylvania. Raymond, adding bigamy to his long list of crimes, married Henne on 28 February 1948. Strangely, his 'sister' Martha joined them for their honeymoon. The marriage lasted less than a month, giving Raymond and Martha ample time to empty Henne's bank account. Once all the money was gone, Ray scared the poor woman away. 'I began to hear stories in our apartment house about how he went to Spain with a woman and she died, so I decided to leave,' she told the *New York Times* after Ray's arrest. According to Henne, Ray had been polite during his courtship and for the first four days of their marriage. 'Then he became irritable and gave me tongue lashings because I wouldn't sign over my insurance policies and my teacher's pension fund.' She also thought his alleged sister acted 'too lovingly to be a relative'. Frightened and broken-hearted, the poor woman left with most of her money gone. But at least she was still breathing.

Myrtle Young of Green Forrest, Arkansas, was not so lucky. Fernandez, using the name Raymond Martin, married the 42-year-old Chicago widow on 13 August 1948. The newlyweds spent the next three days in a cheap rooming house in Chicago. Strangely, Martha – 'Ray's sister' – insisted on sharing their bed, in effect blocking any possibilities of post-nuptial hanky-panky. When Myrtle complained, Martha and Raymond fed the poor woman a handful of barbiturates and put her on a bus to Little Rock. The next day, she was taken off the bus comatose and died in a Little Rock hospital. Though the autopsy report said she had 'cerebral haemorrhage and liver inflammation', the lethal Lothario told police that she died 'from overexertion after a weekend of non-stop sex'. Before Chicago authorities charged him or Martha with anything, the couple took Young's car, her jewellery, $4,000 from her bank account and disappeared.

FRESH CEMENT
After Chicago, Ray and Martha re-emerged in Albany, New York, where they set their sights on Janet L Fay, a 62-year-old widow with whom Raymond had been corresponding. On 30 December the brother-and-sister team moved into the home of the widow and within four days they emptied her bank account of nearly $6,000. Raymond then invited Fay to their apartment in Valley Stream, Long Island. Once there, Martha, who was 'burning up with jealousy and anger', bashed Janet Fay's brains in with a ball-peen hammer. The hammer attack didn't kill her, so Ray garrotted her with a scarf. Then the couple made love next to the dead body before

stuffing it in a trunk and taking it to his sister's home in the Astoria neighbourhood of Queens. Days later, they found an apartment rental near what is now John F Kennedy Airport. They took the body there and buried it in the pit cellar in a four-foot grave, which they covered with a slab of fresh cement.

By 16 January, the murderous lovers left New York for the outskirts of Grand Rapids, Michigan, where Fernandez had been corresponding with Delphine Downing, a 28-year-old widow whose husband had died in a train accident. Delphine and her 20-month-old daughter, Rainelle, lived in a tiny suburban community called Byron Center. Unfortunately for both mother and daughter, Delphine was much younger than Raymond's other lovers, which drove Martha insane with jealousy. Once the brother and his 200-pound sister settled in, Raymond started having sex with Delphine. Not amused by the turn of events, Martha, who was the more dominant of the two, ordered him to kill her immediately.

Things quickly began to unravel when Delphine caught sight of Raymond without his toupee. A struggle ensued and Ray and/or Martha forced an overdose of sleeping pills down Delphine's throat. When she unexpectedly regained consciousness, Ray put a bullet in her head. To appease the crying baby who saw them kill her mother, they bought the girl a puppy. But Rainelle didn't stop crying, so Martha, whose maternal instincts where marginal at best, decided to put an end to the whimpering by drowning the baby in the washtub. Ray then tried to return the puppy, but the former owner didn't take it back.

The killers buried both mother and daughter in the backyard and covered the graves with cement. Neighbours, suspicious about the sudden disappearance of

Delphine and Rainelle, called the police. By then, authorities in New York were searching for the pair after Fay's stepdaughter alerted them of possible foul play involving one 'Charles Martin' and his sister and the disappearance of Fay. Martha and Ray were arrested on 28 February 1949, as they returned home from seeing a movie at the Byron Center theatre. The consummate scammers tried to talk their way out of it, claiming that Delphine and Rainelle had gone on holiday. A search of the home uncovered the fresh cement and detectives quickly unearthed the two victims.

I'M NO AVERAGE KILLER
In custody, Martha and Ray proudly and willingly confessed to the Fay and Downing murders, and many more. Raymond told Kent County Prosecutor McMahon, 'You got me dead rights. I might as well come clean and tell everything.' To which he started by boasting, 'I'm no average killer,' and complained about the meagre $500 they netted from the Downing bank account. In a display of absolute contempt, Fernandez confessed to killing up to nineteen women. Meanwhile, Martha, whose eagerness to please knew no bounds, would chime in with salacious details of their active sex life between murders. Subsequent investigation located most of their alleged victims, many of whom had merely been chiselled by the couple. In a telephone conversation with DA Irwin Shapiro of Queens, Ray admitted to the killing of Janet Fay and directed police to her basement grave.

Prosecutors, realising they could not implement the death penalty in Michigan, quickly motioned to extradite the couple to New York, where they could. Facing the possibility of a change of venue, both killers recanted their non-stop litany of swindle and murder, saying that they confessed only because they thought they would be tried in Michigan. Martha, looking for compassion, told the press, 'I'm afraid of the electric chair. I hope they keep us here.' Ray, more resigned to his fate, said, 'I ought to be killed. I deserve it.'

On 9 March New York's Governor, Thomas Dewey, signed an extradition agreement in which, if the killers were not convicted in New York for the hammer-and-scarf slaying of Janet Fay, they would be returned to Michigan to stand trial for the two Downing murders. On 15 March, Michigan's Governor, G Mennen Williams, released the prisoners to the custody of US marshals, who flew them to New York's La Guardia airport. There they were placed in custody of New York State police officers, who drove them under heavy guard to the Mineola Jail.

THE BRONX COUNTY COURT

Once they were in New York, the wheels of the law kicked into high gear. On 22 March Beck and Fernandez were indicted of the murder of Janet Fay by the Bronx County Court. Two days later, their attorney, Herbert Rosenberg, pleaded not guilty by reason of insanity. He also filed a writ of habeas corpus calling for the immediate dismissal of all charges under the premise that the lonely-hearts slayers were illegally extradited. Judge Ferdinand Pecora, who presided over the case, rejected all motions to dismiss and set the trial to begin on 1 July.

The trial, which became one of the most sensational of the time, was reported by the tabloid press in lurid detail. Even fashion reporters showed up to describe Martha's outfits. The press seemed obsessed with Martha and her weight to the point that she said, 'What am I being tried for, murder, or because I'm fat?'

Headlines frequently called her 'loathsome monstrosity' and an 'overweight ogress', while Raymond was referred to as 'virile', 'handsome' and 'a seedy version of Charles Boyer'.

The first of the lethal lovers to testify was Ray, who drew a crowd of women – romance-novel types – to the courthouse. He said that his confession in Michigan was false and he had made it to protect his lover. Ray, who a psychiatrist said 'suffered from an atrophy of the conscience', repeatedly expressed his love for Martha. At the same time he added that she had 'many disabilities as a woman'. He talked about her obesity, her chronic halitosis, her repeated suicide threats, and blamed her for the killings. But then he would show Martha's noble side by mentioning that she was the caring and loving mother of two. However, he failed to mention that she had not seen her kids since he had met her two years before. He also admitted to the murders of Delphine and Rainelle Downing, describing them as a 'frightful dream beyond control'. Finally, he placed the blame for the Fay murder squarely on Martha's wide lap, claiming that he was out of the room when the widow was killed. 'Me, I never killed anyone. I could never hurt a fly. But that woman, she is evil. She should die.'

After two days of Raymond's assuming and denying all guilt, it was Martha's turn to take the spotlight. The excitement and expectation of seeing and hearing her testify led to the 25 July near-riot outside the Bronx County Courthouse, in which 150 people tried to push their way inside. As her captivating four-day run in the witness box demonstrated, Martha clearly enjoyed her fifteen minutes of fame. Like Raymond, she claimed she confessed to the Fay killing because in Michigan she couldn't be sentenced to death. But, unlike Raymond, she did it with conviction and using flowery and melodramatic language. Poor Martha said that she tried to commit suicide six times because of Ray's serial philandering. Her lawyer, Herbert Rosenberg, pointed out that she had genuine difficulty distinguishing between truth and fantasy and asked her if she still thought about killing herself. In tears, Martha answered, 'Every day.'

On the day of the Fay murder Martha said the two women had been quarrelling over Ray's affections. Janet Fay then slapped her and her mind went mysteriously blank. When she came out of her daze, she found that 'Fernandez had me by the shoulders and was shaking me'. She also noticed the victim lying next to her feet, 'slumped over a suitcase'. And, of course, as dead as a doornail. She stated that Raymond – whom she always referred to as 'Honey', 'Sweetheart' or 'Darling' – did not tourniquet Fay's throat until after she was dead. They did so to avoid soiling the rug with blood. However, the official autopsy report states that Fay died of a fractured skull and a fractured larynx.

The jury of ten men and two women did not believe her momentary lapse of sanity. Instead they ruled in favour of Nassau County Assistant District Attorney, Edward Robinson, who said that together they strangled and brained Janet Fay and robbed her of her savings. On 22 August, after a trial lasting 68 days and costing New York State close to a million dollars, the Lonely Hearts Killers were sentenced to death. Justice Pecora ordered the murdering sweethearts be moved to Death Row in New York's Sing Sing Prison to await their fate.

TRUE LOVE

For the next two years Martha and Ray lingered in prison as their appeals played out and occasionally titillated the tabloid press with tales of Martha's insatiable libido and rumoured Death Row sexcapades. Justice Pecora's original execution date, set for 31 August 1950, was quickly appealed and the execution was postponed. On 11 July the New York Court of Appeals upheld the conviction and assigned new counsel to Fernandez, citing that a single counsel could not represent both defendants without conflict. On 18 August, the State Supreme Court delayed their execution once again. By January 1951 a new date of execution was set and a new series of appeals were filed. On 8 March 1951, after having their last two appeals rejected by the US Supreme Court and the Court of Appeals, the two lovers had their date with death courtesy of Joseph Francel, the Sing Sing executioner.

For her last meal, Martha had two servings of fried chicken, potatoes and a salad. Conflicting accounts of Fernandez's last meal state that he had a Spanish omelet and almond ice cream or that he refused to eat and smoked a Cuban cigar. Two hours before heading for the chair the Death Row Romeo sent a note to his Martha professing his eternal love. According to the *Citizen Register*, the final love note read, 'I want to shout it out. I love Martha. What do the public know about love?' Martha, overcome with joy, hugged the prison matrons and stated, 'Now that I know that Raymond loves me I can go to my death bursting with joy.'

As her final statement Martha wrote:

What does it matter who is to blame? My story is a love story, but only those tortured with love can understand what I mean. I was pictured as a fat unfeeling woman. True, I am fat, that I cannot deny, but if that is a crime, how many of my sex are guilty? I am not unfeeling, stupid or moronic. The prison and the death house have only strengthened my feeling for Raymond, and in the history of the world how many crimes have been attributed to love? My last words are and my last thoughts will be: He who is without sin can cast the first stone.

Raymond was less flowery, writing, 'I am going to die. That is all right. As you know, that's something I've been prepared for since 1949. So tonight I'll die like a man.'

There were four executions scheduled for that night. The first was at 11.02 and the last was at 11.24. Because of the sensational nature of the case, newspapers from all over the nation sent correspondents to cover the electrocution. The first to go was John J King, then Richard Powers, both 22. Together, they were sentenced to death for the 15 March 1950 murder of a radio technician, William Hupe. Next came Raymond, who was walked to the chair by a Catholic priest and was quickly jolted to oblivion. At the time of his death, Raymond Fernandez was 35. Twelve minutes later, Martha was led to the same chair by a Protestant chaplain. As the prison matrons tried to squeeze her into the seat, they discovered that she was too fat to fit and had to be partially seated on the armrest. Nevertheless, the chair did its job, killing her after jolting her four times and flushing two million volts of electricity through her body. Martha was 32 years old. She was the thirteenth woman executed in the state of New York and the eighth one electrocuted. Francel, the executioner, made $600 for the day's work.

CODA
Nearly half a century later, the love between Martha and Ray survives in the form of two movies. The first, *The Honeymoon Killers*, is a 1969 classic directed by Leonard Kastle. The original director, Martin Scorsese – fresh out

of film school – was fired two days into production because of a personality clash with the producer. The film featured the imposing Shirley Stoler and Tony LoBianco playing the cooing killers. Though banned in several countries for its gritty and unflinching look at violence, it is still remembered as a B-movie masterpiece featuring powerful performances by both Stoler and LoBianco. The second and most recent adaptation of the tale, *Profundo Carmesí*, was made in 1996 by the celebrated Mexican director Arturo Ripstein. A less faithful interpretation of the Martha-and-Ray saga, the film was a huge success south of the border. In 1997 it won eight Ariels (the Mexican equivalent of the Oscar), including both Best Female Actor and Best Male Actor for Regina Orozco and Daniel Giménez Cacho for their roles as the Lonely Hearts Killers.

BIBLIOGRAPHY

Brown, Wenzell, *Introduction to Murder*, Greenberg, 1952.

Everitt, David, *Human Monsters: An Illustrated Encyclopedia of the World's Most Vicious Murderers*, Contemporary Books, Chicago, 1993.

Hickey, Eric, *Serial Murders and their Victims,* Second Edition, Wadsworth Publishing Company, Belmont, California, 1996.

Newton, Michael, *Bad Girls Do It! An Encyclopedia of Female Murderers*, Loompanics Unlimited, Washington, 1993.

Newton, Michael, *Hunting Humans: An Encyclopedia of Modern Serial Killers*, Loompanics Unlimited, Washington, 1990.

New York Times, 1 July 1949 to 24 August 1951.

3. NUMBERED FOR THE BOTTOM – CHARLES STARKWEATHER AND CARIL ANN FUGATE

INTRODUCTION

America in the mid 1950s – an era of conformity and rebellion, of Cold War paranoia and B-movie monsters – the era that gave birth to the teenager. Elvis Presley and James Dean typified the surly nonchalance of the rebel teen, and their world was one of hot-rodding and heavy petting, with overtones of greasy lawlessness guaranteed to outrage staid parents. To be a teenager was to be a rebel, but some took it further than others. This is the tale of the most iconic teen killers of them all – the couple whose exploits inspired films such as *Badlands*, *Wild at Heart*, *Kalifornia*, *True Romance* and *Natural Born Killers* – Charles Starkweather and Caril Ann Fugate.

CHARLES STARKWEATHER – REBEL WITH A CAUSE

Lincoln, Nebraska, 1938. The Depression had trapped many in a vicious cycle of poverty, eking out a meagre existence in hovels on the edge of town. Guy Starkweather was a carpenter by trade, although he wasn't ideally suited for the work. Lacking physical stamina, he suffered from a weak back and arthritis, and wasn't able to work regularly. His wife Helen worked as a waitress to supplement the family income and ensure that the Starkweathers were never without food or shelter, even if the latter was characteristically a 'shack'. Charles Starkweather was born on 24 November, their third child of seven.

Charles was an outsider from birth: not only was he poor, bow-legged, red-haired and short, but he also suffered from a speech impediment and chronic short sight, neither of which was dealt with until his teens. While he was happy at home during his early childhood, his school experiences opened up a new world for him – one of trauma and pain. He was treated as an academic failure – not surprisingly, considering that he was unable to see the blackboard even from the front row – and shunned by his peers, many of whom referred to him as 'Red-Headed Peckerwood'. Starkweather was later to pinpoint his first day at school as the day hatred replaced happiness in his heart, describing in *Rebellion*, his prison-penned autobiographical rant, how the other children laughed at and ostracised him.

Starkweather's social frustration soon manifested itself in violence, and he would attack anyone who he believed was making fun of him. He derived most of his self-esteem through being well co-ordinated and strong; his only successful school subject was gymnastics. He saw himself as having a reputation as a mean fighter, an impression belied by the Starkweather remembered by his teachers: a quiet, shy young man whose school 'citizenship record' was above average. But for all of the self-mythologising that was to come later, Starkweather's sensitivity to the circumstances of his poverty was understandable:

> It didn't matter that we all loved each other, that my mother worked hard away from home to help support us children, and washed our clothes and cooked and got us off to school. All these goddamn kids cared about was 'What kind of job does your old man have? What kind of a house do you live in?' [1]

Despite Starkweather's alienation, his interests were generally similar to those of his peers in the Midwest. He enjoyed reading comics, particularly the EC horror and crime comics that would later be considered a prime cause of juvenile delinquency, and watching movies. He was a keen fan of the B-movies that played at local cinemas, particularly horror films, with their powerfully ham-fisted metaphors of social injustice, and westerns, hammering home an escapist ethos of self-determination through violence. He grew up to be a hot-rodder, and the owner of a 1949 Ford, which he'd painstakingly stripped down. But his principal passion was for hunting and firearms, his father having taught him to shoot early on: 'I rather hear the crack of a firearm than have or drive the finist car in the whole wide world'.[2]

Starkweather became more delinquent as he grew older, fighting more and occasionally hot-wiring cars to go joyriding, and was forced to transfer to a new school at the beginning of the ninth grade. Here he was to meet another delinquent, Bob Von Busch, and after the inevitable fight the two became firm friends. Both shared a love of James Dean, the contemporary icon of rebellious youth, and Starkweather, having seen Dean in *Rebel Without a Cause* at the local drive-in, began to dress like him. But extreme poverty has never helped fans keep up with their movie idols, and Starkweather was forced to scour thrift stores and second-hand clothes shops to fulfil his obsession.

Wanting financial independence, and seeing no reason to stay within an institutional system that had only brought him misery, Starkweather left school at sixteen. He soon found work at the Western Newspaper Union warehouse, loading and unloading trucks. Shortly after starting work he was knocked out in an accident involving a heavy machine lever. He later claimed that this injury left him with continual headaches and periodic bouts of confusion. But his co-workers were unsympathetic, considering him ridiculous in appearance and stupid in behaviour – his boss later described him as 'the dumbest man we had'. Because of this, and the stratified job structure at the warehouse, the new employee was landed with the worst jobs going, and felt that the persecution he'd tried to escape at school was, if anything, worse in the workplace.

But home life was looking up. Von Busch had a girlfriend, Barbara Fugate, and introduced Starkweather to Barbara's younger sister, Caril. Although Caril was only thirteen at the time, Starkweather was smitten, and the four of them went on to double-date on a regular basis.

TRUE LOVE

Caril lived in the Belmont district of Lincoln with her mother Velma, stepfather Marion Bartlett and younger sister Betty Jean. She was a pretty brunette with a rebellious attitude, which had already led to her enjoying a local reputation as 'jailbait'. She was considered a slow learner by her teachers, and had already failed a grade in elementary school.

Caril was impressed by Charles's bad-boy stance, and their relationship seemed all the more attractive the more it was opposed by her parents, who didn't consider Starkweather an eligible suitor for their middle daughter. Starkweather was, in turn, besotted with his young lover, who gave him something to live for:

Don't know why it was but being alone with her [Caril] was like owning a little world all our own . . . lying there with our arms around each other

and not talking much, just kind of tightening up
and listening to the wind blow or looking at the
same star and moving over each other's face . . . I
forgot about my bow legs when we was having
excitement. When I'd hold her in my arms and do
the things we done together, I didn't think about
being a red-headed peckerwood then. We knowed
that the world had given us to each other.[3]

Shortly after they started dating, Starkweather had
asked Caril's mother and stepfather if they would
consent to his marrying their daughter. They were
horrified at the prospect, and forced Caril to wait until
the age of majority. Charles went ahead and told his
colleagues that they were getting married anyway, word
of which got back to Velma and Marion; but the couple
were far more concerned when Starkweather started the
rumour that Fugate was pregnant with his child, a
rumour that had no basis in fact.

Charles wanted to spend more time with his lover,
and as his job wasn't working out he left and became a
garbage man; he'd now be able to leave work at 3 p.m.
and spend the rest of the day with Caril. The new job
was exceptionally badly paid, however – a mere $42 a
week – which led Starkweather back into the grinding
poverty he'd sought to escape.

Caril had been slightly injured in a crash while
driving Charles's car, and Guy Starkweather, as part
owner of the car, had been obliged to pay for damages
to the other car involved. Guy thought his son stupid
for letting Caril, a minor, drive the car, and the two had
a bitter argument, which ended in Charles's eviction
from the family home. He slept for a few nights on the
floor of newly-wedded Bob and Barbara Von Busch's
apartment, and soon had his own room in the same

boarding house. But his pay couldn't cover the rent, and he soon fell behind on his payments.

Starkweather's bitterness and sense of ill-treatment were exacerbated during his working hours, as his collection route would take him through the most affluent parts of Lincoln. Why should these people have so much when he had nothing? He at least once hurled abuse at pedestrians while driving the truck through richer areas, and began to believe that robbing a bank was the only way out of his predicament. But this alone wouldn't put these people – the haves and the people who'd mocked him all his life – on his level. As he would later state, only death was the true leveller of class and status – 'dead people are all on the same level'. [4]

THE FIRST KILLING

The trigger, the event that finally pushed Starkweather over the edge, was his inability to buy a stuffed toy dog. He'd gone to a local gas station on the last day of November to buy Caril a toy, but realised he didn't have enough cash – when he asked to buy the stuffed animal on credit, the assistant, Robert Colvert, refused.

That night, at 3 a.m., Starkweather returned to the gas station. He had with him a 12-bore shotgun he'd taken from Bob Von Busch's cousin and as many shells as he'd been able to afford. Possibly indecisive at first at the thought of actually killing somebody, he bought cigarettes and a packet of chewing gum from Colvert and then drove off. When he returned he was wearing a bandana around his face and a hunter's hat to hide his red hair, carrying the shotgun and a bag; Colvert was working on a car and didn't realise anyone was even at the station until he felt the muzzle of the shotgun between his shoulder blades.

Starkweather made Colvert fill the bag with the till's takings, which amounted to $108, then told him to open the safe – Colvert protested that only the manager had the combination, which excuse Starkweather accepted. They then drove to a nearby teenage petting area, where local teens claimed a woman known as Bloody Mary would shoot anyone who came within range of her house; the truth of this story was that the old lady was frequently pestered by teens and would discharge shotguns loaded with rock salt in their direction.

Colvert was then taken from the car. Starkweather claimed that his hostage attempted to snatch the gun from his hands, and in so doing was accidentally shot. As Colvert then attempted to stand, Starkweather shot him again at point-blank range in the head. Starkweather's claims of self-defence and accidental killing, which are common to virtually all of the slayings, are implausible to say the least, and often directly contradicted by forensic evidence, let alone by the circumstances of the killings. If Colvert hadn't been taken to Bloody Mary's neighbourhood to be killed, with the murder blamed on the old lady, then why *had* he been taken there?

The next day, after collecting Caril from school, Charles told her that he'd been involved in the robbery of the gas station, which was a major local news event. He also told her that he wasn't responsible for the murder, but later admitted that 'she was not fooled'. He painted his car a different colour, but made no other efforts to avoid detection; it was widely reported that the money stolen from the till had been all in coins, and Starkweather paid for a new set of clothes using a large amount of change.

But it didn't matter – as far as he was concerned he'd got away with it, and the shared secret intensified the bond between them. Police suspected a transient of being responsible, so Starkweather was off the hook for the time being. As a massive manhunt spread through Lincoln and the surrounding countryside, Charles spent his afternoons in his apartment with Caril, having sex, dancing and practising their knife-throwing techniques. He even bought her the stuffed toy dog he'd tried to buy earlier. Life was beautiful – until the money ran out.

THE FUGATE SLAYINGS

Six weeks after killing Colvert, Starkweather was broke again, and had been fired from his job as a garbage man. His landlady had also kicked him out of his apartment and he'd taken to sleeping in his car. It was a bitterly cold winter, and after a week he'd had enough. On 21 January he borrowed a .22 rifle from a friend, claiming that he'd arranged to go hunting with Marion Bartlett, Caril's stepfather, in an attempt to repair their relationship. The account that follows is based upon Starkweather's recollections after his arrest.

He drove to Caril's house and showed Velma a selection of carpet samples he'd picked up on his garbage route; but she was singularly unimpressed by this peace offering. He asked whether Marion was ready to go hunting or not, and, upon hearing that he wasn't, asked why. Velma told Charles that they didn't want him to see Caril any more, and they argued until Velma slapped him.

He left the house without the rifle and returned shortly afterwards to pick it up. This time Marion was there waiting for him, and literally kicked him out of the house. Hurt and incensed, Starkweather drove to a nearby public phone and called Marion's employers, explaining that Marion was ill and would be taking a few days off work. He then drove to a relative's house and parked the car, returning to Caril's house on foot. He waited, unnoticed on their back porch, for Caril to come back from school – a return heralded by a huge argument between Caril and her mother.

Starkweather went into the house again and was immediately accused by Velma of getting Caril pregnant; she hit him, as she'd done before, but this time he hit back, slapping her so hard that she fell. Marion then picked up the delinquent by the scruff of the neck and marched him to the door, but Starkweather struggled violently and kicked him, at which the two fell to the floor. Marion fled, and Charles assumed he'd gone to get a weapon; with this in mind, he loaded the .22.

When Marion ran back in clutching a claw hammer Starkweather shot him in the head. Velma then ran at him with a kitchen knife. Caril attempted to take the rifle from Charles – not because she wanted to save her mother, but because she herself wanted the privilege of blowing her 'to hell' – but he still managed to shoot Velma in the face as she tried to stab him. Dazed and bleeding heavily, she stared at her husband's killer as she clutched her youngest daughter. Starkweather responded by clubbing her with the rifle butt repeatedly until she was dead.

He then hit Betty Jean, then two and a half, who was screaming hysterically. When Caril told him that Marion still wasn't dead, he went to investigate, picking up the kitchen knife on the way. But the child wouldn't stop screaming, so Starkweather spun around and threw the knife into her throat – all those hours of practice had finally paid off. Having dispatched the youngest member of the family, Starkweather finished off Marion Bartlett by driving the same knife into his throat, 'but the knife wouldn't go in, and I just hit the top part of it with my hand, and it went in.'[5]

The adrenaline rush of killing Caril's family had left them hungry, and Caril made sandwiches while Charles watched TV, to fill the deathly silence left in the aftermath of the slaughter. But there was still some work to do: murder is a messy business, and they soon set to work clearing up the blood and disposing of the bodies. Velma was stuffed into the toilet bowl of the disused outhouse in the garden; Betty Jean was put in a small box and left on top of the same bowl; and Marion's corpse was hidden in the chicken coop, where they covered it with old rags and newspapers.

DOMESTIC BLISS

Finally they had the place to themselves. They stayed in the house for six days, discouraging visitors by way of a sign Caril had put on the front door: 'Stay a way Every Body is sick with the Flue'. They welcomed the visits of the milkman, however, from whom they could buy bread and milk on credit; Charles went into town a few times to buy essential groceries, and also got Caril a few presents, including a puppy and the latest hit records.

Other visitors were less welcome. A school friend of Caril's came on the morning of their first day playing house. She was told that Caril had flu, but she tried calling again, every day of the week; Charles and Caril didn't open the door to her after her first visit. Marion Bartlett's boss and a colleague came one day to see if Marion was well enough to go back to work, but were successfully put off by Caril, who explained that he was still ill. Barbara and Bob Von Busch also came over, but were shown Caril's sign and put off. Their suspicions had been roused, however, and Bob returned later that day with Rodney Starkweather, one of Charles's brothers.

This time Caril changed her story, tearfully begging Bob and Rodney not to come in for fear of endangering her mother's life. Bob and Rodney immediately went to the police. When the officers of the law arrived, Caril reverted to her previous story of flu; she claimed that she hadn't let the relatives in for fear that Barbara's newborn baby would catch flu. When the police asked why Bob and Rodney would have come to them over the matter, Caril complained of Bob's nosiness, and said that he did not get along well with her family. The police believed her and left, telling the Von Buschs later that there was no cause for concern.

Bob and Rodney were unconvinced, and sent a friend of Caril's over to check. The friend was told a third story – that Charles and another man were in the house, armed and holding Caril hostage. The friend told her father, who waited until the following day, a Monday, before notifying the police. That same Monday Caril's grandmother, Pansy Street, alarmed at tales of flu coming from the house, paid them a visit. Caril told her grandmother that Velma's life was in danger if the grandmother came in; Street didn't believe this, and went to the police immediately. The police visited again, found what appeared to be an empty house and left, judging Street to be a busybody.

Bob Von Busch and Guy Starkweather finally persuaded the police later on that day to take them seriously, pointing to Caril's conflicting stories and Charles's disappearance – nobody had seen him for a week – as cause for suspicion. Caril's grandmother returned to the house accompanied by two officers, who this time ignored the flu sign and entered to search the house, which they found empty. Shortly afterwards Bob Von Busch found his father-in-law's body decaying in the outhouse, and a warrant was issued for the arrest of Charles Starkweather for suspected murder.

ON THE RUN

The couple knew it was time to get out of town, but they were badly prepared. Starkweather's car was in poor condition, and had a flat tyre. Charles tried to repair it quickly the best he could, but by the time they'd reached Bennet, sixteen miles out of Lincoln, he knew the car wasn't going much further. Fortunately, he had a hunting buddy who lived nearby – 72-year-old August Meyer – whose farm could be a good place to hole up.

As they approached the farm, on 27 January 1958, their car got stuck in the thawing mud. Irascible after their unsuccessful attempts to push it, they went up to the farmhouse, where Meyer met them on the back porch. Following an argument during which, according to Starkweather, Meyer fetched a rifle and shot at him, Starkweather shot his old friend at point-blank range with a shotgun. Caril claims to have stayed on the track for the killing, although Starkweather was later to claim, 'She said we ought to go up and blast the shit out of him because he didn't shovel his lane.'[6]

He then hid the body in an outbuilding near the farmhouse, covering it with a blanket; when Meyer's dog began to bark at him it too was killed. They ransacked the house, stealing the $100 they found along with Meyer's gun, eating and then resting. After a short sleep they went out to try moving the car again. A neighbour drove past and offered to help; the killer couple accepted the offer, had their car towed out, and paid the neighbour $2 for his trouble.

They drove up to Meyer's house using a different route and parked the car. Charles ran into the outbuilding to check on Meyer's corpse, but to his horror saw that the blanket was missing. Convinced that somebody had found the body, they drove away at speed, but on pausing for food at a roadside café Charles realised that the blanket could have been moved by the wind. They decided to return to Meyer's farmhouse, but used their original route and were soon once again stuck in the mud.

They didn't bother moving it this time, but grabbed the guns and walked back to the main road to hitch a lift. They didn't have to wait long – seventeen-year-old Robert Jensen and his fiancée, sixteen-year-old Carol King, preppy kids a million miles away from the white-trash lovers, stopped and promised to drive them to the nearest phone. But Starkweather had other plans. As soon as they were in the car he jammed the barrel of the shotgun into Jensen's neck, robbed the couple, then ordered Jensen to turn the car around and drive towards Meyer's farm. They stopped by a disused storm cellar, just before the farm. Starkweather forced the pair from the car and down the steps leading to the cellar, shooting Jensen six times in the head en route. Typically, Starkweather was later to claim that he'd been acting in self-defence.

The events surrounding the death of Carol King are less clear. When the bodies were found, Carol was lying on top of Robert, and had also been killed with a shot to the head; but she'd been partially stripped, with her jeans and knickers around her ankles, and her top around her neck. Her torso was smeared with mud and blood, and her genitals had been repeatedly stabbed with a sharp object. The autopsy would show that there was no semen present.

Starkweather changed his testimony regarding Carol King several times, claiming first that he'd killed her, and subsequently that Caril had. In the latter version, he claimed that he'd stripped the corpse so that he could have sex with it, but had been unable to do so owing to the cold. When he returned to the car, Caril thought he'd gone ahead with the necrophile act, and had attacked Carol's corpse in a fit of jealousy. It is also conceivable that Starkweather, unable to rape King, stabbed the body in a frustrated sublimation of the sex act. Caril claimed simply that she'd stayed in the car while Charles killed both Robert Jensen and Carol King.

THE WARD MASSACRE
Thanks to Jensen and King, Starkweather and Fugate had a new car, and planned to leave Nebraska – they could stay with Charles's brother in Washington. But this new car wasn't running too well, either, and Charles was tired, and perhaps homesick, for they drove back to Lincoln, their hometown. They checked out the Bartlett residence and, seeing it surrounded with police cars, drove into the wealthy part of town and slept in the car.

The next day Starkweather's Ford had been spotted near the Meyer farm. Police raided the Meyer residence, and soon found the bodies of the farmer and the young couple. The manhunt spread to Bennet and the countryside nearby. None imagined that the couple would have returned to Lincoln.

One night in a cold, cramped car was enough for Starkweather, and the next day they drove around looking for a suitably opulent place to stay; Starkweather was familiar with the area and many of its residents from his days as a garbage man. They eventually decided on the home of C Lauer Ward, president of the Capital Steel Works. When they rang the bell at around 8.30 a.m. Ward had already gone to work, and Lillian Fencl, the 51-year-old deaf maid, let them in. The couple forced Fencl to the kitchen at gunpoint and, realising that she was deaf, wrote notes instructing her to continue preparing breakfast for Mrs Ward, and to lock one of the family dogs in the basement.

When 46-year-old Clara Ward, Lauer's wife, came down for breakfast, she kept her cool and agreed to co-operate. Caril was left on guard in the kitchen as Charles wandered around the house, marvelling at the lifestyle of the rich couple. Upon finding the library, he called to Mrs Ward to fix him pancakes and serve them to him there. This done, he decided that he didn't want pancakes: he wanted waffles. Mrs Ward acquiesced to his every demand – the master waited on the servant. Starkweather was jubilant.

In the early afternoon she asked permission to go upstairs and change her shoes. Starkweather agreed, but after a few minutes grew suspicious and started up the stairs after her. As he climbed, Mrs Ward appeared, armed, so Starkweather would claim, with a .22 rifle, which she fired at him. She then turned to run, but Starkweather threw a knife, which plunged between her shoulder blades. As he dragged her into the master bedroom, he was irritated by the yapping of a poodle, the Wards' second dog, whose neck he duly broke with the butt of Mrs Ward's .22. He then bound and gagged her with strips of torn sheeting.

Starkweather then rang his father, to inform him that Bob Von Busch was next on their hit list, for having come between the star-crossed lovers. He then wrote a long note to the police, attempting in a barely literate rant to explain why he'd gone on the rampage – Bob Von Busch was one of the principal targets of the rant, which is curious considering that he seems to have been one of Starkweather's only friends. Perhaps Starkweather blamed Von Busch for having drawn the police's attention to the odd goings-on at the Bartlett residence.

As they waited for Mr Ward to come home, they hid the car they'd stolen from Jensen and prepared the

Wards' Packard for a getaway, filling it with food and washing and changing their clothes. The *Lincoln Journal* was delivered during the afternoon, and the pair were impressed with their new-found celebrity – they'd made the headlines.

Mr Ward appears to have been the best prepared of all the couple's victims, as on his return home he leaped upon Starkweather before the killer had a chance to shoot. The two struggled, and Starkweather managed to push Ward down into the basement; but in the struggle he'd dropped his gun, which had followed Ward down the stairs. Starkweather rushed down to fetch it, and, as Ward forced his way up the stairs, shot him in the back. Seriously wounded, Ward managed to make it to the front door, which he opened just as Starkweather shot him again. This time Ward was dead, although it didn't stop one of the homicidal pair stabbing him in the neck – just to be sure.

Their mute witness, the maid, was next. They forced her upstairs to a bedroom and tied her to a bed. What happened next is contested, with a substantially different version of events offered by Starkweather and Fugate. Starkweather claimed that Fugate killed the maid by stabbing her in a frenzied attack, and that Caril had also finished off Mrs Ward, mutilating the body in the process. Fugate claimed the responsibility for both killings belonged to Starkweather. Whatever the case, the two then fled in the stolen Packard.

The bodies were discovered by one of Ward's cousins the next day. When Governor Anderson, a friend of Ward's, was notified, he called out the National Guard. Armed troops roamed the streets, the city was sealed off, and aircraft were sent in to scout the area for the Wards' Packard.

CAPTURE AND ARREST

With the Packard Starkweather felt that he could make it to Washington. They drove through the night, and stopped on the Wyoming border at first light, spending what little money they'd found in the Ward house on soft drinks and petrol. As they drove into Wyoming, they looked for another car, worried that a description of the Packard would have been sent out; they were in fact twice reported to the police as acting suspiciously, but neither call was followed up.

It was still early when Starkweather spotted a Buick, a far more discreet car than the Packard: this would suit his needs perfectly. He pulled up alongside and woke the driver – a travelling salesman named Merle Collison – announcing that he wanted to swap cars. Collison's reply evidently didn't suit Starkweather's mood, as the salesman was then shot repeatedly in the head and body.

The shotgun blasts had left Collison's corpse jammed at the front of the car, and Starkweather was unable to release the brake and drive away. As he tried to wrest the body from the car, a passing motorist, Joseph Sprinkle, stopped and asked if he could help. Starkweather turned, gun in hand, and replied that he could – he could help move the body, or he'd be killed too. As Sprinkle walked towards Starkweather he tried to grab the gun from the killer and the two struggled in the middle of the road.

Unluckily for Starkweather, Deputy Sheriff William Romer happened to be driving past. When he saw the men fighting he stopped and approached them, where-upon Caril ran towards him, shouting out that one of the men was Starkweather, and that she'd been kidnap-ped by him. Starkweather ran for the Packard and fled, while Romer couldn't shoot with Caril in the way. The policeman shoved Caril in the back of the car and started to chase the rampaging teen.

Starkweather drove east at high speed towards the town of Douglas, and Romer called for reinforcements, which duly joined the chase. By the time they went through Douglas, Starkweather was hitting a hundred miles an hour, and beyond the town he reached a hundred and twenty. But the police cars kept up with him, shooting all the while. One shot shattered the rear windscreen, and almost immediately Starkweather stopped the Packard. He'd seen blood and thought he'd been hit, but there was only a small wound where he'd been cut by shards of flying glass – arresting officers were later to refer to him as a 'yellow son of a bitch'. Starkweather climbed out of the car, smoothed his hair and tucked in his shirt, then lay down, taking his time over following the orders of the police, who shot at his feet.

ON TRIAL

Starkweather, when arrested, claimed initially that Caril hadn't been involved in any of the murders. He was charged with first-degree murder, for having killed Robert Jensen, and jailed in Wyoming, but was soon moved to Nebraska at his request, possibly to avoid the Wyoming gas chamber. Starkweather was by now a minor celebrity, and his enterprising father sold signed photographs of the murderous youth outside the jail and then later the courtroom.

The trial began on 5 May, with much of the debate concerning Starkweather's sanity. Starkweather's defence team wanted to show that the killer was insane and suffering from abnormalities of the brain, but to the teen and his family the stigma of insanity was a step too far, and they insisted that Starkweather be treated as sane; in any case, Starkweather appreciated his new-found celebrity status, and felt that 'nobody remembers a crazy man'. The defence, notwithstanding Starkweather's protests, entered a plea of 'not guilty by reason of insanity' and Starkweather was subjected to a series of psychiatric tests, by the end of which he was found by the prosecution to be 'legally sane'. If Starkweather were to be committed to a mental institution, they argued, he'd be out in no time, having escaped paying the price for his crimes.

As the trial progressed, the relationship between Starkweather and Fugate deteriorated irremediably; when he discovered that she'd accused him of taking her hostage, he pointed out that she could have 'escaped' at any time, and implicated her in the mutilations of certain victims. Whatever the truth of this, Starkweather's guilt didn't seem to be in question, and on 23 May, after less than 24 hours of deliberation, the jury found him guilty of first-degree murder, and specified that he pay the highest price – the death penalty.

But Starkweather wouldn't be executed until June the following year, and he spent his time at the Nebraska State Penitentiary writing his autobiography, *Rebellion*, and drawing and painting. His psychology was of interest to the prison psychiatrist, James Reinhardt, who conducted a series of interviews with his homicidal subject, which would later form the basis for a book on the case. Two points from the interviews are of particular interest. The first is that Starkweather displayed no remorse at all for the killings, and the second that the killer had an anthropomorphised image of death, a female figure who would appear to him in his dreams:

All I could see would be the part from the waist up. It was a kind of half human and half bear . . . only it didn't have no neck. It just tapered off from a big chest to a small pointed head . . . it didn't have no arms and no ears.[7]

Starkweather's relationship to this figure is clarified here: 'Eleven people dead who wasn't expecting her and me here waiting.'[8] That Starkweather had a death wish appears likely – why, otherwise, did he return again and again to the scene of his crimes, in an apparent bid for capture?

When Caril Ann Fugate was tried as an accomplice in the Jensen slaying, her defence maintained that she had been held against her will for the duration of Starkweather's rampage. One of the points used to prove this was that she'd been buggered by Starkweather, which was considered evidence of an abusive, nonconsensual relationship. But the jury didn't buy it – Charles's accounts of Caril's responsibility for the mutilation of certain victims were too convincing, and the fourteen-year-old had damned herself by contradicting key statements over the course of her interrogation and trial: she was found guilty of murder on 20 November. 'Even fourteen-year-old girls must realise they cannot go on eight-day murder sprees',[9] said the prosecuting attorney in summing up. But Fugate's youth meant that she couldn't be sent to the chair, and she was given a life sentence, to be served at the euphemistically named Nebraska Center for Women. She maintained her hostage story until her release on parole in 1976, a born-again Christian.

Starkweather, nonchalant to the last, was executed on 25 June 1959. He had no final words. Despite his conviction that the chair was a relatively painless and efficient dealer of death, it took three pulls of the switch before Starkweather was finally killed, taking him to a world he believed 'couldn't be as bad as this one'. His body was claimed by his family and buried at Wyuka Cemetery.

That Starkweather's exploits were to be immortalised in celluloid decades after his death is fitting considering his own love of exploitation movies. He can be seen as a patchwork construct of different movie personae: the western anti-hero, defining his rugged individualism through violence; the *Wild One* rebel, a hot-rodding teen with a hatred of authority expressed through posture and rock 'n' roll; and Frankenstein's monster, a creature damned from birth by the society that created him, a monster whose love could never be understood. Despite the fact that it took a long time for Hollywood to exploit the Starkweather and Fugate story, Charles's stardom was recognised by some at the time of his death: a group of thirty-odd denim- and leather-clad teens hung out by the prison walls, drinking beer, revving their cars and playing their car radios full-blast, come to pay tribute to an original rock 'n' roll rebel.

NOTES
1. Starkweather, quoted in Sargeant, Jack, *Born Bad*, Creation Books, London, 1996, p. 14.
2. Ibid., p. 15.
3. Ibid., p. 25.
4. Ibid., p. 21.
5. Starkweather, quoted in Reinhardt, James, *The Murderous Trail of Charles Starkweather*, publisher unknown.
6. Sargeant, op. cit. p. 37.
7. Ibid., p. 71.
8. Ibid., p. 71.
9. Ibid., p. 72.

4. OH, MANCHESTER, SO MUCH TO ANSWER FOR* – IAN BRADY AND MYRA HINDLEY

'I know that what I was involved in was indefensible in every respect'

— Myra Hindley, *Guardian*, 18 December 1995

'I led the life that other people would only think about. That's why they are so obsessed with the case for over twenty years. They relate to it: the hideousness, fascinating and horrible'

— Ian Brady, to author, in *Brady and Hindley – Genesis of the Moors Murders*, 1986

INTRODUCTION

The names of Myra Hindley and Ian Brady elicit equal measures of repulsion and fascination, even now, over three decades after they committed their heinous crimes. Details of the appalling death of Lesley Ann Downey – stripped, tortured, raped and then suffocated, with much of her ordeal recorded on a tape recorder, and her obscene humiliation captured on Brady's camera – shocked the British public when they were first published, and continue to do so to this day. The callous treatment of the bodies of the children – their first four victims dumped on the bleak Yorkshire Moors with the intention of denying their parents a body to bury – has also caused reactions of outrage and horror.

The lives of the incarcerated Brady and Hindley have been reported in detail in the British tabloid press, who will not let us forget they are monsters beyond redemption who should never be freed. Any legal moves by

---

* From the Smiths' 'Suffer Little Children'.

Hindley to challenge the terms of her life sentence are reacted to with outrage by the newspapers, ready with a condemnatory quote from a victim's relative or a Tory MP. Reports on the killers' poor health (Hindley's cancer, Brady's self-inflicted damage caused by years on hunger strike) are accompanied by cries of glee.

As icons of evil, the police mugshots of Brady and Hindley, aggressively eyeing the camera with a decadent arrogance, are without parallel. Like David Bailey's portraits of the Krays, from roughly the same period, these photographs have gained an almost iconoclastic quality in their ability to portray the flipside of the optimistic 1960s. The image of Hindley continues to inflame. A portrait of her by the artist Marcus Harvey, replicating the infamous photograph by the use of hundreds of children's handprints, was physically attacked and damaged when it was shown as part of London's controversial 'Sensations' exhibition at the Royal Academy in 1997.

Unsurprisingly, the tabloids had a field day – appalled that this image was being exhibited as 'art' – and produced shock-horror headlines echoing decades of similar outrage to such phenomena as 'No One Is Innocent', a hit record by Ronnie Biggs and the Sex Pistols in which Brady and Hindley are mentioned, Moors Murderers T-shirts which were for sale in London, and the Smiths' song 'Suffer Little Children', which explicitly refers to Hindley and several of the victims by name.

It is conceivable that the legacy of Hindley and Brady will be that their acts are remembered as a manifestation of the ultimate evil, a dark cloud obscuring the optimism of the 'swinging' decade in which their crimes were committed.

IAN BRADY

Ian Duncan Stewart was born on 2 January 1938 in the Rotten Row Maternity Hospital, Glasgow. His mother, Margaret Stewart, was a 28-year-old waitress. On Ian's birth certificate the father was described as 'Husb. Deceased', which was certainly untrue, as Margaret had never married. She always maintained that Ian's father was a journalist on a local newspaper who had died before the child was born. Margaret found it difficult both to keep working and to look after her baby; she put an advert in a shop window offering the child for adoption.

A couple named John and Mary Sloane responded, and Ian, who was less than six months old, was passed into their care. The Sloanes, who had four children of their own, lived in a tenement in Camden Street in the Gorbals district; Margaret agreed to pay for her child's upkeep and said she would visit each day. Ian was given the name Ian Sloane; he called Mrs Sloane 'Auntie' and his mother, when she was able to see him, he called 'Peggy'.

His mother's visits became less and less frequent. The young Ian was an intelligent child, but was antisocial, felt alienated from other children and was prone to violent tantrums. He also differed from other children in that he had no religious beliefs: aged five, when his class were asked by a teacher whether they believed in God, Ian was the only child to reply that he did not. A contemporary of his at school recalls sadistic incidents including habitual cruelty to cats and an occasion when the young Ian tied him up with string and attempted to set his clothes on fire with burning newspapers.

When Ian was twelve, his mother married a man named Patrick Brady; the couple moved to Manchester and no effort was made to see Ian until he was sixteen. A year after his mother married, Ian found out that he was illegitimate and his outlook on the world around him became markedly more negative. He also formed a fascination with Nazism and Hitler that would continue well into his adult life. He started stealing from shops and breaking into houses. On several occasions the police apprehended him, and he appeared in court three times between the ages of thirteen and sixteen. The final time Ian escaped a custodial sentence, but only on the condition that he move down to Manchester to live with his mother and her husband. For three years before his departure from Glasgow, Ian had a regular girlfriend, a girl named Evelyn Grant, but the relationship ended when he pulled a knife on her in a fit of jealousy.

In December 1954 the youth arrived at his mother and stepfather's home in Moss Side, Manchester. During 1955, the Brady family moved home twice, ending up in Cuttell Street, less than a mile from Bannock Street in Gorton, where a thirteen-year-old schoolgirl named Myra Hindley was growing up. During that year the Glaswegian obtained gainful employment: he was for a short time a porter at Smithfield Market, but this came to an end in November 1955 when he was caught stealing lead seals from boxes of bananas. On this occasion the court was not so lenient and Ian Brady, as he was now known, was sentenced to two years in borstal. Now aged seventeen, Brady had his first spell of incarceration in Strangeways Prison, a two-month spell in which he mixed with hardened adult criminals. He was then sent to a borstal camp in Hatfield, Yorkshire, where he was involved in brewing illegal alcohol. After an incident in which Brady had a punch-up with a warder, he was moved to a borstal within Hull Prison. During his time there Brady received an education in crime from his contacts with other inmates. He tried to gather accomplices in order to organise safe-breaking and bank jobs on his release; he dreamed of becoming a big-time criminal.

Brady served his time at Hull and was released in November 1957. Returning to his mother's home in Manchester he managed to get a blue-collar job in a brewery, where he was employed between April and October 1958. He then saw an office job advertised that interested him. Wearing the suit he had been bought by his mother and stepfather for his 21st birthday, in early 1959 Ian was interviewed for a clerical job as a bookkeeper at Millwards Merchandising, a company involved in the wholesale trade of chemicals. Despite his inexperience and criminal record, he was given the job.

MYRA HINDLEY

Myra Hindley was born on 23 July 1942 in the working-class district of Gorton, Manchester. She was the product of a mixed Catholic–Protestant marriage. Her mother, Hettie, worked in a local factory, and her father, Bob, had been conscripted into the British Army's Parachute Regiment, where his service continued until the end of war with Germany in May 1945. On his return home Myra's father got a job labouring and continued his participation in amateur boxing, and his pugnacious nature resulted in his being frequently involved in fights and brawls in local pubs, where he was a habitual drinker. His violence extended into his home life: Hettie, Myra and her sister Maureen (born in 1946) were frequently physically attacked by Bob. Myra Hindley gives her version of the results of this violence and bullying in her 1995 letter published by the *Guardian*; she notes that her father's behaviour had taught her 'lessons in dominance and control' and that her upbringing had resulted in her feeling that 'emotions should not be openly displayed otherwise I would be vulnerable'.

After Maureen was born, the Hindleys found it difficult to cope with the demands that two children put upon them. Myra was encouraged by Bob and Hettie to spend more time at her maternal grandmother Ellen's house, a few minutes' walk away from her parents' home. Ellen Maybury made a bedroom for Myra in her house, and was responsible for bringing up the little girl herself, although Myra made daily visits to her parents' house. She was a pupil at Peacock Street Primary School, but, with an IQ of 109, Myra was not academically gifted, although she showed promise at English and was proficient at sports, particularly netball and athletics. She failed her eleven-plus exams (taken when a child was eleven years of age to determine which type of school he or she would be sent to), and was educated at Ryder Brow Secondary Modern School, where a school report assessed her behaviour as 'satisfactory' but her attendance 'consistently unsatisfactory'.

A traumatic event occurred when Myra was fifteen: in June 1957 a friend named Michael Higgins drowned in a reservoir. Myra, distraught with grief, turned to religion and took instruction in Catholicism. She left school and during the next few years endured a series of dull clerical jobs. She had the usual spare-time pursuits of other teenagers in the late 1950s – going to coffee bars and pubs, listening to pop music and going out with boys. Myra changed her appearance to look more fashionable: she now had her hair dyed pink or white and put on layers of make-up and mascara.

In 1959 she became engaged to a local boy, Ronnie Sinclair, who worked at the Co-op, but six months later the couple parted. Myra was looking for a more exciting life than marriage to Ronnie and having his children, but she did not know exactly what it was she wanted or how she could obtain it. She investigated the possibility of moving away from Manchester and getting a job in London, but to no avail. She applied for, and was offered, a job at Millwards Merchandising.

In January 1961 she started work there, to be paid wages of £8.10s (£8.50) per week. On her first day she was introduced to her new workmates. Ian Brady's Scottish accent and fastidious black clothing made him stand out from the others. On that first day Myra learned that Brady would be one of the men she would be taking shorthand dictation from. In her 1995 *Guardian* letter she writes of feeling 'an immediate and fatal attraction' towards Brady. This attraction would soon become more intense.

FATAL ATTRACTION

Ian Brady appeared an aloof, fascinating and mysterious character to Myra. He seemed detached from those around him and unwilling or unable to take part in the social life of the office. At lunchtimes Brady would either go off alone to place bets on horses, or would be seen at his desk reading books. Ian would dictate letters to Myra, but when she attempted conversation he was not forthcoming. Occasionally he would direct withering remarks at her, but most of the time he ignored her. This caused Myra Hindley to suffer 'a year of emotional torture' while she fantasised about being married to the sullen and moody Scot.

Myra wrote a diary in which she logged her feelings for Ian. During the seven months in which she wrote it, she moved between curiosity as to whether he was 'courting', declarations of her love for him ('I hope he loves me and will marry me some day') and her disillusion at being again rejected by him ('He has killed all the love I had for him'). Towards the end of the year, Ian's attitude towards the infatuated blonde appears to have softened: she would join him in his office to eat her packed lunch, and they would talk.

Following the Christmas party at Millwards on 22 December 1961, Ian asked Myra if she would like to go out with him later that evening for a drink; the delighted girl agreed. The following night they went to the cinema. The film was Ian's choice: *Trial At Nuremberg*. The relationship progressed and Myra learned more about Ian's interests. He was fascinated by the Nazis and by German culture; Myra copied Ian by attempting to learn German. He would discuss Nazi theories of race with Myra. Brady expressed a violent dislike of blacks and Jews and the love-struck Myra Hindley found herself agreeing with him.

Brady had records of Hitler's speeches, to which they would listen in rapt attention. He encouraged Myra to read his favourite books, which, apart from an English translation of *Mein Kampf*, included Dostoyevsky's *Crime and Punishment* and works by de Sade. Brady had strong views on other matters. An atheist, he mocked religion and criticised Myra's Roman Catholic beliefs; he also spoke of his dislike of children and antipathy towards being a father.

Myra had been a virgin when they met. She had sexual intercourse with Brady on their second date, but Ian's demands quickly became sadomasochistic: as well as whipping her bare buttocks, he demanded anal sex and on several occasions made her put objects into his rectum while he masturbated. Brady had several cameras and the equipment to develop and print his own black-and-white photos. He took a series of pictures of himself and Myra in explicit pornographic poses.

Myra Hindley has claimed that the only time these photographs could have been taken was when she was drugged by Ian, and accused him of having given her alcohol laced with his grandmother's sleeping pills; but, as there are several series of photographs that appear to be taken on different occasions, this seems unlikely. Hindley claims that she became furious with him after he admitted drugging her against her will, and as a consequence of this, and in an attempt to leave Brady, she went to London to be interviewed for a job in Germany. She also claims that on her return to Manchester Ian was waiting for her at the railway station, and that he persuaded her not to accept the job abroad and to continue the relationship.

Soon they were virtually living together, and Ian moved many of his belongings into Myra's grandmother's house. Ellen Maybury went to bed early, so usually the couple had the place to themselves. If they were not at home in the evenings, they would be at the cinema – usually watching X-certificate or horror films. Myra would get on the back of Ian's motorbike and they would go on a journey, out to the desolate Yorkshire Moors, which Ian felt so drawn towards, because they reminded him of the Scottish countryside he had visited as a child.

As their relationship developed, Myra started wearing the boots, short skirts and leather jackets that Ian found attractive. Her hair was now dyed in increasingly flamboyant and garish colours. Brady showed his affection for Myra by giving her the nickname 'Hessie', a name redolent of both the concert pianist Myra Hess and Hitler's deputy Rudolph Hess. She called him 'Neddy', after a character in the BBC radio series *The Goon Show*.

Ian and Myra discussed how pleasurable it would be to abduct and rape someone; for Myra it may have been an enjoyable and perverse fantasy, but Ian was deadly serious. The pair discussed bank jobs they would pull off; like Ian, Myra now had fantasies of becoming a big-time criminal. To this end, and at Ian's suggestion, she took driving lessons and bought a van. She also joined a shooting club in order that she and her lover could gain access to firearms, and after a few practice sessions was able to buy two pistols from members of the Cheadle Rifle Club. She was becoming moulded to Brady's desires as her own self became dominated and fractured; as Myra put it in the *Guardian* letter, 'He had a powerful personality, a magnet-like charisma into which my own personality, my whole self, became almost totally subsumed'.

12 JULY 1963 – THE MURDER OF PAULINE READE

Sixteen-year-old Pauline Reade had been in the year below Myra's sister Maureen at school. She lived with her brother Paul and her parents Amos and Joan in a house two doors away from David Smith, who was her ex-boyfriend and was now going out with Maureen. At around 7.30 on the evening of Friday, 12 July, she said goodbye to her parents and left home, intending to go to a dance in a local club. Shortly after she had left home, Myra shouted out to her from the parked van, and asked the teenager to accompany her to the Moors, where she wanted help finding a glove that she had lost, promising to recompense the girl for her efforts by giving her some pop records that she said were in the back of the van.

Myra drove off towards the Moors, with Ian following at a distance on his motorcycle. Hindley's account of what followed after their meeting up on the Saddleworth Moor is that Ian and Pauline went off together, Ian then returning by himself to the van to inform Myra that he had raped the child and then killed her by slitting her throat. Using a spade that had been put in Myra's vehicle, they dug a deep hole and buried the body.

Ian Brady gives a different version of events: in a letter to newspapers published in 1990 he mentions Myra's 'physical participation' in both the sexual attack and murder of Pauline Reade.

Pauline Reade's body remained on the Moors until July 1987, after Myra Hindley had agreed to help police and indicate where the child was buried.

23 NOVEMBER 1963 – THE MURDER OF JOHN KILBRIDE

Twelve-year-old John Kilbride lived in Ashton-Under-Lyne, a town just outside Manchester. Patrick Kilbride, his father, was an Irish labourer who worked on building sites. His mother Sheila had seven children to bring up, John being the eldest. That Saturday, the day after the world had been shocked by the assassination of the US President John F Kennedy, John Kilbride spent the afternoon at the cinema with a friend named John Ryan, and the pair then went on to a nearby market. At around 5.30 p.m. that afternoon the boys separated, with Ryan catching a bus home. Myra and Ian were in a hired Ford Anglia car; Myra wore a black wig at Brady's suggestion – he thought her bright blonde hair made it more likely that she would be recognised by any possible witnesses.

According to Hindley, Ian approached Kilbride in the street and lured him into the car with the promise of a bottle of sherry. Once again, a search for a missing glove was suggested and Myra and her passengers headed for the Saddleworth Moor, where Kilbride was assaulted and anally raped by Ian Brady, who then strangled the boy with a length of string after finding that the knife he had brought with him was not sharp enough to cause fatal injuries. As with the previous murder, Myra helped him bury the body. The rented car was then thoroughly cleaned, inside and out, in an attempt to ensure that no forensic evidence was left behind.

John Kilbride's body was found by police on 21 October 1965.

16 JUNE 1964 – THE MURDER OF KEITH BENNETT

At around 7 p.m. on that Tuesday, Winifred Johnson said goodbye to her son Keith Bennett, a bespectacled twelve-year-old, as they were leaving their home in the Longsight district of Manchester: Winnie to go and play bingo, and Keith to go and stay overnight with his grandmother, who lived less than a mile away. The boy was never to return home. He was picked up by Hindley and Brady in Myra's own vehicle – a second-hand Mini van that she had recently bought. They asked the boy if he could help them move some boxes from an off-licence, and Keith agreed. According to Hindley, on arrival at Saddleworth Moor, Brady went off with Keith Bennett and raped and murdered him by strangling him with string. He also took a photograph of Keith with his naked buttocks exposed and covered in blood. Brady buried the body alone, using a spade he had concealed nearby for such a purpose. The pair drove back to Granny Maybury's house, where they washed their clothing and burned their shoes. Myra's van was given a thorough cleaning.

Keith Bennett's body has never been found, despite apparent efforts by Hindley in 1987 and in 2001 to direct police to his grave.

BRADY, HINDLEY AND THE SMITHS

Born in 1948, David Smith was illegitimate, the son of Joyce Hull and John James Smith. During his early childhood he was brought up by his grandparents, receiving occasional visits from his alcoholic father. When David was nine, John James Smith took him to live in a filthy room in a lodging house in Wiles Street, Gorton. By his teens David Smith was a young man with a string of convictions for violence and larceny behind him. He succeeded in one legitimate field, becoming a skilled boxer, before being expelled from school at the age of fifteen following an assault on the headmaster.

Myra's younger sister Maureen, aged eighteen, married sixteen-year-old David Smith at a register office in August 1964. At the time of the wedding, Maureen was seven months pregnant with Smith's child. The newlyweds moved into David's lodgings in Wiles Street. Smith was a good-looking young man who wore the teen fashions of the time – in Smith's case 'rocker' clothing: black jeans and leather jackets.

Brady saw a potential acolyte in Smith, and the two couples would often meet up and go off in Myra's car to the Moors, where Brady would engage Smith in long discussions about how to commit the perfect bank robbery. In wine-fuelled conversations in Wiles Street and at Myra's grandmother's home, Brady would hold forth on his philosophy of life, his view on the pleasures of crime, violence and pornography, his admiration for de Sade and Hitler and hatred for Jews and blacks. The pair would go out on the Moors together and have target-practice sessions using Myra's pistols. David Smith was intrigued, impressed and flattered by the older man's attentions. In Fred Harrison's book, *Brady and Hindley – Genesis of the Moors Murders*, Smith hints at a physical attraction between himself and Ian Brady:

. . . the buzz of teasing a friend, arms around
shoulders like buddies, only Myra didn't like it too

much, relegated to girls' talk with baby sister . . .
even that was part of the buzz and tease.

During one of their late-night debates, a drunken
Brady, testing Smith as to how far he would go in the
course of a robbery, told him that he had killed three or
four people and that he had taken photographs of his
victims after they had been killed. Speaking to Smith for
the first time of the murders that had been committed,
Brady described how he and Myra lured young people
into their car before taking them home to be killed, after
which the bodies were buried on the moor. Testing
Smith further, Brady offered to kill one of David's
enemies, a man named Tony Latham. The murder plan
fell flat when a photograph of Latham that Smith planned
to take in a pub to show to Brady failed to materialise.
David Smith had forgotten to put any film in the camera.

An incensed Brady planned to kill Smith because he
felt he could no longer trust him; allegedly Myra made
him change his mind because the death of Smith would
hurt her sister Maureen. Brady relented; Smith would be
kept as a potential ally. Smith's loyalty to Brady and
willingness to participate in murder would be tested at
a later date.

During 1964 Ellen Maybury, along with Ian and
Myra, were relocated to 16 Wardle Brook Avenue, a
house on a newly built estate. Their home in Gorton, ten
miles away, was to be demolished as part of a modern-
isation programme by Manchester City Council. Ian and
Myra were pleased with this new home, and set about
decorating and furnishing it. He would move in with
Myra completely by early 1965. Granny Ellen made no
complaint about this, despite the fact that in Manchester
in 1965 it was rare for unmarried people to be openly
living together.

26 DECEMBER 1964 – THE MURDER OF LESLEY ANN DOWNEY

On Boxing Day 1964, Ian and Myra had the house in Wardle Brook Avenue to themselves. Granny Maybury was out visiting her son Jim; there had been an agreement that her granddaughter would drive her back home that evening, but on arriving at her Uncle Jim's house around mid-afternoon Myra refused to take her, saying that the roads would be too dangerous to go back on. The old lady slept on Jim's living-room floor that night.

Lesley Ann Downey was the ten-year-old daughter of Ann Downey. Her father Terry had separated from his wife. Lesley lived with her mother, her then boyfriend, Alan West, and her three brothers in Ancoats. At around 4.30 that afternoon Lesley Ann, together with her brothers and some friends, went off in a group to a funfair at nearby Miles Platting. After about an hour, the children had spent their pocket money and started off on the walk home. But Lesley Ann didn't go with them – she wanted to stay and enjoy the atmosphere.

Hindley and Brady had planned the murder of another child for that day, and had noticed the posters around Manchester advertising the funfair. Myra, wearing her black wig, drove off in her car with Ian in the passenger seat. They took some packages with them, and on arrival at the funfair took these with them. They then approached Lesley Ann, telling her they needed help getting these parcels back to the car and then to their house. Promising her that they would give her some money and drive her home afterwards, they accompanied Lesley to the car. The little girl got in and was driven to Wardle Brook Avenue.

As they went into the house and took the child up to their bedroom, Ian switched their portable tape recorder on and carried it with him. The sixteen-minute tape, later played in court during their trial, details the events leading up to Lesley Ann's death. This obscenely horrific and harrowing but very telling recording pointed to the full and apparently willing participation of Myra Hindley in the abuse and torture of the child. The tape is mostly concerned with Hindley forcibly trying to get Downey to put something into her mouth. The recording ends with what sounds like a camera tripod being opened.

At their trial in 1966 Brady told the court that he alone had gagged the child, and that Hindley had played no part in this. In a confession to prison aquaintance Rena Duffy in prison twenty years later, Myra Hindley said that she had placed the gag – a handkerchief – in Lesley Ann's mouth. In Peter Topping's interviews with Hindley published in 1989 (see bibliography), she gives her account of events. (Topping was the detective who led the reinvestigation into the Moors murders in the 1980s.)

Hindley says that, after the tape recorder was switched off, Brady made the child undress and took photographs. He then told Myra to go and run a bath for the little girl, and not to come into the bedroom until he told her. When she came in some twenty minutes later the girl was dead. She was on the bed, naked apart from a scarf. There was blood running down her legs and strangulation marks on her neck.

Contrary to Hindley's accounts in her interviews with police, when cross-examined at her trial and in her statements to the media, Brady said in a written statement to the press in January 1990 that Hindley had insisted on strangling Lesley Ann Downey herself, using a silken cord.

Downey's body was washed in the bath; at around 8 p.m. Hindley and Brady carried the corpse out of the house and into Myra's Mini van. They drove off to Saddleworth Moor, where they buried her, along with her clothing and the bloodied sheet from the bed.

Lesley Ann Downey's body was recovered by police on 10 October 1965.

6 OCTOBER 1965 – THE MURDER OF EDWARD EVANS

Brady was still keeping David Smith close to him, hoping that he would prove himself as an ally. In late September 1965, the pair plotted to rob an electricity board showroom. Part of the plan involved concealing all evidence of criminal activity that Brady had amassed in Wardle Brook Avenue. To this end, on 5 October, three days before the robbery was planned to take place, Smith helped Brady deposit two suitcases at the left-luggage department at Manchester Central railway station. The contents of these suitcases included sadistic and Nazi literature, Brady's notebooks, photographs taken on the Moors and inside Wardle Brook Avenue, and several reels of quarter-inch audiotape, including the recording of the gagging and torture of Lesley Ann Downey.

On 6 October, David Smith appeared at Wardle Brook Avenue, asking Brady for money to pay off the back rent that he owed. Brady replied that he would deal with it. Late that afternoon Ian and Myra drove off towards the city centre, and Brady was dropped off at the Central railway station, where he encountered Edward Evans, a seventeen-year-old boy whom Brady recognised, having encountered him in the gay bars that he frequented. Offering Evans a drink back at his place, Brady led him to the car and introduced him to Myra, who he said was his sister.

At Wardle Brook Avenue, where Myra's grandmother was by now in bed and asleep, Evans and Brady started drinking wine together; it may also be assumed that Brady buggered Evans as forensic tests found that hairs matching those found on the settee in the living room were found in Evans's anus. The two men were left alone when Myra Hindley then went to pay her sister a brief visit; as she left Maureen's house to go back home, she asked David Smith to accompany her on the walk back because she claimed she was frightened of the dark. Smith and Hindley entered the house, where Ian greeted them and then disappeared, leaving them both in the kitchen. The next thing they heard was a terrifying scream. Smith ran into the living room and saw Brady violently attacking Evans's head with an axe.

As the dying Evans writhed in agony on the floor, Brady cursed him as he continued hitting him, calling out, 'You fucking cunt' and 'You dirty bastard'. When the bloodied form of Evans finally lay still, Brady put a cushion over his head and strangled him. After Evans had breathed his last Brady announced that this murder had been 'the messiest yet'. David Smith and Myra then cleaned the living room of all traces of the murder; Evans's body was wrapped up in a blanket and locked in a room upstairs. It was planned to drive the corpse out to the Moors the following day. Brady, Hindley and the terrified Smith then had a meal in the kitchen, during which Brady alluded to other killings and the burial of bodies on the Moor.

ARREST AND TRIAL

Returning home to Maureen, David Smith was in a shocked state. Sick with fear, he started vomiting uncontrollably, and then told his wife what had happened. She advised him to contact the police, and Smith made the call from a phone box in the early hours of 7 October. He advised police that there were guns in the house, so extra precautions were put into place. He gave police a full account of Ian and Myra's other activities, and told them of the existence of the two suitcases that had been deposited in the left-luggage office.

At 8 a.m. that day, Superintendent Robert Talbot, wearing a bread delivery man's outfit and holding a basket of loaves – a disguise deemed necessary in order that whoever was in the house would respond – knocked on the door of 16 Wardle Brook Avenue. He was accompanied by Detective Sergeant Alexander Carr, with a further 25 police officers ready for action in a nearby street. When Myra Hindley opened the door, Talbot informed her that he was a police officer and asked if there was a man in the house, to which she replied that there was no man there. Not satisfied with this reply, Talbot entered the house, where he found Brady sitting on the settee in the living room. Announcing that he was here because of reports of acts of violence that had taken place during the previous evening, Talbot and his officers began searching the house, only to find that the door of one of the bedrooms was locked.

After some prevarication by Myra, the police were given the key. Entering the room, police found the bludgeoned Evans, the bloody axe and two loaded pistols. Brady was immediately arrested and taken to a police station; Hindley remained free, but was interviewed on several occasions, during which she refused to discuss anything until she had consulted Ian Brady. On 11 October, Hindley was arrested and charged with the murder of Edward Evans.

Acting on Smith's information that a number of children had been killed, they combed their missing-persons files. The house in Wardle Brook Avenue was thoroughly searched and a large amount of potential evidence removed, including 149 photographic negatives, 170 photos, a photograph album, tape recordings and two tape recorders. In the spine of Myra's bible, which she had been presented with on the occasion of her first communion, police found the ticket from the left-luggage office.

On opening the suitcases, police found several items, including nine sickening photographs of Lesley Ann wearing only socks, shoes and a scarf. They also found two reels of quarter-inch tape. One spool included an edition of the BBC's *The Goon Show* and a sports commentary taped from the radio, as well as some unidentified music. The other contained the horrifying tape recording of the torture of Lesley Ann Downey, followed by two songs performed by the Ray Conniff Singers: 'Jolly St Nicholas' and 'The Little Drummer Boy'. During October 1966, the bodies of Lesley Ann Downey and John Kilbride were found, police having been guided to the buried children by photographs they had found of various parts of Saddleworth Moor.

On being interviewed by police, Brady and Hindley denied killing Lesley Ann Downey. Ian claimed that two men whom he declined to name had brought her to Wardle Brook Avenue to be photographed and then left with her when she was still alive; Myra stated that David Smith had brought Lesley Ann to the house and had left with her. They also told police that Smith had been responsible for killing Edward Evans.

On 27 April 1966, the pair appeared at Chester Assizes, where they were formally charged with the murders of John Kilbride, Lesley Ann Downey and Edward Evans. They pleaded not guilty to all charges. During the trial, Brady repeatedly minimised Hindley's involvement. Both Hindley and Brady repeatedly accused Smith of being responsible for the murders. Appearing as a key prosecution witness during the trial, Smith graphically described the murder of Edward Evans: 'My first thoughts were that Ian had hold of a life-sized rag doll and was just waving it about ... the lad groaned and Ian lifted the axe over his head and brought it down upon the lad's head.'

He also told the court how Brady had repeatedly referred to other murders and victims whose bodies were buried on the Moors. Searching Smith's home, police found notes in his handwriting in which he had parroted Brady's philosophy: 'People are like maggots, small blind, worthless fish bait ... Rape is not a crime, it's a state of mind ... Sadism is the supreme pleasure ...'

Under questioning in court, Brady admitted hitting Evans with an axe but insisted that it was David Smith who had killed him.

On 6 May 1966 the jury found Brady guilty of all three murders, and Hindley guilty of the murders of Lesley Ann Downey and Edward Evans. They were both sentenced to life imprisonment. Had their crimes been discovered earlier, they might have paid with their lives, the death penalty in the UK having been abolished in November 1965.

IMPRISONMENT

Brady was sent to Durham Prison, Hindley to Holloway in London. Owing to the hostility of other prisoners, they each asked to be put on Rule 43, by which prisoners can ask to be placed in solitary confinement for their own protection. Attempts by the pair to establish the right to visit each other – based on the premise that they had in fact been married according to common law – ended in failure, despite Myra's efforts in persuading the campaigning Labour peer Lord Longford to make representations to the Home Office on their behalf. Hindley and Brady maintained contact via letter until 1970, when Myra's renewed interest in Roman Catholicism came between them, and, after some barbed replies from Brady in which he mocked her religious beliefs, communication between them came to an end.

Ian Brady spent most of his time in prison confined to his cell, not showing any remorse or regret for his crimes. During his incarceration – in various locations, including Durham Prison, Parkhurst, Albany on the Isle of Wight and Gartree – he has expressed much rage and anger against the prison system. His politics have radically changed – Ian Brady is extremely left-wing, and has expressed a particular loathing of the Conservative government under Margaret Thatcher. He has never sought parole and in a public statement in 1978 stated that he had

accepted [that] the weight of the crimes both Myra and myself were convicted of justifies permanent imprisonment, regardless of expressed personal remorse and verifiable change.

He has gone on hunger strike on many occasions, and in 1985 he was examined by psychiatrists who 'sectioned' him under the Mental Heath Act and ordered that he be kept in a maximum-security hospital. Having been sent to Ashworth Hospital in Liverpool, he learned how to transcribe books into Braille. According to Longford, Brady also volunteered to donate a kidney for transplant, apparently as a compensatory act for the pain he has caused. When the authorities declined the offer of the kidney and then told him that his Braille work was to end, Brady became depressed and made several suicide attempts. He also embarked on another series of hunger strikes.

Brady has never confessed formally to the murders of Pauline Reade and Keith Bennett. The detective Peter Topping describes in his autobiography an offer made by Brady in 1987: 'all the facts about the killing in return for the means to take his own life'. Topping turned this deal down. In July that year, after the body of Pauline Reade had been discovered following a confession by Myra Hindley, Brady, handcuffed and wearing a long overcoat and dark glasses, was taken to Saddleworth Moor in an attempt to help find Keith Bennett's grave. During the ramble on the Moor accompanied by a posse of police officers, Brady told of how he and Hindley had buried Bennett's body, but failed to locate the spot.

Brady's mental and physical condition deteriorated during the 1990s. Repeated hunger strikes, during which he came close to death, weakened him considerably. Brady has found a creative outlet: he has written his autobiography, rumoured to be locked away in the vaults of a major British publishing company, to be published after Brady's death.

In the mid-1990s he completed a factual book on the subject of serial murderers, *The Gates of Janus*, which was published in the USA in 2001. The force of Brady's rage blows through the pages as he attacks organised religion, the authority of politicians and the press, all of which he still heartily detests. His scholarly analysis of serial killers makes for compelling reading.

In the opening chapters of his book Brady gives some clues as to his own predilections and motivations: 'being in a position of having tasted both fantasy and deed, I can candidly testify that fantasy is invariably more hedonistically superior, its creator having the advantage of omnipotence'.

He refuses to show any remorse for his crimes: 'You contain me in a concrete box that measures eight by ten and expect public confessions of remorse as well? . . . Remorse is a purely personal matter, not a circus performance'.

In a letter sent to this writer in December 2001 Brady crystallised his view of the comparative magnitude of his own crimes: '. . . you can't beat "respectable" people when it comes to serial global slaughter'. He criticised Ashworth Hospital as 'a bullshit factory exploiting "patients" exclusively for commercial gain'.

It would seem that Myra Hindley has had a somewhat happier time in prison than Ian Brady. In Holloway, Durham Prison and Cookham Wood, where she is held at the time of writing, she has embarked on lesbian affairs and, despite some vicious physical attacks on her by other prisoners, seems to have achieved a degree of social integration within these institutions. She has gained an Open University degree, is well read and considers herself a feminist. It is a considerable under-statement to say that she has never been forgotten by the British tabloid newspapers. There was uproar in the press in 1972 when the governor of Hollaway, Dorothy Wing, took Myra in her car one afternoon for a walk on Hampstead Heath. In 1974 Hindley, another prisoner named Maxine Croft and a lesbian prison officer with whom she was having an affair, Pat Cairns, were charged with plotting to allow Hindley to escape from Holloway – Hindley was given an extra twelve months added to her existing sentence.

Until his death in 2001 Lord Longford was a continual presence in Hindley's life behind bars, en-couraging her in her Roman Catholic faith and making representations to the Home Office requesting that she be made eligible for parole. Longford's reasoning was that the original tariff of thirty years should be binding. A succession of politicians have failed to agree with Longford, even after the watershed year of 1996. Two recent Home Secretaries, Michael Howard and Jack Straw, have resisted any notion of considering freeing Hindley. Hindley's letter to the *Guardian*, published on 18 December 1995, details the relationship with Brady and his effect on her. She writes that her 'greatest regret' was that she met Ian Brady, documents how she has changed during her time in prison and analyses her perceived role as 'a national scapegoat'. She also claimed that she had become 'a political prisoner serving the interests of successive Home Secretaries who have placed political expediency and, effectively, a lynch-mob rationale before the dictates of basic human rights'.

In 1997, following the election of a Labour government, Hindley made a bid in the Court of Appeal to overturn the ruling made by the previous Conservative Home Secretary, Michael Howard, that she should never be released from prison. This bid failed. In late 2000, Hindley was admitted to hospital for cancer treatment.

The murders have had catastrophic effects on the victims' families: Lesley Ann Downey's mother, Ann West, documented her haunted life in her book *For the Love of Lesley*; Keith Bennett's mother, Winifred, has pleaded that Brady and Hindley reveal the spot where her son was buried; the families of John Kilbride, Pauline Reade and Edward Evans have also suffered immeasurably.

THE MURDERERS' RELATIONSHIP
The inevitable question remains – would these murders have taken place if Brady and Hindley had never

encountered each other? Jonathan Goodman, in his study of the case, *The Trial of Ian Brady and Myra Hindley*, interprets the meeting of Brady and Hindley in 1961 as creating 'synergy, a sum of evil far greater than its parts'. Hindley herself refers in her *Guardian* letter to her 'fatal weaknesses' regarding Brady, claiming that when they met she was 'emotionally immature' and, as we saw earlier, as their relationship progressed she fell further under the spell of Brady's 'powerful personality' and 'magnet-like charisma'. In *The Gates of Janus* Brady claims, 'I have never seriously set out to corrupt anyone'.

The killings have been frequently interpreted as a classic *folie à deux*. When they met, they were an unlikely couple. Brady's background – his Scottish upbringing, turbulent childhood, sexual abuse when a boy and criminal activity as an adolescent – was certainly far different from Myra Hindley's. And undoubtedly, when they met, she was the one who changed her political beliefs, her religious practices, her sexual behaviour and even her physical appearance to please Ian Brady.

Their behaviour since being imprisoned has also radically differed: Brady refusing to show remorse of any kind, nor wishing for release; Hindley expressing her regret and sorrow for the suffering she has caused, praying to her Catholic God for forgiveness while using every legal avenue possible in her efforts to be granted parole.

For Ian Brady, and to some degree for Hindley, the killings had a sexual element. It is likely that all the victims were raped by Brady – a fetishist in the extreme – either vaginally or anally, before being murdered. Brady's literal interpretations of Nazi philosophies and those of de Sade – his carrying the logical conclusions of these ideologies into his personal life and that of Myra Hindley – ended in the tragic loss of young lives.

BIBLIOGRAPHY

Brady, Ian, *The Gates of Janus*, Feral House, Los Angeles, 2001.

Goodman, Jonathan, *The Trial of Ian Brady and Myra Hindley*, David and Charles, Newton Abbott, 1973.

Hansford Johnson, Pamela, *On Iniquity*, MacMillan, London, 1967.

Harrison, Fred, *Brady & Hindley – Genesis of the Moors Murders*, Grafton, London, 1987.

Jones, Janie, *The Devil and Miss Jones*, Smith Gryphon, London, 1993.

Ritchie, Jean, *Myra Hindley – Inside the Mind of a Murderess*, Angus & Robertson, London, 1988.

Topping, Peter, *Topping*, Angus & Robertson, London, 1989.

West, Ann, *For the Love of Lesley*, Warner, London, 1993.

Williams, Emlyn, *Beyond Belief*, Hamish Hamilton, London, 1967.

Wilson, Robert, *Devil's Disciples*, Express Newspapers, London, 1986.

5. HEADS & TAIL – DOUGLAS CLARK AND CAROL BUNDY: THE SUNSET STRIP KILLERS

'You're the one for me, Fatty.'[1]

Its full name in Spanish is El Pueblo de Nuestra Señora la Reina de los Ángeles de Porciúncula. In English that means 'The Town of Our Lady the Queen-of-the-Angels of the Little-Piece-of-Land'. 'The Angels', for short, or, rather, Los Angeles. But if the religious connotations of Los Angeles are not unusual in California, then neither are the ironies that attach to them. There is, for example, San Francisco, city of 'St Francis' and base for the infamous and still unidentified Zodiac killer and the somewhat less infamous Zebra killers – black cultists who murdered whites during the 1970s. Then there's Sacramento, city of the 'sacrament', and base for the serial killers Richard Chase, the so-called 'Vampire of Sacramento', and Gerald and Charlene Gallego, the 'Sex-Slave Killers' whose killing spree in a 1973 Dodge van is examined elsewhere in *My Bloody Valentine* (see 'Killing in Company'). Last but not least, there's Los Angeles, city of 'the angels', and base for Douglas Clark, the 'Sunset Strip Slayer', and his myopic partner Carol Bundy.

So, at least, says the official version of the crimes. According to Clark himself, the nickname should be plural, not singular: not 'Sunset Strip Slayer' but 'Sunset Strip Slayers'. Two of them, to be precise. Furthermore, neither of them was called Douglas Clark, because the crimes, according to Clark, were committed not by him but by Bundy and a former lover of hers called Jack Murray. Bundy, like the police, denies this, but Murray is unable to corroborate what she says. Bundy herself is to blame for his silence, because she had already shot and decapitated him by the time of her arrest in 1980. She described the crime to the police as 'fun' and as the interview drew to a close told the interviewing officer that she was sexually aroused by him. From which one can see that Clark's accusations are not wholly implausible.

Clearly, Carol Bundy was no ordinary woman, but then even the most rabidly misandric disciple of Andrea Dworkin would find it hard to claim that Clark was an ordinary man. He had been born in 1948 in Pennsylvania to a naval officer called Franklyn Clark whose peripatetic career took his young family not just from city to city in the United States but also overseas, to Japan. The taste for travel that Frank Sr seems to have acquired in the navy did not leave him when he left it in 1958, and the following year he moved with his wife and five children to the Marshall Islands, where he worked for an American transport firm based in Texas.

PORTRAIT OF THE SLAYER AS A YOUNG MAN

The family led a privileged existence on the atoll of Kwajalein, perhaps nourishing a taste for luxury and self-indulgence in Douglas Clark that was only increased when he was sent with his brother Walter to board at the Ecolat, an exclusive school in Geneva that catered for the children of diplomats, film stars and European and Middle Eastern royalty. It was in Geneva, Clark later claimed, that he acquired a taste for 'kinky' sex, and, though that remains unproven, it is certainly true that his behaviour away from the bedroom attracted attention. Among other things, he got drunk, stole a bicycle, and wrote an obscene letter to a female teacher, and by the time he was sixteen the authorities at the school had had more than enough of him.

And so he was expelled. Although his parents already had a reputation for defending their wayward son in the teeth of the evidence, the brute fact of his expulsion seems to have made them realise the need for discipline and Franklyn Clark, as an ex-navy man, may naturally have concluded that training in the armed forces might provide it. Clark was duly dispatched to Culver Military Academy in Indiana, where he stayed for the next three years while his parents and younger siblings continued to travel around the world.

But, if his parents' hopes had been that the military should make a disciplined and sober man out of him, those hopes were thoroughly dashed. Clark continued to defy authority and pursue his own pleasure at the academy, and the first faint indications of what the future held for him became apparent in his predilection for recording his sexual exploits on audio tape. Sex itself wasn't enough: he needed some souvenir of it too. In 1967 he left Culver and was drafted for the war then being fought in Vietnam. For someone of Clark's intelligence it was easy enough to avoid frontline service, and he found his way into the Air Force, where he was trained to monitor Russian radio communications.

He served most of his time in Anchorage, Alaska, and is known to have been an *habitué* of the city's many nightclubs and bars, like the serial killer Robert Hansen, who killed prostitutes from Anchorage in the early 1980s as part of a hunting ritual that he followed according to whether or not they satisfied him with oral sex.[2] Like Hansen's, Clark's crimes would involve oral sex and prostitutes; unlike Hansen's, Clark's would add decapitation and necrophilia. It must remain uncertain whether he had acquired those tastes by the time he left the Air Force with an 'honourable discharge', but it is true that he left Alaska with the intention of driving to Mexico, long a Mecca for American men with unconventional sexual tastes.

EARTH-MOTHER GIRLS ARE EASY

En route, however, he stayed in California with his sister Carol-Ann, who was then living in the Los Angeles suburb of Van Nuys with her husband. Apparently liking what he saw of the state, he decided to settle there and in 1972, at the age of 24, he married a woman called Beverly whom he had met in a bar in North Hollywood. Beverly, like Carol Bundy, was overweight and blonde and it was with her, if not in some earlier relationship, that Clark may have realised how to exploit the low self-esteem and vulnerability of a woman who is anxious and unhappy about her looks and her weight. Clark was handsome, articulate and, on the surface at least, full of self-confidence and bravado, and, for a little investment in affection and flattery at the beginning, he could reap a lasting reward in devotion and self-sacrifice from the right woman.

And so, after his divorce from Beverly in 1976, he undertook a series of such relationships, securing free board and lodgings from a succession of overweight and underloved women whom he flattered and then battened on until either he or they grew bored or disillusioned. In those days, he was at least a serial exploiter of women; by the time he met Carol Bundy, he may have been well on the way to being a serial killer of them too.

Bundy was six years older than Clark, born in August 1942 to Charles and Gladys Peters. Her father was an alcoholic and, like Clark's father, he moved frequently with his wife and their two daughters, Carol, the elder, and Vicky, the younger. However, it was Gladys Peters who was the disciplinarian of the family, handing out severe beatings to her daughters, particularly Carol, whom she is said to have disowned at the age of eight. Gladys died while Carol and Vicky were still children, but the relief of no longer receiving beatings from her was destroyed by their father, who demanded that his two daughters provide him with sex while he searched for a new wife. Prematurely introduced to sex by her own father, Carol learned to associate it with protection and shelter, and while still at high school she began using it to try to win the affection and loyalty of men.

It is hardly surprising, therefore, that she left home at the age of seventeen to marry a 56-year-old man, nor is it surprising that he too should have sought to exploit her by trying to force her to work as a prostitute. Carol left him and went to live with a 32-year-old writer of science fiction and pornography called Richard Geis. Geis, who recognised her intelligence and potential, might have been the saving of her, but by then she had acquired too great a taste both for sex and for the abuse that so often accompanied it. By the time they had moved to Oregon she had begun to sleep with men for money and when Geis learned of this on their move to Santa Monica, California, he paid for her to attend nursing school, perhaps in an attempt to guide her away from a career in prostitution.

If so, his plan worked: on graduation Carol began a career as a nurse that would end only with her arrest and imprisonment for involvement in the Sunset Strip murders. She was no longer living with Geis and it was at work that she met and married the man whose surname would give the crimes a macabre echo of another infamous series of serial killings. Grant Bundy was a fellow nurse with whom she had two boys; henceforth, Carol was known as Carol Bundy. Like all of Carol's previous relationships, the marriage did not last, beginning to founder under the strain of Carol's increasingly bad eyesight until in 1979, in response to what she claimed was her husband's increasing violence, Carol left home with her sons and settled in Van Nuys, Los Angeles.

She and Clark were now living in the same city and their meeting would not long be delayed, but in the meantime Carol had one more painful relationship to endure. Jack Murray was a British-born Australian citizen who had emigrated to America in the hope of fashioning a career in showbusiness on the strength of his singing voice and his good looks. Overconfidently christening himself the 'Australian Tom Jones', he had failed in his ambitions and had instead married and become a handyman at the apartment block where Carol was now living. Such a job is an excellent choice for a gregarious male egotist with a high sex drive, for it furnishes a constant supply of new female acquaintances, and when Murray carried out repairs in Carol's apartment he discovered that she was eager not only to listen to his stories but also to share his bed. As their relationship developed Murray, whether out of good nature or gratitude, gave her advice that enabled her to seek successful treatment for her eye condition, which had by then reduced her to near blindness, and Carol's infatuation deepened, and darkened, into obsession.

WHEN DOUGLAS MET CAROL
Such was the strength of this obsession that she pursued Murray and dreams of eventual marriage to him through

months of disappointment, allowing him to exploit her for money and sex, though it must have been obvious to any halfway impartial observer that he had no intention of leaving his wife Jeanette and children. Finally, when she visited a nightclub in the hope of persuading him to leave his wife and instead saw him dancing happily with her, she may have realised that her hopes of a life shared with him were over, though her feelings for him remained very strong. Frustrated and lonely, overweight and unhappy, she was now a perfect target for Douglas Clark as she sat in the nightclub – had he happened to be there, of course.

And in fact, if one version of the story is correct, he was. He introduced himself, charmed her for the rest of the evening, and then left her with a promise that he would be in touch again. As he had so often in the past, Clark was making the initial investment in a relationship that he hoped would repay him many times over in accommodation, sex and money. He called Carol within two days, invited himself for dinner at her apartment and ended up staying the night and treating her to passionate but considerate sex and a hefty dose of flattery and affection. However, the following day, as he left, he made a strange request, asking her to lend him a pair of her cotton underpants. Perhaps used to male perversity by now, and not wishing to jeopardise their newborn relationship, Carol agreed but when she presented a pair to him Clark baulked at their size and left without them.

The episode is yet another indication of Clark's need for some lasting souvenir of sex: something through which he could relive and revive his pleasure. So far it had taken him no further than fetishism and an obsession with women's underwear; in the near future, it would perhaps take him into deadly felony. His relationship with Carol quickly developed, helped when Carol left the apartment block she shared with Murray and his wife and moved to a new apartment some three miles away. Despite his refusal to break up his marriage for her sake, Murray was not prepared to break off their relationship altogether, and after helping her move he called on her regularly for sex.

The strength of Carol's sex drive, or the depth of her need for male attention, or both, can be gauged from the fact that she was simultaneously having regular sex with Clark. But sex with Clark, if the police and Carol herself are to be believed, was a quite different proposition, for Clark gradually initiated her into the polymorphous perversity of his fantasy life, whose full extent Carol had by no means glimpsed when he asked her for a pair of her cotton underpants. It was 1976 and many miles north in Sacramento a brain-damaged recidivist called Gerald Gallego may already have begun to describe his fantasies of 'young, disposable sex slaves' to his infatuated young wife Charlene. In Los Angeles, Douglas Clark was doing the same to the infatuated Carol Bundy. He fantasised, he told her, about kidnapping and imprisoning a young girl for sex. He also fantasised about murder and necrophilia.

But fantasies were gradually ceasing to satisfy him: like Gerald Gallego, he wanted to turn fantasy into fact. And he wanted Carol to help him do it. There are suggestions that he had already embarked on a career of serial murder by the time he met Carol, or that he embarked on it while he was still grooming her as his partner. Certainly he had the tools for the job: after Carol bought a blue 1973 Buick station wagon for the two of them to use, she discovered a large knife hidden behind the sun visor. It was for self-defence, Doug reassured her, and he suggested she buy a gun for herself. In fact, he suggested she buy two: .25 Raven automatics from a pawnshop in Van Nuys. Both were registered in her name.

By now the affection and charm he had initially invested in their relationship were long gone: he was living on dividends paid by Carol on valueless stock, and Carol was happy to continue paying them. Perhaps she felt more comfortable in an abusive relationship, knowing from copious experience in the past exactly how to maintain one, and, when Clark refused to have sex any more, perhaps she felt that a man and no sex were better than no man and no sex. Or perhaps, if Clark's version of events is correct, he had simply tired of her and her odd behaviour.

But if that was the case it is also odd that he did not leave her completely, and there is evidence elsewhere that Carol was right when she later told the police of Clark's sex-and-death fantasies. In April 1980, a 22-year-old prostitute called Charlene was working in a supermarket car park on Sunset Boulevard near Le Brea Avenue. A man driving a blue station wagon pulled in. The young prostitute approached him and they agreed a price for oral sex, whereupon she got in the car and was driven by him to a less public spot on De Longpre Avenue.

But, as she prepared to fellate him, he grabbed her and began to stab her with a knife. After a severe struggle, she managed to kick a door of the car open, break free and throw herself on to the sidewalk, bleeding badly. She would later identify her attacker as Douglas Clark. If so, she would have been his second known victim. The first, an unidentified teenage girl, had been found dumped in the Saugus-Newhall district of Los Angeles County on 2 March 1980, shot to death with a pistol whose calibre matched or was close to that of the .25 Raven automatic pistols bought under Carol's name the previous year.

TWO STEPS TO HEAVEN

The failure of the attack on Charlene and the possibility of later identification did not deter Clark and in June, according to Carol and the police, he went hunting again. In the pungent phrase of a letter purportedly written by Jack the Ripper, it was a 'double event': a pair of stepsisters, Gina Marano, sixteen, and Cynthia (Cindy) Marano-Chandler, fifteen. Their naked bodies were found dumped off a freeway on 12 June, and forensic examination soon established they had been shot in the head. Carol would later tell the police that at that time she came across a duffel bag full of bloodstained female clothing in the Buick station wagon. Oddly, she had taken the clothing to a laundromat to be washed without knowing the full story behind it, which emerged, she went on, when she met Clark a few days later and he described what he had been up to.

He had picked the stepsisters up in the station wagon on the afternoon of the 11th from a bus stop on the Sunset Strip, persuading Gina to accompany Cindy when the latter was reluctant to accompany him alone. After forcing Cindy to begin fellating him and ordering Gina to 'look away', he had taken out one of the pistols, shot Gina behind the left ear, and then shot Cindy in the head too when she raised her head from his crotch, doubtless startled by the gunshot that had fatally wounded Gina. He then drove them both to a garage he rented in Burbank, where he noticed that, although badly wounded, neither was dead. He shot them again, and then, finally satisfied that they were dead, began to realise some of his necrophilic fantasies, arranging their bodies so that they performed post-mortem cunnilingus on each other before inserting his penis into Cindy's mouth and vagina and sodomising Gina.

Carol's reaction to the story was, she claimed, to ring the police department in Van Nuys on 14 June. Using the false name of 'Betsy', she told them that her lover was responsible for the murders but the officer who spoke to her, mistaking her for a crank, refused to take her seriously and assumed when she was cut off at the police switchboard that she had tired of the game and hung up. Less than a week after trying to turn Clark in for murder, however, she accompanied him on a hunt for what would be his fourth known victim. On Highland Avenue in Hollywood, he and Carol invited a prostitute whom Carol could later identify only as 'Cathy' into the station wagon. They had previously agreed a code whereby, without alerting the victim, Carol would signal her willingness to murder a prostitute: she was to announce, 'Boy, am I having a blast!' and one of them would shoot the prostitute in the head as she raised her head from fellating Clark.

In the event, it was Clark who carried out the actual killing, shooting Cathy with a gun handed to him by Carol. Like Gina and Cynthia Marano, she did not die instantly and she bled heavily in the car as Clark and Carol drove it along the Hollywood Freeway in search of a spot to dump her. They found one near the Magic Mountain amusement park, dragged her from the car and left her partly concealed beneath some bushes. They then drove home, arriving there early on the morning of 21 June. Carol later accompanied Clark to a car wash in an attempt to get rid of the blood that was now staining the car. Killing was a messy business, but if Carol is to be believed Clark had by no means had enough of it.

HEADLESS CORPSE DUMPED IN A CAR PARK

That night he went hunting again, and it was with his fifth victim, a prostitute from Little Rock, Arkansas, called Exxie Wilson, that he created the most macabre and distinctive aspect of the Sunset Strip murders. He had seen three prostitutes standing together, perhaps already alerted to a killer on the loose and banding together for mutual protection. If so, their strategy worked, for when Clark tried to persuade one of them to accompany him they all refused. He drove off but when he drove past the spot a little later he found only one of the prostitutes left: a slim blonde in a pink dress. She agreed to accompany him for oral sex and, when Clark had found a quiet spot in a nearby car park and parked the car, she lowered her head towards his crotch.

Clark then shot her but in her death throes she bit him, adding weight to Clark's assertion that he would never have been foolish enough to mix oral sex and bullets, for fear of being bitten on the penis. However, from the accounts given by Carol of the crimes, he did not shoot his victims while they were actually performing oral sex, but when they were lowering or raising their heads to his crotch and so unable to watch his hands. Whether or not he was bitten therefore depended on how well he timed the shot; on this occasion he timed it badly and his pain and anger were such that he wanted revenge on Wilson's corpse.

And so he cut her head off with the knife from the 'kill bag' of paper towels, rubber gloves and chemical cleaners Carol had put together for dealing with the aftermath of a crime. He then stripped her, dumped her naked headless body on the tarmac of the car park and drove off with her head in a plastic bag. The brazenness of the crime did not mean he had abandoned all caution, however, and, realising that he might be identified by one of the other prostitutes he had propositioned earlier, he returned to the spot where he had seen them. Like Exxie Wilson, one of them, identified by the police as Karen Jones, had returned on her own, and like Exxie Wilson she agreed to accompany him in the car for sex, unaware that Wilson's severed head was sitting near her on the floor of the car.

When Clark stopped the car, he quickly shot her in the head. He then stole her earrings and what money she had on her, doubtless to make the murder look like robbery, dumped her body on the street and drove to Carol's new apartment on West Verdugo Avenue, still with the severed head of the day's first victim sitting on the floor of the car. Later on in the day he would return yet again to the pickup point where he had seen the three prostitutes, two of whom he had now killed, in search of the third, a black woman whom, luckily for her, he was unable to find. The police had already found Karen Jones's body and would soon make the macabre discovery that awaited them in a nearby car park: the naked headless corpse of Exxie Wilson.

This is undoubtedly the most notorious aspect of the Sunset Strip murders. Decapitation and the eerie power of the severed head are ancient motifs in myth and religion, most famously making an appearance in the New Testament tale of the anonymous daughter of Queen Herodias who danced before King Herod:

> But when Herod's birthday was kept, the daughter of Herodias danced before them, and pleased Herod. Whereupon he promised with an oath to give her whatsoever she would ask. And she, being before instructed of her mother, said, Give me here John the Baptist's head in a charger. And the king

was sorry: nevertheless for the oath's sake, and them which sat with him at meat, he commanded it to be given her. And he sent, and beheaded John in the prison. And his head was brought in a charger, and given to the damsel: and she brought it to her mother. [Matthew 14:6–11.]

Extrabiblical tradition gives Herodias's daughter the name of Salome, and the story of her destruction of John the Baptist has echoes in pagan mythology. The loudest of them sounds from the *Metamorphoses* of the Roman poet Ovid (43 BC?–AD 17), which tells of the death of the poet-musician Orpheus in Thrace at the hands of maddened female worshippers of the god Dionysus, who tear him limb from limb and throw his head in a river, down which it floats still singing. In John Dryden's translation the relevant lines run:

His mangled limbs lay scatter'd all around,
His head, and harp a better fortune found;
In Hebrus' streams they gently roul'd along,
And sooth'd the waters with a mournful song.
Soft deadly notes the lifeless tongue inspire,
A doleful tune sounds from the floating lyre;
The hollow banks in solemn consort mourn,
And the sad strain in echoing groans return.
Now with the current to the sea they glide,
Born by the billows of the briny tide;
And driv'n where waves round rocky Lesbos roar,
They strand, and lodge upon Methymna's shore.

The head was retrieved and preserved in a cave sacred to Dionysus at Antissa, where it made prophecies that were so successful and well regarded that they began to draw business from the oracles at Delphi and other cult centres of Apollo, who therefore visited the head and successfully ordered it into silence.[3] Both strands of the tradition, Christian and pagan, exercised a powerful attraction on the symbolist painter Gustave Moreau (1826–98), who returned again and again to them in such works as *Jeune fille thrace portant la tête d'Orphée* (Young Thracian Girl Carrying the Head of Orpheus) of 1866 and *Salomé dansant avant Hérode* (Salome dancing before Herod) of 1876.

And so an obsession with severed heads, although doubtless rare, can be fed easily enough from European literature and art. At least, an obsession with the severed heads of *men* can be so fed; Clark's obsession, if such lay behind his decapitation of Exxie Wilson, had rather scantier nourishment, but a police search of his belongings after his arrest is reported to have uncovered a textbook, perhaps of anthropology or morbid psychology, containing a picture of a severed penis in the mouth of a head impaled on a stick. However, whether or not any long-lasting psychopathology prompted Clark to sever and retain the head, the deed is of a piece with his need to retain some souvenir of an event that had affected him powerfully or given him great pleasure: the audio recordings of sex he made at the military academy, for example, or the pair of cotton underpants he requested from Carol after their first night together.

SEVERED HEAD IN A FREEZER

And when, finally, the head was dumped, retrieved by the police and subjected to forensic examination, it would provide evidence backing up Carol's claims that Clark had oral sex with it while it was kept in her apartment, for traces of semen were discovered in the mouth and throat. Carol herself had played with the 'souvenir' in less degrading but almost equally disturbing fashion, making it up with cosmetics while they discussed what to do with it. In the end, having kept it refrigerated in Carol's freezer for days, they decided to dump it. Worried that her and Clark's fingerprints might be on it, Carol scrubbed it thoroughly with detergent, then wrapped it in old clothing and put it into a wooden jewellery box she had recently bought, before she and Clark drove off to dump it on the street.

It was not a sensible thing to do, but perhaps, like those of many serial killers before and since, the crimes were committed at least partly out of a desire to shock and outrage the world and gain some of the attention which the swollen egos of such criminals crave. They dumped the box near the car park where Exxie Wilson's decapitated body had been found and it was discovered the following day, 27 July 1980, by a man who was soon on the telephone to the police with news of its horrifying but not unexpected contents. The police had already found a body minus a head; now they had found the head too.

But whatever satisfaction Carol had gained from her involvement in the murders quickly evaporated when she realised that her help had not, as she had hoped, brought her and Clark closer together. On 29 July she perhaps made another kind of bid for his attention when she attempted suicide. Her failure suggests that this reading is correct: it was a bid for attention rather than a serious attempt to kill herself. As a trained and still practising nurse, she could very likely have found more effective and quicker means of suicide than the tranquilliser pills and insulin injection she actually used.

Clark did not take the attempt seriously and it also failed to gain the sympathy of Jack Murray, who was still seeing her for sex. But Carol had another means of gaining Murray's undivided attention: by telling him about her involvement in the crimes being committed by Clark. Whether or not Murray took her seriously – and it seems unlikely, in view of the fact that he did not immediately call the police – Carol soon decided that she had made a serious mistake. Murray now knew far too much and though, like Orpheus, he had been a singer in life, unlike Orpheus, he would not continue to sing when he was dead. In Clark's version of the crimes, of course, Murray's failure to go to the police is perfectly explicable, because he had known about them all along, as one of the two perpetrators.

As Carol planned a way of keeping Murray quiet, however, Clark was creating more for him to be kept quiet about: on 1 August he went hunting again, picking up a prostitute later identified only as Jane Doe #18.[4] So at least runs one version of events. In another, Jane Doe #18 was picked up a few days earlier, around the time of Exxie Wilson's and Karen Jones's murders. But if when Clark (or Carol and Murray) picked her up is uncertain, what he (or they) did to her after doing so is not. She was shot, stripped and dumped near a tall oil-storage tank in the San Fernando valley. In the summer heat of California her body decomposed quickly and when she was discovered towards the end of the month she was unrecognisable. In the absence of other clues to her identity she has remained so.

It was Clark's last known killing, for within a few days both he and Carol would be in police custody, beginning the long series of accusations and counteraccusations that would see her imprisoned for life and him waiting to face the death sentence. The end of their affair and the Sunset Strip murders came when Carol finally solved the dilemma she had been facing over Murray's knowledge of the crimes, whether that knowledge was indirect, through her incautious tale-bearing, or direct, through his participation in them with her.

CHEVVY PETTING

She solved the dilemma by inviting Murray to have sex with her in a Chevrolet van he owned and where he had had sex with her many times before. The windows of the van were heavily tinted and it was very difficult to see the interior clearly from outside. This made the van highly suitable both for sex and for what Carol was planning: murder. When Murray began to lower his trousers preparatory to sex, she shot him once in the head, then, finding his pulse still beating, shot him in the head again. He was now dead, but there was more to the killing than a simple silencing of a potentially dangerous police witness, because she continued to attack his body, stabbing him in the buttocks and back with a knife.

Finally, she cut off his head. Murray's rejection of her had been avenged. So the decapitatory theme of the Sunset Strip murders was both underlined and returned to its more traditional form: when Carol fled the murder scene, abandoning the body, she was carrying with her the severed head of a man, rather than that of a woman. The head itself would never be recovered: according to Carol she and Clark dumped it in a 'trash can' later in the day, and it presumably ended up in one of the city's rubbish dumps and was soon irretrievably buried in rubbish.

It remains odd, however, that Carol should have shared this aspect of psychopathology with Clark. In his case, it may have something to do with the curious appearance of his own head and face: his head is large and rounded and his eyes widely spaced and prominent. Looking at him, one can, in TS Eliot's phrase, see the 'skull beneath the skin'. In Carol's case, it may have something to do with her extreme short-sightedness. When she was standing near someone, she would have seen their head and face most clearly: other parts of the body would have been more blurred, and so less 'real', perhaps, the further they were from the head. Murray's head may therefore have represented the most 'real' part of him and so the part she chose to take with her when she abandoned the body.

But that body was soon succumbing to the same California heat as was making Jane Doe #18 unidentifiable in the underbrush of the San Fernando valley. On 9 August, the police received a call about Murray's van, which had remained parked in the same spot for over a week and was giving off an increasingly bad smell. When they arrived and opened it, they found Murray's decapitated corpse, heavily blistered with decomposition and, in an unpleasantly surreal touch, wearing women's underwear. Murray, like Clark, had been a fetishist, and, although the police at first considered a possible homosexual motive, the post-mortem cuts on the back and buttocks revealed by forensics were characteristic of a female murderer.

Their enquiries soon led them to Carol Bundy and her lover Douglas Clark. After her first interview with the police and release subsequent to further investigation, Carol began to break down completely and reverted to the confessional mode in which she had told Murray of the crimes she and Clark had committed together. This time, however, she told too many people too convincingly, and on 11 August 1980 she and Clark were arrested for the first and what would prove to be the final time. The Sunset Strip murders were over, and the circus of the police investigation and trial was about to begin.

NOTES
1. Line from Morrissey's song of the same name.

2. For further information on Robert Hansen, see Wilson, Colin, and Seaman, Donald, *The Serial Killers: A Study in the Psychology of Violence*, Virgin Books, London, 1997.

3. Graves, Robert, *The Greek Myths*, Book 1, section 28, 'Orpheus'.

4. In American jurisprudence unidentified bodies are traditionally identified, depending on sex, as John or Jane Doe, followed by a number giving the order in which they were discovered by a particular police force in a particular year. Jane Doe #18 was, therefore, the eighteenth unidentified female body discovered in Los Angeles in 1980.

BIBLIOGRAPHY

Farr, Louise, *The Sunset Murders*, Pocket Books, New York, 1993.

Kerekes, David J. 'It's Fun to Kill People!' Critical Vision: *Random Essays and Tracts Concerning Sex, Religion and Death*, Critical Vision, Manchester, 1996.

6. DEAD MAN'S CURVE – CHRIS WORRELL AND JAMES MILLER

'I knew that I had come face to face with someone whose mere personality was so fascinating that, if I allowed it to do so, it would absorb my whole nature, my whole soul . . . I did not want any external influence in my life . . . I had a strange feeling that Fate had in store for me exquisite joys and exquisite sorrows.'

The Picture of Dorian Gray, Oscar Wilde, p.28, Penguin Books, 1985.

In Oscar Wilde's novel *The Picture of Dorian Gray* (1891) the title character becomes, through Faustian wish-fulfilment, the enigmatic young man that all of London society revolves around. A price is paid for this, of course – one that Wilde soon got to know all too well. He acknowledged that of the three main characters in the novel, Lord Henry Wotton represented the world's perception of him; the artist Basil Hallward was who he thought himself to be; and Dorian Gray was who he would have liked to have been, in another age.

There is the veiled suggestion in *Dorian Gray* of an after-dark world of sin and perversity visited by Lord Henry and Dorian, the world-weary hedonist and the beautiful pupil; in youth there lies the vicarious means of extending pleasure's lifespan. This was no mere fiction for Wilde, as his infatuation with Lord Alfred Douglas (sixteen years his junior) – whom he had met just after *Dorian Gray* was first published in book form – proved.

In the intense, distanced reality of the artist, such attachments are commonplace: William Beckford, the author of *Vathek* (1786), was the corruptor of eleven-year-old William Courtenay, a boy whose beauty became his pursuer's ruin; the French poets Paul Verlaine and Arthur Rimbaud had ten years between them, but wandered nineteenth-century Europe together, a highly emotional relationship that ended with Verlaine wounding Rimbauld with a pistol; the failed writer Kenneth Halliwell watched as his prodigy Joe Orton – only a few years younger – overtook him in terms of talent, success, popularity and promiscuity. Halliwell murdered Orton in 1967 and then took his own life.

Appropriately, these are the Greek tragedies of the older lover: envy and attachment, seeing something they once, or never, had, in close range. For the other party, it's a thin line between rejection and tolerance, the self-sacrifice of one part for something 'greater'. Jack Kerouac's 1957 novel On The Road has Dean Moriarty as one of its speed-tripping, conformity-defying characters. Moriarty was modelled on Kerouac's real-life Beat Generation friend Neil Cassady, an infuriating live wire admired and despised in equal measure. He was a heroic figure to Kerouac and the poet Allen Ginsberg, the latter forcing himself physically on to Cassady, something that he didn't so much reject as tolerate: 'I don't really know how much I can be satisfied to love you,' he once wrote to Ginsberg. 'I mean bodily, you know I, somehow, dislike pricks and men . . .'[1]

This is the view from the other side of obsession and desire: the pursued may not exactly share the same feelings as their pursuer. There are ways and means to deal with this: you can be thankful for what you've got, and take what you can when you're offered it; or you can alter and change what you desire, so it fits into your way of thinking. The American serial killer Jeffrey Dahmer once attempted this, by drilling a hole in the head of one of his (deceased) victims and pouring in corrosive fluid in the vain hope of making the corpse his obedient sex slave. Killing for control. In England, Dennis Nilsen, a lonely civil servant, occasionally killed the young men he invited back to his home for a drink. He would then wash the body and leave it in bed or sitting around, just like a lover. There was no love up for grabs, so Nilsen altered the rules. He had and desired, in his own words, 'a sense of total social isolation and a desperate search for sexual identity'.[2]

To Dahmer and Nilsen, there was nothing wrong in their search for the right way to satisfaction. In Australia in the 1970s, James Miller never went so far in his own search to belong: he took what he was offered, staying the obedient partner throughout the crimes that the object of *his* obsession, Christopher Worrell, committed. Between 23 December 1976 and 12 February 1977 Worrell sexually assaulted and murdered seven women in areas around Adelaide, South Australia.

THE LOSER AND THE RAPIST
James William Miller was an older man attracted to a younger, more reckless person of his own sex, and, as in some of the aforementioned examples, his attraction was reciprocated in an offhand, casual manner. This was love to him: love through the non-reflective side of a two-way mirror.

Miller was born in 1940, one of six children. A natural loner, he left school at a very early age, turning his back on education for a life of petty crime: at eleven he was sent to reform school, the first in a long line of prison sentences. On the outside, when he wasn't successfully stealing to live, Miller worked as a casual labourer for whoever would employ him. By his mid-thirties, Miller's track record as a petty criminal was a success, of sorts: he had accrued over thirty convictions, mostly for car theft and burglary. It was during one term in Adelaide Jail in 1973 that James Miller met twenty-year-old Christopher Robin Worrell. Miller was doing three months – his shortest sentence ever – for breaking into a gun shop. Worrell was awaiting trial on a charge of rape; at the time of his arrest he was under a two-year suspended sentence for armed robbery. The pair hit it off immediately, and within a week were sharing a cell. To James Miller, who had spent years living by and for himself, the young Chris Worrell must have been a dream come true: someone he could get on with, someone who liked him; not only that, but compared with the rodent-featured, thin, balding Miller, whose physical condition seemed to advertise his loser status, Worrell was a handsome man, with long dark hair, a strong build and boyish good looks.

Born in 1953, Chris Worrell told Miller that he had never known his biological father; when he was six, his mother remarried. One time he told Miller that he had served in the Royal Australian Air Force. Truth or otherwise, it would have only heightened the image the older man had of him: that of the good-looking, serious criminal action man. For the rape charge, Chris Worrell was sentenced to four years, with an additional two for breeching his suspended sentence. He was transferred to Yatala Prison, and James Miller went with him to finish his own three months. They no longer shared a cell, but stayed friends until Miller was released.

In the autumn of 1974, Miller was sent back to Yatala to serve an eighteen-month stretch. An indication of his criminal-loser status comes with the crime that got him sent down: stealing 4,000 pairs of sunglasses and attempting to sell them in hotel lobbies. After his release, Miller went to live with his sister and her family back in Adelaide. In 1976, Worrell was granted early parole, and left Yatala to join up with Miller. The older man was delighted to be in the outside world with his best mate. They decided to rent a flat, and soon ended up working together in a labouring gang for Unley council.

Free from the confines of prison life, there were more opportunities for Miller to attempt to take his infatuation further. Possibly unable to tempt Worrell into a full physical relationship, Miller had to make do with what he was offered. Worrell liked girls; the best way he could maintain his heterosexuality was to allow Miller to perform oral sex on him every now and then – a non-committed act for the recipient. It made a relationship, of sorts, and all that Miller could possess of his young friend. Worrell, like Neil Cassady's attitude towards Allen Ginsberg, 'disliked pricks and men'. He was a convicted rapist, a man with an intense sexual appetite: while Miller went down on him, Worrell would read bondage magazines. But James Miller could see that he was no competition in Worrell's eyes compared with a good-looking woman. What sex life they had soon disappeared and the relationship returned to the same brotherhood-like position as before, with Miller still the adoring older man.

Away from prison, other things could be seen more clearly, as well. Despite being besotted with him, Miller began to witness a different side in Chris Worrell. Miller had seen nothing of the mood that bagged Worrell a rape charge; the fact that he had been convicted of sexually assaulting a woman meant little to Miller, a passive homosexual. But Worrell's temper was unpredictable, fraying over the slightest inconvenience, and Miller took on the mantle of the mate who could calm him down. This was the side that landed Worrell in Yatala, the side that walked hand in hand with his sexual needs.

Chris Worrell was now 23 years old, with a golden gift when it came to meeting and picking up girls. By December 1976, every night after work, Miller would drive around the Adelaide districts in his old 1969 blue and white Valiant with Worrell sitting in the passenger seat, checking out the talent. He would approach girls at bus stops, outside hotels, in railway stations, while Miller – who at 36 probably resembled to many of Worrell's dates the archetypal 'creepy older friend' – waited obediently in the car. Once Worrell had scored, Miller would drive them to a remote spot outside the city, then go for a walk while they had sex on the back seat. Other times, Miller would sleep in his car while Worrell had full use of their apartment. Worrell told him that he sometimes tied girls up during sex. Not once was James Miller confronted with anything odd about his friend's sexual preferences: the girls came and went, and Miller – knowing he could never satisfy Worrell as they did – was just happy to help out in any way he could. It was an uneven arrangement, but the only solid thing in Miller's life. Elsewhere there was nothing.

OFF SWAMP ROAD

On 23 December 1976, Adelaide city centre was in the grip of late-night shopping fever. As had happened before, Chris Worrell told James Miller to drive around the outskirts of the main shopping centre while he went for a walk through the crowds. Miller made the journey twice before he spotted Worrell standing outside the Majestic Hotel, talking to a dark-haired teenage girl. Eighteen-year-old Veronica Knight had become separated from a friend in the crowded city arcade, but, after Worrell introduced himself, she had accepted his offer of a lift home – she was living in a nearby Salvation

Army hostel. While Miller drove in the direction of the hostel, Worrell persuaded her to go with them out to the Adelaide foothills. For some reason, probably because of Worrell's good looks and confident manner, she agreed.

At their destination, Miller pulled the car down on to a sidetrack. When Worrell forced Veronica into the back seat, Miller got out and went for a walk. He let the usual amount of time pass – thirty minutes – before returning. But this time, something was different: there was no post-sex straightening of clothes or embarrassed female glances. Worrell was sitting in the passenger seat, Veronica was on the floor in the back, motionless, still fully clothed. Her hands were tied. When Miller asked him what had happened, Worrell calmly replied that he'd just raped and strangled the girl. Enraged, the normally calm Miller grabbed Worrell, but soon let go when the younger man pulled a knife and held it to his throat, threatening to kill him if he didn't back off.

From that moment, the dynamic of their friendship changed: not only would James Miller now help Chris Worrell because he loved him, but because he was frightened for his life. It was a broad step up from the dark moods he had previously witnessed. It was also the last step in the hierarchy between the two: now there was no doubt that Worrell was in charge. He told Miller to drive the car to Truro, a small town just north of Adelaide.

Going down a dirt track known locally as Swamp Road, Miller eventually stopped by a wooded area. When he refused to help pull Veronica Knight's body out of the car, Worrell again threatened him with the knife. They dragged the corpse under a fence, covered it with leaves and branches and left the area quickly. The total concealment of Veronica's body was not important: Swamp Road was so called because it was a track that divided an expansive flood plain into two paddocks. An occasional clump of trees broke the flats. In an area inhabited by mosquitoes and frogs, the only sign of human occupation was the wire fence running alongside the track. James Miller drove back to Adelaide in silence. Worrell had lurched into a foul mood, and Miller now knew better than to open his mouth.

The next day, when they reported to work as usual, Worrell was back to his usual self. Over the Christmas holiday the murder was never discussed, or even mentioned. Miller had now seen what the man he loved was capable of, and perhaps knew that Worrell could turn on him if angered.

On the morning of 2 January 1977, Miller obediently dropped Worrell off outside Adelaide's Rundle Mall, saying he'd pick him up at the other end. Worrell eventually turned up, accompanied by fifteen-year-old Tania Kenny. Tania had just hitchhiked up the 70-odd kilometres (about 45 miles) from Victoria Harbour, and was looking for a place to stay or people to hang out with. She drove off with the men to Miller's sister's house. After checking that no one was home, Worrell took Tania inside. Miller knew the score and waited in the car; but, when Worrell eventually came back out alone, he knew something was wrong. In the room that his sister's children used as a play area, Tania's lifeless body was bound up with rope, a strip of sticking plaster over her mouth. She was naked apart from a shirt. Worrell said he'd strangled her. Any argument that Miller tried to start was cut short by the fact that he didn't want his sister to find out what had happened. It was a mixture of this and his still-strong feelings for Worrell that made him help dispose of Tania Kenny. They stuffed the body into a cupboard, and then drove out to the Dean Rifle Range at Wingfield. Behind the range, they dug out a shallow grave, and then returned to Adelaide.

Later that night, with Miller's sister and family still absent, they transferred Tania's body to the car and drove back out to Wingfield to bury it. It was James Miller's first complicit act in the killings. Driving home, he made some vague suggestion that Worrell should see a doctor, but he didn't want to risk losing him: Chris Worrell was the only real friend he had ever had, and he would rather Worrell continue with his violent sexual desires than not be with him at all.

But not every night was murder night for the pair. Throughout January 1977 Worrell continued to pick up girls, using his looks and confident chatter. He would wander around his favourite locations: Adelaide railway station, the Rundle Mall and various hotels, including the Mediterranean, the Buckingham Arms and the Ambassador's, where, on 21 January, he met Juliet Mykyta. Sixteen-year-old Juliet had a job in the school holidays selling jewellery from a pavement stall. She was waiting for the 9 p.m. bus, and had just telephoned her parents to tell them she was going to be a little late coming home, when Worrell started chatting to her. He offered her a lift home. On the Port Wakefield road Miller stopped off at a secluded spot to allow Worrell to get on with his business. It was now only a matter of chance whether his friend went too far with a girl. He watched as Worrell forced Juliet into the back seat and, despite her resistance, started to tie her hands up. It was an act Miller had seen many times before, so he got out of the car and went for a walk.

A fair distance away, Miller heard raised voices. Turning back, he saw Juliet on the ground, as if she had been kicked in the stomach. Worrell was standing over her. He rolled her on to her back, knelt down on her stomach and started to strangle her with a length of rope. (At his trial, Miller would claim that he grabbed Worrell's arm in an attempt to stop him strangling the girl; but, when he was threatened, he simply shook his head and walked off. Such an attitude, as if he were turning a blind eye to a friend's drug habit, would have a deciding effect on his case.) When it was over, Worrell had sunk into his post-kill mood. Knowing what to do, Miller drove to Truro, avoiding the area where they had buried Veronica Knight just before Christmas, taking another track off Swamp Road. Near a deserted farmhouse, they carried the body into a clump of thick trees, and covered it up with leaves and branches. Then, as before, they drove back to Adelaide in silence.

South Australia's population makes up less than 10 per cent of the country's total. It is the fourth largest of eight states, and its land mass stretches to 984,000 square kilometres (380,000 square miles). There was little likelihood that Chris Worrell and James Miller would ever be caught for their crimes. Because of that, perhaps it was inevitable that the killings settled into a sort of comfortable pattern, with Miller accepting his place as the lapdog to his friend's violent desires. Within a seven-day period, five more girls would be murdered, homicides that stopped only through unforeseeable chance.

On 6 February 1977, sixteen-year-old Sylvia Pittman was waiting for a train at Adelaide station when she met the wandering Worrell. Parked up in the Windang area, Miller went for his customary walk. Half an hour later, he returned to find Sylvia face down in the back seat with a rug over her. She had been strangled with her own tights, but was still fully clothed. As before, Worrell had slumped into a black mood. They dumped the body off Swamp Road and covered it with leaves before heading back home.

On the evening of 7 February, Miller picked up Worrell and 26-year-old Vicki Howell outside the main Adelaide post office. To Miller, Vicki was different from the other, younger girls Worrell usually targeted. She seemed comfortable in their company, mentioning that she was separated from her husband. Even Worrell seemed to treat her differently: at Nuriootpa, 60 kilometres (37 miles) northeast of Adelaide, he got Miller to stop the car so that Vicki could use a roadside restroom. When the time came for Miller to leave them alone in the car, he quickly returned with some excuse: in reality he wanted to check that Vicki was all right. But, for once, Worrell was calm and his usual chatty self. When Miller returned again, relieved that Vicki wasn't going to be harmed, he found Worrell covering her lifeless body with a blanket. He had strangled her.

Unable to fathom his friend's unpredictability, Miller vented his anger. He was incapable of understanding Worrell's hair-trigger psychopathic personality any other way. Miller had taken to Vicki: maybe he saw in her the seeds of another friendship, and therefore an open avenue along which to take a step away from Worrell's crimes. But Worrell refused to answer his questions, instead ordering him to drive to Truro. The fact that Miller did as he was told showed how quickly he reverted to his subservient self. Off Swamp Road, Vicki's body – clad only in shorts – was hidden just like the others.

Sixteen-year-old Connie Iordanides was picked up in Adelaide city centre on 9 February. Worrell asked her if she wanted a lift. Connie gladly sat up front with him and Miller, but became frightened when the car drove off away from the direction she said she wanted to go. They eventually stopped at a secluded spot in Wingfield. As Worrell forced the now-hysterical girl into the back seat, Miller ignored her pleas and got out of the car. When he returned her body was covered with a blanket: Worrell had raped and strangled her. They dumped the fully clothed body under bushes off Swamp Road, and spent the night sleeping in the car at Victoria Park racecourse.

In the early hours of 12 February, Worrell got talking to a twenty-year-old hitchhiker, Deborah Lamb, in an amusement arcade, suggesting that he could take her to Gawler, her destination. At the beach there, Miller disappeared into the scrub. On his return, Worrell was standing in front of the car, pushing sand into a shallow hole with his feet. Deborah was nowhere to be seen. Worrell had this time erased any evidence for Miller to get angry over.

It was the last time Worrell would rape and murder: a week later, on 19 February, he was killed in a road accident.

Deborah Skuse had been the girlfriend of a man Worrell and Miller had known in Yatala prison. When they had finally got round to visiting him on the outside, they found that he had walked out on Deborah. In an attempt to help her get over the relationship, the three of them drove 370 kilometres (230 miles) southeast to Mount Gambier for the weekend. But, by the Saturday afternoon, Worrell had fallen into one of his black moods, possibly because he wanted to have sex with Deborah, possibly because he knew it wasn't the ideal situation in which to do to her what he'd done to the other girls. Miller must have sensed this, and they decided to return to Adelaide.

For once, Worrell was driving, recklessly. He had been drinking lager all day and, as they sped through the country north of Millicent, Deborah pleaded with him to go more slowly; this just prompted Worrell to shout back at her. Within seconds, the car went out of control, into oncoming traffic. To avoid a head-on collision, Worrell spun the car off the road, flipping it on to its roof before it eventually stopped. Chris Worrell and Deborah Skuse died instantly. Other drivers rushed to the scene, and James Miller was taken to hospital in shock. He escaped with a fractured shoulder.

Now Miller carried the twin burdens of having his best friend, the man he loved, die and being the only person alive who knew what he had done. At Worrell's funeral, Miller met a girl – Amelia – whom Chris had been seeing for a short time before his death. She was almost as upset as Miller over the loss and, perhaps because it was the only thing he could think of to say, Miller told her that Chris might have had a blood clot on the brain; the emotion of the funeral probably led him to tell Amelia that Chris had murdered girls around Adelaide, that they were buried near a place called Blanchetown, that he had also boasted of killing two women in Western Australia; that perhaps the 'clot' was responsible for his killings. Such high emotions just upset Amelia even more, especially Miller's suggestion that it might have been a good thing that Chris had died. She tried to forget about it for the time being, unable to cope with such wild claims, Miller talking of clots to explain away his friend's sadistic tastes. She kept the confession to herself for two years, until the discovery of a number of female remains became a news item.

WORRELL'S LEGACY

After the funeral, James Miller went back to the loner anonymity that had been his life before meeting his 'best mate'. He was a man with no record of violence or sexual offences, and yet had spent nearly two months passively watching as Worrell assaulted and killed innocent women: half scared of being killed himself, half scared of losing him. To Miller, their deaths were a small price to pay. Shouldering the secrets of a dead man, and probably thinking nothing of his emotional confession to Worrell's girlfriend, Miller became another South Australia transient, moving from town to town, sleeping in abandoned cars and homeless hostels, lost and directionless without the man he loved.

Just over a year after Chris Worrell's death, on 20 April 1978, William Thomas, a mushroom picker, was working in one of the desolate paddocks off Swamp Road. There, stuck in the ground, he discovered what looked like a leg bone. Not investigating too deeply, he carried on with his work. On 25 April – Anzac Day – Thomas returned to the paddock with his wife. For five days he had been thinking about the bone, initially guessing it to be that of a cow; but something did not seem quite right. Finding the spot again, he turned the bone over to discover that it was part of a human leg, the buried half still covered in well-preserved skin, the toenails painted. Further searching around the area turned up more bones, clothing and a skull. After the police were called in, they used these and other found items to identify the remains as those of Veronica Knight, missing for almost a year and a half. Believing it to be a one-off incident, the police made no further searches in the paddock.

Swamp Road, one year later. On 15 April 1979, in the same paddock where Veronica Knight was found, four walkers discovered a skeleton. A police search amassed clothing and jewellery, which eventually led them to identify the remains as those of sixteen-year-old Sylvia Pittman. A reopening of missing-persons files clearly showed that five other young women had disappeared around the same time as Knight and Pittman. Detective

Superintendent Keith Harvey, now in charge of the initial enquiry, had always had his suspicions over the disappearances. Marshalling seventy police officers, he ordered a thorough search of the paddocks. On 26 April, in the paddock on the opposite side of Swamp Road, the remains of Connie Iordanides and Vicki Howell were found. With nothing to explain why these bodies were so close together, the police made a public appeal.

In May, Worrell's girlfriend Amelia read in a newspaper about the discoveries: a map showed how close to the Blanchetown area they were, just as James Miller had told her at Chris's funeral. She contacted the police, telling them all he had confessed to her. On 23 May, after round-the-clock surveillance, plain-clothes police officers picked up James Miller in Adelaide. He had tried to run after realising he was being followed. Still destitute, he was doing odd jobs for the Central Mission in return for a bed and food. The officers took him to Angas Street Police Headquarters, where he was questioned by Detective Sergeant Glen Lawrie and Detective Peter Foster of the Major Crime Squad.

At first, Miller denied all accusations the officers threw at him. He gave vague or false answers to their questions and, most of all, he denied ever having met anybody called Amelia. Miller had spent most of his life behind bars; filtered through courtrooms and interview cells, his petty criminal status equipped him with a slippery skin of denial. But then they showed him two things: a photograph of Chris Worrell and Amelia together, and her statement retelling everything he had told her at the funeral. Suddenly, Miller said that he *did* know them, and that perhaps the girl had done all this in order to pick up the $30,000 reward on offer. Such inconsequential answers just made the officers more determined. Finally, at the end of a six-hour interview, Miller went back on everything he had said, and gave them a statement:

> I drove around with Chris and we picked up girls around the city. Chris would talk to the girls and get them into the car and we would take them for a drive and take them to Truro and Chris would rape them and kill them. But you've got to believe that I had nothing to do with the actual killings of those girls.

After the confession that he had carried inside him for over two years came the evidence. Later that same night, James Miller was driven under police escort to Truro's Swamp Road, the beach at Gawler, and the Dean Rifle Range at Wingfield. At each, police uncovered the remains of Juliet Mykyta, Deborah Lamb and Tania Kenny. Before his eyes, James Miller was seeing the wreckage of a dead man's psychosis, evidence that painted him as a murderer's accomplice: there was no one else alive to say otherwise.

EPILOGUE: MURDER OR MAD LOVE?

At his trial in February 1980, James Miller pleaded not guilty to seven counts of murder. But the Crown Prosecutor, BJ Jennings, was convinced of Miller's total complicity in the crimes: 'If a man assists another by driving him to a place where a girl is going to be raped and killed,' he stated, 'then he is guilty of murder.' Disposing of those women was the easiest option. On the one hand Worrell was the man who had bound and raped them; on the other, Miller was the man who turned and walked away while such acts were happening. Accusing fingers could point to both of them.

Claims by the defence counsel, KP Duggan, that Miller did not play any part in soliciting and abducting the girls before their deaths, were rejected by the Crown. Miller's loyalty to his dead friend meant nothing in the legal arena; his obsession with a younger man and the desire to maintain it at the cost of other human lives painted Miller as a misogynistic cold fish. Duggan noted that 'Miller had found himself in one of the oldest relationship problems in the world, that of the involvement in the wrongdoing of someone else. He was trapped in a web of circumstance. Although Miller admits that he handled the situation incorrectly, he maintains that he is not a murderer.'

But mad love was no defence against a murder charge. On 12 March 1980, James Miller was found guilty on six counts of murder. The Crown judged him not guilty of the murder of Veronica Knight, as the jury agreed that he did not know what Chris Worrell intended to do to the girl. The judge, Mr Justice Matheson, sentenced James William Miller to the maximum term of six life sentences. He was sent back to Yatala Prison, this time without the company of Chris Worrell.

In July 1984, James Miller went on a 43-day hunger strike. It was one of many protests citing his innocence, and, as with the others, the authorities ignored it. He was paying the price of friendship, but still harboured no animosity towards his dead friend. In an interview around the time of the protest, he claimed, 'Chris Worrell was my best friend in the world. If he had lived, maybe 70 would have been killed. And I wouldn't have ever dobbed [turned] him in.'

In 1999 Miller applied to have a non-parole period set against his sentence, prompted by the fact that at the time of his conviction the law made no provision for the fixing of non-parole periods. In March 2000 he lost his bid to have the jail term shortened; this followed the granting of a non-parole period in February. Chief Justice John Doyle set it at 35 years from the date of his arrest.

In 2014 James Miller will be eligible for release at the age of 74. The unrequited love for a dead man will have cost him the majority of his life. The past was dug up, and, through it, his future was raked over, but he still breathes while seven women do not.

NOTES

1. Morgan, Ted, *Literary Outlaw: The Life & Times of William S. Burroughs*, The Bodley Head, London, 1991, p.139.
2. Wilson, Colin & Seaman, Donald, *Encyclopaedia of Modern Murder*, Pan Books, London, 1989, p.259.

BIBLIOGRAPHY

Ferguson, Anthony, 'Serial Killing Down Under', *Headpress* 19.

Kidd, Paul B, 'Christopher Robin Worrell and James William Miller: The Truro Murderers', www.crimelibrary.com

7. KILLING IN COMPANY – GERALD AND CHARLENE GALLEGO

As though . . . the ironic fates had decided to set up a standing,
frightful example of the natural qualities of man and woman,
of their basic aptitude to fuse together; a label on the packing case
'These chemicals are dangerous'.[1]

DODGE VAN MAN
In 1974 a comic called *The Broken Cross* was published
by Christian evangelists in Chino, California. It opens
with a fourteen-year-old girl called Donna hitchhiking
alone to Los Angeles. By the fourth frame a van has
stopped for her. There is a man at the wheel with a
woman by his side. The two of them invite Donna
aboard. She thinks, 'It looks safe! . . . There's a girl with
him!' So she accepts their invitation and gets aboard,
and within a few hours she is dead, sacrificed to Satan
by a coven of witches.

In 1978, secular reality begins to imitate Christian art,
when a Californian couple called Gerald and Charlene
Gallego climb into a van and drive off to fulfil what was,
according to Charlene, Gerald's long-held fantasy of
'young, disposable sex slaves'. According to Gerald, it
was Charlene's fantasy too. The van is a roomy 1973
Dodge with airbrushed paintings of mountains on its
sides: harmlessly romantic, one might think, until one
notices that the mountains have vultures circling above
them. The couple drive to the Sacramento Country Club
Plaza shopping mall and Charlene gets out with careful
orders from Gerald. She is to find and bring back two
young women.

Hesitant at first, according to her later testimony, she is driven on by Gerald's threats and begins to walk through the crowds looking for a suitable pair of victims. Eventually she comes across Rhonda Scheffler, aged seventeen, and Kippi Vaught, a year younger at sixteen. She invites them to join her in a pot-smoking session and the two of them, mistaking the petite blonde 21-year-old for a girl of their own age, accept the invitation and follow her to the car park where the van waits.

As do Gerald and a .25 pistol. It is the beginning of 26 months during which Charlene, according to her testimony, is a terrified and unwilling accomplice in ten murders, nine of them involving prolonged rape and sexual assault. According to Gerald, she is an excited and more than willing participant. It is a familiar pattern: the couple who kill in company and then divorce on detention. Myra Hindley's initial claim of her relationship with Ian Brady was that 'Wherever he has gone, I have gone'. Soon she would begin to distance herself more and more from Brady, until by the 1990s she was claiming he had beaten and intimidated her into helping him with crimes in which she had been no more than a peripheral participant: making the initial contact, luring a child who might otherwise have been suspicious into her and Brady's car: 'It looks safe! . . . There's a girl with him!'

The Canadian Karla Homolka, arrested in the 1990s for murders involving her partner Paul Bernardo, would not wait so long to claim the status of victimised victimiser. Like Myra, like Charlene, she would try to use domestic violence to lever her way out of prison. It did not work for Myra, who seems likely to die behind bars, and as yet it has not worked for Karla. For Charlene, however, it worked four years ago in July

1997, when she was released from prison in Nevada after serving seventeen years on a plea bargain against her former husband, who is now in the final stages of a protracted legal fight against death by lethal injection. Reverting to her maiden name of Williams on her release, Charlene appeared on *The Leeza Gibbons Show* claiming to be a battered wife who had participated in the crimes out of fear, not in fellowship.

But, if Charlene was following a familiar pattern in the 1990s, so was Gerald, whose defence has drawn on a history of head injury backed by a CAT – computerised axial tomography – scan revealing 'significant damage' to his brain. In the record of court action no. 35291, *Gerald Armond Gallego, Appellant, vs. The State Of Nevada*, one finds the following testimony by the psychiatrist Dr David V Foster concerning Gallego's childhood: 'Mr Gallego was severely tortured, beaten, humiliated and at times starved and deprived of food, affection, warmth, and suffers severe post-traumatic stress disorder as a consequence.'

And so Charlene was a victim of Gerald; Gerald was a victim of his childhood. But both, perhaps, were also victims of partnership. There is a very ancient myth, recorded most famously in Plato's *Symposium*, that describes how human beings were once oddly shaped creatures with three sexes: conjoint male-and-female; wholly male; and wholly female:

The primeval man was round, his back and sides forming a circle; and he had four hands and four feet, one head with two faces, looking opposite ways, set on a round neck and precisely alike; also four ears, two privy members, and the remainder to correspond. He could walk upright as men now do, backwards or forwards as he pleased, and he could also roll over and over at a great pace, turning on his four hands and four feet, eight in all, like tumblers going over and over with their legs in the air; this was when he wanted to run fast.[2]

But the human race, revelling in the strength of its sensory and locomotory powers, grew arrogant, made war on the gods, and tried to storm Mount Olympus. Zeus, the father of the gods, decided to handicap the human race by slicing each human being in half and forcing them to go on just two legs with a correspondingly reduced complement of faces, ears, and privy members:

Each of us when separated, having one side only, like a flat fish, is but the indenture of a man, and he is always looking for his other half. Men who are a section of that double nature which was once called androgynous are lovers of women; adulterers are generally of this breed, and also adulterous women who lust after men: the women who are a section of the woman do not care for men, but have female attachments; the female companions are of this sort.[3]

The myth survives in English when we talk of 'searching for our other half'. Charlene might be said to have found hers in Gerald, and Gerald to have found his in Charlene: they complemented each other in a sinister way uncovered by an FBI survey into the female partners of male 'sexual sadists': the women were 'uniformly better educated and [more] intelligent than their men'.[4] Charlene was an only child born, on 10 October 1956, into a prosperous upper-middle-class family in Sacramento, California. Her IQ is reported to have touched near-genius levels at 160, and she showed great talent on the violin, an instrument that is, of course, expensive both to acquire and to learn. However, the familiar trajectory of wealth and success faltered in her high-school years, when she began to study the fateful trivium of drugs, drink and sex. She graduated from high school with difficulty, failed college and quickly entered and just as quickly left two marriages. And then she met Gerald.

Gerald's life had also followed a familiar trajectory since his birth in 1946, but in his case it was the trajectory of poverty and failure. Almost every biography of him, no matter how brief, notes that in 1955 his father, Gerald Albert Gallego, was the first man executed in the newly installed gas chamber in Mississippi, where Gerald Sr had killed two policemen and whither he had fled from California after serving time in the notorious San Quentin jail. The biographies usually go on to add that Gerald Jr followed in his father's footsteps by committing his first known serious crime at the age of thirteen, when he raped a six-year-old girl who lived nearby. When he left juvenile prison he continued where he had left off and by the age of 32 he had been jailed several times, and had accumulated seven marriages, two of them to the same woman, several of them bigamous. He had also accumulated a daughter called Mary Ellen and outstanding warrants for arrest on charges of incest, rape and sodomy. And then he met Charlene.

BEAUTY AND HER BEAST

The aforementioned FBI study notes that the criminal *folies à deux* all formed 'relatively quickly', despite the way the female halves of them recognised the 'sinister' personality of the male halves. Or perhaps *because* of the way the female halves recognised this. The Gerald and

Charlene who met in September 1977 were so dissimilar that perhaps it is true that they were made for each other: separate halves of a single whole. If Gerald, dark-haired, saturnine, and built like an ape, was the Beast, Charlene, blonde, ethereal, and doll-like, was certainly the Beauty. Their attraction was as strong as it was mutual, unlike calling to unlike, and a few days after their first meeting in a poker bar in Sacramento Gerald sent Charlene roses with a card reading 'To A Very Sweet Girl'.

The sweet girl was living with her ape-man within weeks, working happily in a supermarket to support him and, Gerald would later claim, eagerly helping him to fulfil his sexual fantasies of power and domination. Gerald installed a runaway teenager in their small house on Bluebell Lane and Charlene formed part of a *ménage à trois* that unbeknown to Gerald was occasionally turning into a *ménage à deux*: Charlene was having sex with the teenager behind his back and destroying the neatness of Plato's theory of sexual attraction. Charlene, like Rosemary West, wasn't satisfied with sex of one conventional kind: she wanted sex with women too.

When Gerald discovered her lesbian secret he threw the teenager out of the house and gave Charlene the first of what she would claim were repeated beatings, though Gerald counterclaimed that she would sometimes give as good as she got: if he broke a finger punching her in the face, she would split his head open with a piece of wood. In the meantime, knowledge of her bisexuality had made Gerald impotent when he attempted consensual sex with her, and he resorted to forcing himself on her as part of an escalating fantasy of sexual violence and domination. Charlene, he claimed, was more than happy to play along and in July 1978, on his 33rd birthday, she presented him with a special present: not a *ménage à trois* involving Gerald, Charlene and a teenage runaway, but a *ménage à quatre* involving Gerald, Charlene, Gerald's teenage daughter Mary Ellen and a teenage friend of Mary Ellen's.

But Gerald, according to Charlene, wanted more. According to Gerald, Charlene did too. She had long listened to his sexual fantasies about young sex slaves; now she had helped him fulfil them. His fantasies about young disposable sex slaves remained; now she would help him fulfil them too. On 11 September 1978, around the anniversary of their first meeting, the two of them climbed into their Dodge van and set off to turn the fiction of a Christian comic into secular reality. As already described, Charlene enticed Rhonda Scheffler and Kippi Vaught back to the van with promises of a pot-smoking session, but when she opened the back the only thing that promised to smoke was the barrel of Gerald's .25 pistol.

SHOT IN THE BACK OF THE HEAD

Terrified into mute obedience, the two girls were bound with tape and laid in the back of the van. Gerald then climbed into the front seat, leaving Charlene, by then two months pregnant, to watch over them as he drove east from California, the 'burning furnace' of early Spanish settlers, towards the mountains of Nevada, the 'snowy' state. He was searching for an isolated spot to rape the girls, and when he found one in the woods of the Sierra Nevada foothills he left Charlene in the van while he marched them away with the gun and a sleeping bag. He was away some hours; when he returned with the girls he ordered Charlene to return alone in the van to Sacramento, establish an alibi, and return in an Oldsmobile that the Gallegos were able to borrow from Charlene's parents.

So, at least, runs one version of the first crime. In another version, Charlene takes part in the rapes, forcing the girls to perform oral sex on her and biting their defenceless bodies. The two versions converge later, when it is agreed that Gerald knocks the girls unconscious with a tyre iron and shoots them in the head with the pistol. Their bodies were then dumped, to be discovered two days later by migrant farm workers. Forensic examination would reveal that one of them had been shot twice, the first bullet merely grazing her skull near the left ear, the second fired at close range into the back of her skull. Perhaps if she had played dead, she would have stayed alive; perhaps she remained unconscious after her beating with the tyre iron, and the second bullet had been a follow-up after the first was fired casually and in haste.

Beauty and the Beast had cruised, caught, and conquered; and they celebrated the success of their first murders, hostile commentators would later claim, when they drove to Reno, Nevada, the marriage-and-divorce capital of the United States, on 30 September 1977. Divorce would come later, when both were behind bars; now was the time for marriage with Beauty's doting parents Charles and Mercedes Williams as witnesses. Charles Williams, a grocer who had worked previously as a supermarket butcher, had already unwittingly helped the murders by sharing the cost of a loan on the Dodge van with his daughter; after the four of them returned to Sacramento he helped again by using his contacts to find Charlene a job in a meat-packing plant. Gerald, as ever, was happy to use Charlene's earnings as he pursued his chief interests: sex and domination.

But he was also interested in staying out of jail, and as the police hunt for the killer or killers of Rhonda Scheffler and Kippi Vaught continued in Sacramento, he and Charlene left California for a time to live in Houston, Texas. Charlene's parents, still happy to indulge their daughter's whims and not realising quite how far those whims extended, had helped their delinquent son-in-law to obtain false documentation in the name of Stephen Robert Feil. In German, *feil* is an adjective meaning 'venal' or 'mercenary'. It is also a homonym of the German noun *Pfeil*, meaning 'arrow'. These are appropriate meanings to add to those of Gerald's real surname, which is derived from Spanish, where it means 'Galician', and which splits in English into the highly appropriate 'gall' and 'ego'.

FUN AT THE FAIR

Having returned to Sacramento, Gerald displayed both in abundance in June of the following year, 1979, when the memories of his first success were no longer enough and he decided to do it all over again. He chose Reno as a hunting ground this time, less likely on a romantic whim than because he didn't want the Sacramento authorities to realise that they had a serial killer on their doorstep. He drove to the scene of his and Charlene's marriage and forced his by-now thoroughly subdued and dominated wife to trawl the crowds at the Washoe County Fair for two more young victims. As before, Charlene had a story ready: she was offering work putting advertising leaflets on the windscreens of cars at the fair. She met fourteen-year-old Brenda Judd and thirteen-year-old Sandra Colley, told her story and waited for their response. When the two girls agreed, Charlene led them to the van, telling them that they needed to collect the leaflets there.

Gerald, who had been following at a distance, then arrived at the van with a pistol. The two girls were bound, gagged and loaded into the van, and Gerald headed off along the Interstate 80 highway, stopping en route at a hardware store to buy a hammer and shovel. He had learned from the previous murders that casual dumping led to speedy discovery; this time he wanted to make it harder for the police. He resumed the wheel of the Dodge but, soon after, he stopped, handed the wheel to a frightened Charlene, ordered her to drive on and climbed into the back to rape the two girls. So at least runs one version of the second abduction and rapes. Another version says Charlene was so angry that Gerald had started the rapes without her that she drove off the road, braked hard, seized another pistol and exchanged shots with him before Gerald, wounded in the arm and complaining that the abrupt braking had bruised his penis, agreed to let her take part. As before, the two versions converge when the rapes are completed and Gerald beats the two girls unconscious with the hammer, shoots them in the back of the head and then uses the shovel to dig graves that concealed their bodies so successfully that they were listed as 'runaways' and presumed still alive until Charlene's confession in 1982 (in 1999 their graves were finally discovered and their identities confirmed by DNA tests).

KILL 'EM MALL

Back in Sacramento, life then resumed its normal course *chez* Gallego: violent sex, beatings and adultery. But the normal course of life now included annual hunts for disposable sex slaves and, in April 1980, Gerald and Charlene set off in their van again. Predators go where there is prey and for lions, interested in gazelle or zebra, hunting might take place at a waterhole; for Gerald and Charlene, interested in teenage girls, it was the car park at Tower Records in Sacramento. They were scared off by the presence of police and, like lions reverting to a tried-and-tested hunting place, decided to try their luck at a shopping mall again.

They drove to the Sunrise Mall at Citrus Heights and Charlene again went off on her own in search of a pair of girls. She soon found one: Stacy Ann Redican and Karen Twiggs, both seventeen, and both willing to believe Charlene's story of free drugs and a ride in an attractive, airbrushed van. There seems little doubt that if they had been three or four years younger Charlene would have tried the 'advertising leaflet' story again, and equally little doubt that she would have been believed. She was blonde, beautiful and petite, and she dressed and looked just like a teenager herself. Like called to like, and like did not realise its mistake until it was too late.

Because again, when Charlene had taken her new friends back to the van, Gerald and a gun were waiting. It was a .357 Magnum this time, its calibre swelling either with Gerald's ego or in compensation for it, and the two girls obeyed the stocky, dark-haired man standing behind it. They were forced into the back of the van and Gerald raped them repeatedly there as Charlene drove along the I-80 into the Nevada desert. When the rapes were over Gerald took the girls away one by one, killed them with a hammer and buried them in shallow graves. Whether the hammer was the same as that used in the murder of Brenda Judd and Sandra Colley is now uncertain, because it was thrown from the van by Charlene as they drove back to Sacramento.

Was she getting frightened and trying to destroy evidence? Or was she simply asserting herself in the partnership and readying Gerald for what she thought would be bad news? The bad news was that she was pregnant for the second time. The first time, in the previous year, Gerald had forced her to have an abortion at her own expense; this time, to Charlene's surprise, he welcomed the news. Perhaps he too was having doubts and felt a child would help create a suitably misleading air of domesticity in the Gallego household. What he and Charlene did next certainly supports that reading, because they visited Reno again and remarried, this time under the alias of Feil that Gerald had illegally assumed in 1978.

DEATH ON VACATION

To celebrate their newlywed status, the Feils took a holiday with their van in Oregon, the state that borders California and Nevada to the north. It was June 1980, a month before the bodies of Stacy Ann Redican and Karen Twiggs would be discovered in the Nevada desert to the south, and eight or nine months too soon for the Gallego's annual sex-slave hunt. But the Gallegos weren't the Gallegos any more: they were the Feils, and with a change of name came a quickening in murder rate. As they drove in the van down the coastal highway Gerald spotted a 21-year-old woman called Linda Aguilar walking beside it. He stopped the van and asked her if she wanted a lift. Well, she was pregnant, she was carrying groceries home, and 'It looks safe! . . . There's a girl with him!'

And so she accepted the offer and, while Charlene drove the van, Gerald raped her in the back. So at least runs one version of the story. In another, Charlene took part in the rape too. The two versions converge when Gerald strangled their seventh victim and beat her to death with a rock. Her body would be discovered a fortnight later, on 22 June, in a shallow grave dug in sand near the Pacific. Forensic examination would reveal grains of sand lodged in her nose, mouth and throat, suggesting that she was still breathing when she was buried, though probably unconscious from her head injuries. Her rape and murder had broken the annual pattern, because it followed that of Stacy Ann Redican and Karen Twiggs by only two months, but Gerald, like many serial killers before and since, found that cooling off between crimes was happening more and more quickly. He was cold by July, the following month, and he went looking for a new victim, not in Oregon or even in Nevada, but right on his own doorstep, in West Sacramento.

NO JANE DOE

Though whether he went looking for a victim or a victim found him could be debated, because with a quickening of murder rate came a change in murder method. Two changes, in fact: he no longer went cruising in the van and he no longer required extreme youth. And this time, perhaps, he needed to get drunk beforehand. On 16 July 1980, he and Charlene drank heavily all day and by nightfall found themselves in the Sail Inn, a bar in West Sacramento, being served by a 34-year-old barmaid called Virginia Mochel. Gerald was attracted to her, wanted her and was determined to get her, whatever the risk.

When the bar closed he and Charlene were waiting in the car park. It was the early morning of 17 July – a time Gerald's Spanish namesakes would call *la madrugada*, only a few letters from *la mandrágora*, 'the mandrake', or the root that drives men mad. And what Gerald was contemplating certainly seemed mad: he intended to abduct Virginia Mochel and take her back to his and Charlene's home on Bluebell Lane. Previously a combination of good luck and good judgment had kept him from the scrutiny of the authorities: Rhonda Scheffler and Kippi Vaught were murdered and dumped fifteen miles from Sacramento; he chose Reno for his next victims, Brenda Judd and Sandra Colley, and they were young enough for their disappearances to write them off as 'runaways'; he abducted Stacy Ann Redican and Karen Twiggs in Sacramento but murdered and dumped them in Nevada; he abducted, murdered and dumped Linda Aguilar many miles north in Oregon, and she was known to lead a wandering life, which delayed the search for her and then frustrated the search for her killers.

But Virginia Mochel had a settled life and was in paid employment to provide for two small children. Her disappearance would be reported quickly and be investigated thoroughly. Gerald didn't let it stop him. After Virginia Mochel locked up the bar and walked into the car park to drive home, she found herself confronting the same .357 Magnum as Stacy Ann Redican and Karen Twiggs. She was forced into the van and driven back to Bluebell Lane, where she was repeatedly raped by Gerald while Charlene watched television. So at least runs one version of the story. In another, Charlene participated, helping Gerald sodomise his victim and abusing Virginia Mochel herself. As before, the two versions coincide with the murder, performed by Gerald in the van as Charlene drove it towards Clarksburg, where the body was dumped.

Daylight on 17 July announced Gerald's 34th birthday, but if he celebrated it in the complacent knowledge of a bad job well done, his complacency would soon be shattered. Virginia Mochel's body would not be discovered until 30 October, but the police did not need a raped and battered body to know that something had happened to her. They began their investigation where she had last been seen, at the Sail Inn on the evening of 16 July, and regulars soon pointed them towards a couple of strangers called Stephen and Charlene. 'Stephen' was Gerald under his alias of Stephen Feil, but when the police tracked him down and questioned him he denied any involvement in or knowledge of Virginia Mochel's disappearance. When Charlene was questioned too she backed him up, saying that she and Gerald had gone fishing that day, and perhaps her blonde innocence was working its final piece of protective magic, for the police, despite their suspicions, accepted the story.

But when Virginia Mochel's body was discovered in October, the hands bound with fishing line, those suspicions must have increased. By then, however, the end was very near. Perhaps under the strain of the near miss by the authorities, Gerald and Charlene had separated in September 1980, and the sudden spate of murders ceased. At least, so far as is known they ceased, but, if Gerald carried on killing in the time he and Charlene were apart, Charlene did not learn about it and was unable to tell the police about it in the plea bargain she made after her arrest. Gerald left Sacramento for a time but on 1 November, the day after Hallowe'en, he was back and Charlene agreed to see him again.

BUNGLED FINAL ABDUCTION

But not just to see him: to help him find a new pair of victims. Borrowing her parents' Oldsmobile, they went cruising the malls and car parks of Sacramento during the evening and night of 1 November and on into the early morning of 2 November. Finally they reached the Arden Fair mall and Gerald, drunk and carrying a .25 pistol, climbed out of the car and approached a pair of prospective victims. It was an odd break in the routine for Gerald to do his own dirty work at the beginning of an abduction, and there was an even odder break in his choice of victims: not a pair of girls or young women, but a young man and a young woman, Craig Miller, aged 22, and Mary Beth Sowers, 21.

Odder still, however, the abduction did not go well. In fact, it went disastrously. The young couple had been attending a fraternity dance and after Gerald forced them into the car at gunpoint Craig Miller was seen by some of his friends. When they tried to find out what was going on, Charlene, in the driver's seat, shouted at them and drove quickly away. Not quickly enough, however, to stop one of Miller's friends noting the licence number of the Oldsmobile. It was all over, but the Gallegos hadn't realised it yet. Craig Miller was disposed of quickly, shot in the head and dumped in El Dorado county outside Sacramento without any attempt at concealment; Mary Beth Sowers was brought back to Gerald's new home and raped. Then, like Miller, she was taken out into the country, shot and dumped.

Charlene and Gerald then returned to Gerald's home to clean up and dispose of evidence. It was one of the last acts in their partnership, because they found the police waiting for them when they returned the Oldsmobile to Charlene's parents the following day. Charlene spun a tale of drunken confusion to cover the events of the previous night, but they knew it would hold the police for no more than a few hours. That night they tried to find Craig Miller's body and hide it better, but it was gone. The first obvious conclusion was that it had been found by the police; the second was that it was time to go on the run.

With the help of Charlene's parents and money wired to them in Salt Lake City, Utah, they made it as far as Omaha, Nebraska. By then, however, the police had been talking to the Williamses and Charles and Mercedes knew just what kind of man their daughter had married. When Charlene asked for more money to be wired to Omaha, the Williamses told the FBI and Charlene and Gerald were arrested when they turned up to collect their money at the Western Union office. It was the end, or, rather, the beginning of the end. Having killed in company, the Gallegos divorced in detention, and Charlene agreed to a reduced sentence and eventual parole in return for providing evidence against Gerald, who would inevitably face the death sentence not just in California but in Nevada too.

He conducted his own defence in California and lost, being sentenced to death in 1983 for the murders of Craig Miller and Mary Beth Sowers. In Nevada he handed his case over to a public defender and lost again, being sentenced to death in 1984 for the murders of Stacy Redican and Karen Twiggs. Repeated appeals since then mean that, of November 2001, he is still waiting to meet the death sentence in one or the other state. Charlene, as already mentioned, served her sentence and was released in 1997.

NOTES

1. Waugh, Evelyn, *Put Out More Flags*, Penguin Books, London, 1942, chapter 1, part 3.
2. Plato's *Symposium* (360 BC), Jowett's translation of 1871.
3. Ibid.
4. Pearson, Patricia, *When She Was Bad: How Women Get Away with Murder*, Virago, London, 1998, 'What's Love Got To Do With It?', p. 185.

BIBLIOGRAPHY

Flowers, R Barri, *The Sex Slave Murders: The Horrifying True Story of America's First Husband-and-Wife Serial Killers*, St Martin's Press, New York, 1996.

Hoffmann, Eric van, *A Venom in the Blood – The Bizarre True Account of the Husband-and-Wife Serial Killers who Terrorized the California Countryside*, Pinnacle Books, 1999.

Hecox, Walt and Biondi, Ray, *All His Father's Sins: The Shocking Truth About California's Most Gruesome Serial Killer*, Prima Publishing, California, 1988.

8. GHOST OF A GIRL – THE DEAD-END CRIME TRIP OF ALTON COLEMAN AND DEBRA BROWN

Mankind – with the emphasis on 'man' – casts a pretty long shadow, catching within it those who follow him. If he's (in)famous especially, then others who have played a significant part in his life will more than likely have their own lives reduced to nothing more than being a connection: a link that joins together one greater part to the other. It's fair to say that those 'others' caught in these great shadows are usually female. Example: obituaries of the American journalist Martha Gellhorn (1908–98) listed an impressive array of achievements, both personal and professional: war correspondent (from the D-day landings to the Vietnam conflict), travel writer and novelist.

But these were obscured by one solitary event: Gellhorn was briefly married to Ernest Hemingway. The big shadow cast over her belonged to him. In the greater scheme of things, she was just one of the famous writer's wives. Nothing more. Too strong a person, however, to be totally assimilated into a literary legend, Martha Gellhorn was still solid, still mobile: flesh and bone. There were and are others – 'others' in less celebrated shadows, who lack the defining outlines of personality, of individuality. Others lead, they follow. Like ghosts.

In the summer of 1984, Alton Coleman and Debra Brown, black residents of Waukegan, Illinois (a Lake Michigan industrial town twenty kilometres, or about twelve miles, north of Chicago), went on a 53-day rampage in the Great Lakes region – a malevolent road trip that spanned seven states and clocked up eight murders, seven rapes, three kidnappings and numerous armed robberies. 'Rampage', however, might be too strong a word: Coleman and Brown's crimes lacked direction, motivation (rational or otherwise), genuine targets or planning. What they do reek of is boredom: boredom filtered through modern life, homicides committed for the vaguest of reasons. The reasons were Alton Coleman's, a paranoid with a hair-trigger temper, whose violence – for the most part – confined itself to his own ethnic group. Debra Brown, it seems, was there because, in one of the richest countries on the planet, there appeared to be nothing better to do. Everything and nothing. Different levels of social status do not mean that the next step up will be the answer to all problems: those higher levels just create boredom by another name. In the USA, what is constantly at your fingertips can very easily be taken away. It works all ways, through all classes. Example: in May 1998, fifteen-year-old Kip Kinkel, the son of a well-off Oregon family, shot and killed his parents before going to his local school to mow down classmates in the cafeteria. To his mother and father, Kinkel seemed alienated and directionless, and so they financially encouraged any interests he took up. When his interest turned to firearms, the chequebook overruled the heart and Kinkel got whatever he wanted. As long as it made him 'happy'. Punishment and reward. Ghosts and lost souls drift across the social strata of the USA, no more so than in the industrial regions of the Great Lakes.

There are leaders and followers, never an equal partnership: there are those that fool themselves that they are equal and those that know they are in charge. One walks in the other's shadow. Debra Brown was one such follower, a girl lost in the shadows of her partner,

Alton Coleman – one step below him, but one step above the people they murdered together. Brown came out of other shadows when she met Coleman, but it was just a step from day-to-day obscurity to the exciting confines cast by Coleman: she was the ghost of a girl making ghosts out of their victims.

IN THE ZOMBIE SHOPPING MALL

Alton Coleman was born in November 1955, the third child in three boys and two girls. Their mother was a known prostitute in a ghetto area of Waukegan who first gave birth when she was fourteen. Debra Denise Brown was also born in Waukegan, in November 1962, the fifth of eleven children raised in a far more respectable home. Elton, as he was called then, didn't interest his mother, and was soon sent off to live with his maternal grandmother. Mildly retarded, Coleman was nicknamed 'Pissy' in the schoolyard, owing to his habit of regularly wetting his pants. Uninterested in an education, he grew up running with Waukegan street gangs; like them, he carried a knife, indulged in petty vandalism and soon earned himself the more flattering moniker, 'Big Al'. Dropping out of grade school, he began working part-time in the kitchen of an army veterans' home. Some years later, Debra Brown would drop out of high school, the prospect of having to take on more education already a bore to her. Non-aggressive, she had a dependent personality and, like Coleman, was mildly retarded (perhaps because of a head injury sustained as a child). To people like her and Coleman, life was a Sargasso Sea of unformed feelings, ideas, decisions and plans. Coleman's first job was washing dishes in a kitchen, probably the easiest unskilled employment to obtain, to leave, to be fired from. In this zombie shopping mall, every single day is the rest of your life:

tomorrow doesn't matter, so why not drop out? Why look for something better?

Already known to the Waukegan police for an array of minor crimes, Alton Coleman was eighteen when he committed his first major offence. On 27 December 1973, Coleman and an unnamed accomplice kidnapped a 54-year-old woman from a local shopping centre. They raped and robbed her, and then dumped her out of their car – naked but alive – in a local housing project. Two days later, the pair were arrested. The victim refused to testify on the rape charge, and so they could be convicted only on the robbery. This denial or silence from the victim was the first instance in a thin line of courtroom wheedling that Coleman would use in his defence. Intimidation or the spectral threat of violence was usually the cause, but Coleman would later claim that his faith, the voodoo deity Baron Samedi (a.k.a. Ghede), made him invulnerable against conviction. Samedi is the predominant force in voodoo, the wise lord of cemeteries and black magic, clad in black top hat, black tail coat and dark glasses. In voodoo lore, he waits at the crossroads that lead to *guinee* – the home of the gods – to catch souls travelling there.

After serving just two years of a six-year sentence in Illinois's Joliet Prison, Alton Coleman crawled back into the regular world a successful graduate of incarceration sexuality. The time spent inside must have only heightened sexual desires still in their infancy throughout his teenage life. In Joliet, he was accused numerous times by other inmates of assault, usually of a sexual nature. His tastes ran towards dominant, rough sex. An internal psychiatric profile described Alton Coleman as 'pansexual . . . willing to have intercourse with any object, women, men, children'.

Three months after his release, Coleman was in court again charged with rape, but was acquitted when it was implied that the woman consented. The next eight years saw Coleman mapping out a habitual pattern of rape that, for some reason, gave no indication to the authorities of what he would eventually be capable of. In 1980 Coleman got married, a six-month-long entanglement that ended with his teenage bride seeking police protection. During the later trial of Coleman and Debra Brown, she offered descriptions of her former husband's obsession with bondage, young girls and violent sex. The apex of Coleman's violent desires and sentence-dodging abilities came in the summer of 1983, when he was accused of indecent liberties with a child. The charge was filed by one of Coleman's sisters after he had tried to rape her eight-year-old daughter. But, in court, the sister suddenly changed her mind about the accusations. Initially baffled by the turnaround, the presiding judge commented – with perception – that the woman was obviously terrified by Alton Coleman. No witnesses and no victim ensured he was a free man. An unrestrained attitude to sex and a knack of intimidation walked with Coleman through his future crimes.

THE KINDNESS OF STRANGERS

Waukegan, early summer 1984. In a local bar 21-year-old Debra Brown met 28-year-old Alton Coleman. Brown was engaged to be married at the time, just another ghost in the mall, a follower who could not find anything to follow, anything to do. If Brown was anonymous and already dead, then Coleman's shadow was an exciting one to fall into. He offered a step up, a definite direction that would lead to nowhere. The pair disappeared from Waukegan, ending up in Gary, Indiana. Coleman had jumped bail. He was a suspect in the rape and murder of a fifteen-year-old girl from Chicago.

Followers and leaders. The Great Lakes region became a killing ground for Alton Coleman's disorganised mind. This was not an expression of pent-up anger: this was slaughter as a TV dinner, a break between flicking through all those channels and picking up burger and fries at the drive-in. There was no higher purpose to Alton Coleman and Debra Brown's rampage (even Coleman's belief in Baron Samedi could be culturally reduced to nothing more than implying he had watched the James Bond film *Live and Let Die* (1973), where Geoffrey Holder portrays the Baron as the white man's enigmatic enemy): they drifted through landscapes that offered everything and yet nothing, stealing whatever came to hand, lashing out at whoever was close. One led, the other followed.

On 29 May 1984, nine-year old Vernita Wheat persuaded her mother to allow her to go on a trip to Waukegan, fifteen kilometres (some nine miles) over the border from her home in Kenosha, Wisconsin. She was accompanied by Robert Knight – a man who had recently made friends with the mother – and his girlfriend. They were going to Waukegan to pick up a stereo as a belated Mother's Day gift. The next day, neither Vernita Wheat nor Knight and his girlfriend returned to Kenosha. Vernita's mother contacted the local police. At the station, looking through a photographic line-up, she identified Alton Coleman as 'Robert Knight'. Her daughter's body would not be found until 19 June, in an abandoned Waukegan building. She had been strangled. The day after he kidnapped and murdered Vernita Wheat, Alton Coleman appeared at Lake County Circuit Court for a pre-trial hearing on rape charges dating back to Chicago in the early 1980s. On that same day, 30 May, a federal grand jury indicted Coleman and Brown on kidnapping charges. Ghosts and shadows, flitting through the fingers of legal systems. Coleman must have thought his protection by a *loa* was working.

Both Coleman and Brown were now wanted faces, visible images sought by police, the subjects of fledgling investigations by the Federal Bureau of Investigation. In the Chicago town of Evanston, Debra Brown was even questioned by local police over the whereabouts of Coleman, but she gave nothing away about her new love, not even the fact that Coleman (under an assumed name) and she had stayed in a room at the Holiday Inn that stood just one block away from Evanston police station. On 5 June, the couple rented an apartment in Gary. From there on began the burnout spiral that eventually brought Alton Coleman and Debra Brown down, exhausted by random destruction. Their invisible status – the spell sought from Baron Samedi – worked for some time, but not for ever. Through the fact that they mostly kept within their own racial group, they were assured Coleman's voodoo protection. For example, an Evanston man reported to police that on 10 June he was flagged down by a black male (later identified as Coleman) and offered $25 for a ride to Chicago. After stopping off at an unspecified location (believed by the FBI to be where Coleman bought fake ID), Coleman offered more money and the suggestion that the man drive him to Gary, southeast of the city. Reluctantly, the driver agreed. It was the unwanted interruption of a normal day, a blip on the schedule, the significance of it realised only later. Coleman the buddy, the brother. Add the silent Brown, with her blank history and willingness to follow, and you have a couple. A nice couple. No threat. On 17 June, 21-year-old Donna Williams, a hairdresser from Gary, was last seen going to pick up a 'nice' couple from Boston, who wanted to visit her local church. The guide and her guests never arrived at their destination. Two days later, Williams's mother reported her missing. Police enquiries at the salon where Williams worked offered positive IDs on Coleman and Brown: they had been recent visitors to the premises.

Alton Coleman and Debra Brown were building up a legion of ghosts to accompany them. Ghosts of girls. The day after the abduction of Donna Williams, the couple – driving Williams's car – pulled up to the kerb in a Gary street and asked two children for directions. Seven-year-old Tamika Turks and her nine-year-old niece, Annie, were on their way back from the store, but they got in anyway, tempted by offers of money. Once inside the car they were kept quiet with a knife while Coleman drove out twenty kilometres (twelve miles) from Gary, to a wooded area where he said they were going to play a game. Deep in the woods, Coleman and Brown tore up Tamika's shirt and used it to bind and gag her and Annie. When Tamika began to cry and struggle, Brown put a hand over her mouth in an attempt to silence her. Coleman, angered by the noise, stamped repeatedly on Tamika's face and chest; then he raped her, and strangled her with an elastic strip of bedsheet (later found to have come from the couple's apartment). After they had carried Tamika's body to nearby bushes, the couple forced Annie to perform oral sex on both of them. Then Coleman raped and attempted to strangle her. The couple eventually left Annie for dead, but she had only passed out. Staggering out of the woods, she was picked up by a motorist and taken to the local hospital. She later identified Coleman and Brown from photos. The following day – 19 June – Tamika's body was found.

A few days after the brutal murder of Tamika Turks, a woman in Detroit, Michigan, was abducted while getting into her car outside her own home. A couple – who, police later revealed, matched descriptions of Coleman and Brown – threatened her with knives and demanded she drive them the eighty-odd kilometres (more than fifty miles) south to Toledo, Ohio. At one point during the journey, the woman deliberately ploughed the car into a stationary lorry. While the couple lay dazed in the back, she was able to escape on foot. When they came to their senses, her passengers took off in the damaged car.

The only consistent thing about Coleman and Brown's crime trip was its inconsistency, its lack of patience. The pair wanted transport: they found the nearest available source. The pair wanted sex: they found the nearest available source. The rationale between who was a victim and who was a bystander in their eyes was blurred, murky. Debra Brown was only a threat in the presence of her lover; Alton Coleman, who would soon make the FBI's Ten Most Wanted list, was the authorities' worst nightmare: a killer with no motive, who left no clues to why he did what he did. His violence could be summed up in a shrug of the shoulders. As a couple, as leader and follower, they zigzagged in a schizophrenic line. Ten days after her disappearance, on 27 June, Donna Williams's car was located in a Detroit alley. In it police found a forged ID card holding Debra Brown's picture. Local residents told them the vehicle had been there since 19 June. When the petrol ran out, the pair must have simply gone looking for another vehicle to take them on their trip to nowhere. If this was Alton Coleman's way of avoiding police detection, his voodoo must have been blocking some signals to the authorities: for every mode of transport they stole, its owner was left behind, mostly alive and ready to tell the facts. On 30 June, for instance, in Detroit, two men – one an invalid – offered the couple a ride. Once in the car, Coleman pulled a gun. The driver tried to wrest it from him, but failed and instead fled from the car. The invalid was thrown from the moving vehicle, albeit unharmed.

On 2 July, at around breakfast time, Coleman and Brown, roaming the Detroit suburb of Dearborn Heights, broke into Palmer and Maggie Jones's home. The middle-aged couple were beaten with a length of pipe and left bleeding on the floor while Coleman and Brown stole petty cash and their car, finally heading for Toledo. During the beating, police reported, the couple were made to listen to a rambling and inconsequential rant from Coleman on how his fellow blacks were driving him to murder other members of his race. In Toledo, they abandoned the car, only to steal another. They had become like ghosts again, flitting across the peripheral vision of the authorities. One report had it that Coleman exchanged gunfire with the tender of a local bar, after he tried unsuccessfully to kidnap a customer. Whoever was at hand became victim or witness.

The flash fire of attention in Toledo gave form to these silhouettes. To thirty-year-old Virginia Temple, they must have seemed the 'nice young couple' that Donna Williams also saw: she invited them to spend the night of 7 July in the home she shared with her ten-year-old daughter, Rochelle. The next morning, Coleman and Brown robbed her home and left. The bodies of Virginia and Rochelle were stuffed in the crawlspace beneath the house. Both had been strangled, and Rochelle raped. Lives and bodies touched by the couple disappeared and appeared simultaneously.

A Cincinnati resident, Tonnie Story, went missing on 10 July. She had last been seen with a couple resembling

Coleman and Brown. Inexplicably, they had been driven to Cincinnati from Dayton by a 79-year-old minister, the Reverend Millard Gay. Using pseudonyms, the couple had spent an amicable few nights at Gay's home, and he had gladly driven them to Cincinnati for their 'prayer meeting'. Donna Williams's corpse was discovered on 11 July, in an abandoned house near Wayne State University, Detroit, almost 350 kilometres (220 miles) from her home of Gary. She had been strangled with a pair of tights. It's possible that her body lay in the trunk of their car while Coleman and Brown killed Tamika Turks.

Up until the discovery of Williams's corpse, Alton Coleman's homicidal tendencies had been restricted to his own racial group: it was easy to remain anonymous, to travel safely in such a self-imposed ghetto. A white man rampaging through a Waukegan project would be as recognisable as Coleman slaying his way through a WASP suburb. Coleman's superficial reliance on Samedi's black magic, his paranoid insistence that his brothers were pushing him to murder his own kind, had so far boxed in the couple's crimes, compartmentalising them within one social group. But Coleman's only restriction on his wayward frenzy was about to disappear. On 13 July, in the Cincinnati suburb of Norwood, two young blacks turned up on the doorstep of Harry and Marlene Walters, a middle-aged white couple. They had arrived on racing bikes (even these modes of transport betrayed Coleman and Brown's flailing methods, grabbing whatever was within reach) to look at a camper van that the Walters had for sale. Within hours, Harry Walters had been badly beaten, and his wife Marlene bludgeoned to death in the house's basement. Coleman and Brown got away in Harry's car.

Through Harry Walters's description of the criminals' modus operandi, the authorities charged Alton Coleman with the aggravated murder of Marlene Walters, attempted aggravated murder, aggravated burglary, aggravated robbery and grand auto theft. The next day Harry's car was found abandoned in a cornfield, 125 kilometres (78 miles) south in Lexington, Kentucky. By murdering Marlene Walters, Alton Coleman and Debra Brown stepped out of the shadows of their own culture and became one hundred per cent visible. It could only be a matter of time before they were caught. What dictated to Alton who lived and who died was perhaps a matter known only by him. Like Samedi, he took or spared the souls who crossed his path.

The couple's disorganisation as they skidded across seven states could probably be seen from space. Close up, as the 'nice young couple', it was harder to trace. At first. A Lexington resident, Thomas Harris, after his arrest, explained that he was 'kind of forced' to help Coleman and Brown when they kidnapped Oline Carmical Jr, a 44-year-old college professor, on 16 July. They bundled him into the boot of his car and then drove north to Dayton, leaving him there. Later in the day, Carmical was rescued (describing his kidnappers as two black men and a woman), Harris was arrested and Coleman and Brown returned to the home of their friend Reverend Gay. They beat him and his wife, tied and gagged them and stole their station wagon.

Two days later, after dumping the minister's vehicle beside a car wash in Indianapolis, Indiana, Coleman and Brown abducted the business's owner, 77-year-old Eugene Scott, and drove off in his car. After Scott was reported missing, a search culminated hours later when his body was found in a roadside ditch near Zionsville. He had been stabbed repeatedly and shot four times in the head with a .38-calibre firearm. Knife slashes on his hands suggested he may have put up a struggle, or just

GHOST OF A GIRL

futilely tried to shield himself from Alton Coleman's
frenzy.

Coleman and Brown roamed across state borders with
no apparent care for their own anonymity. On 19 July,
Dayton police began a search for a mother and her two
children, a three-year-old boy and a four-year-old girl.
According to a later FBI report, the family had disappeared after being seen with Coleman and Brown earlier
in the month, and it was suggested that they may have
even stayed with the couple at Reverend Gay's home at
the beginning of July. In Cincinnati, again on the 19th,
the body of fifteen-year-old Tonnie Storey was found.
She had been raped, stabbed repeatedly and shot in the
head twice.

Within the 24-hour time span of this discovery, Alton
Coleman and Debra Brown remained visible back in
Evanston. On the night of the 19th, they were seen at
least three times in a four-hour period, within the same
two blocks. On Wesley Avenue, a man drinking with
friends told police that Coleman stopped to have a beer
with the group; a mother reported that she talked to
Coleman for about an hour while eating her dinner on
the porch of her house (with Coleman outside, she
phoned in an anonymous tip, but he was gone when a
squad car arrived); around 11.30 p.m., another resident
in the Wesley Avenue/Foster Street area phoned in a
Coleman sighting but, again, a dispatched car couldn't
find him in the district where, in 1973, Coleman
committed his first major crime.

It was the morning of 20 July before the ghost figures
of Alton Coleman and Debra Brown were finally pinned
down. Their aimless wanderings had to stop somewhere; definition had to be given to those two shells.
Tipped off by a local man who had grown up in the
same area as Coleman, a team of police officers closed

in on the couple. They were sitting in Mason Park watching a basketball game from the bleachers. Both looked scruffy, wearing clothes purchased at a local charity store. Both looked tired and wasted. When the pair got up and walked away from the game, they were arrested. Neither resisted, although both gave false names; separately asked her boyfriend's name, Debra Brown gave a different one from the name offered by Coleman. In Brown's handbag police found an un-loaded, .38-calibre, snub-nosed revolver. They took off Coleman a three-inch pocket knife and a steak knife. Both had blood on them. Possession of the gun and steak knife facilitated a double arrest. In the afternoon, five blocks away, police recovered a car believed to be the murdered Eugene Scott's. Debra Brown's finger-prints were lifted from inside it. Their crime trip had run out of road, no longer watched over by their top-hatted *loa*.

DEATH DEALS FOUR NEW CARDS

Alton Coleman and Debra Brown's arrest was just the beginning for the US legal system. The random trail of crime they left behind cut deep into many states, some with and some without the death penalty. It went unsaid that states that carried the penalty would be first in line to prosecute, whereas states such as Wisconsin – which did not – would have to wait their turn. If it ever came at all.

In July 1984, a Chicago federal magistrate set the bail bond in the forthcoming Vernita Wheat murder trial at $25 million and $20 million for Coleman and Brown respectively. The action effectively imprisoned the couple there and then, although this did not stop them legally entering into a common-law marriage before they were taken away to separate prisons.

The random, lifeless actions of Alton Coleman and Debra Brown returned hard in consequence. In Ohio, the trials for the murders of Marlene Walters and Tonnie Storey resulted in death sentences for the pair. For Walters, Coleman was sent to the electric chair. Brown got a life sentence, even though she boasted about getting a kick out of the murder. For Storey, the pair received death sentences. In Indiana, for the horrific murder of Tamika Turks, Coleman received a death sentence, and a hundred-year stretch for the attempted murder and molestation of her niece, Annie. Brown got death and forty years for murder, attempted murder, and child molestation. In Illinois, Coleman was sentenced to death by lethal injection for the kidnapping and murder of Vernita Wheat. With four death sentences looming, there were no further prosecutions for the four other outstanding homicides. Awaiting their fates, Debra Brown was sent to the Ohio Reformatory for Women; Alton Coleman was sent to the Mansfield Correctional Institution, Ohio.

It would seem that murder was just a by-product of Alton Coleman's sexual desire. The couple's crime trip had no gaps in it: when Coleman could not find a hole to sate himself, Brown probably stepped in, but even she could satisfy him only so far, as Coleman's desires became more and more violent. His boredom, his lack of interest, found no other outlet apart from sex and violence. In his 1960 novel *Ritual in the Dark*, Colin Wilson set this challenge: that the boredom and frustration felt by mankind – with the emphasis on 'man' – are mere facets of a mind not utilising its full potential. This potential, Wilson explains, must be realised in creativity: writing, art and – sometimes – violence. Expression through violence. In *Ritual in the Dark*, the writer Gerard Sorme has brilliant ideas for books but lacks the discipline actually to begin writing them; the painter Oliver Glasp is prolific but lacks the social skills to sell his work and himself; finally, the romantic Austin Nunne is neither writer nor painter. He expresses his frustrations through murder. Of the three characters, Nunne is the most self-confident, yet his inability to fix his mind on One True Thing has led to homicide. Boredom and ennui usually drag the sufferer down to some level; it just depends on the individual mindset whether that level is being slumped in front of the TV or killing another human being.

But these are extraneous circumstances. Unlike Wilson's characters, Coleman and Brown were not using murder as a form of expression, an indication of a higher self. It may be indicative of their cultural surroundings that there are no handy artistic tags to hang on their deeds, no literary comparisons. The viewpoint is different, saturated in consumer excess, pitted with a grab-bag of belief and paranoia. The crimes of Wilson's characters are already a million miles away: they are fighting to escape a boredom set up by their creator. Alton Coleman and Debra Brown were trapped within that industrial sinkhole of the Great Lakes region long before their burnout road trip. Murder to Coleman was the last twitch when orgasm transgressed to violent satisfaction, or disgust. Murder to Brown was a hyper-reality she had never known, played out next to a man she was devoted to. They had not grasped for meaning and so their crimes, and lives – and the lives of their victims – were meaningless. They existed only in the shadows of a superficial culture.

EPILOGUE: A LINE OF GHOSTS
In January 1991, the governor of Ohio reduced Debra Brown's death sentence to life without parole. The

governor commented that she was 'retarded, and dominated by Alton Coleman'. By 1997, Brown had launched her own campaign to overturn her Indiana death sentence. But the legal system's tolerance of Alton Coleman's loophole skills was wearing thin. In August 2000, through an unrelated murder case, the US Supreme Court ruled that a murder defendant is entitled to 'constitutionally adequate legal representation'. Jumping on this, Coleman's attorneys filed for relief under the new ruling. The Indiana Supreme Court was forced to reconsider Coleman's death sentence. Rising to the opportunity, Coleman alleged that during his sentencing his then counsel were inadequate because they did not make clear mitigating factors that might have spared him the death penalty. His current attorneys stressed that their client had suffered from a troubled childhood, personality disorder and brain dysfunction. But not even Coleman's voodoo could magic such claims out of nowhere: Indiana rejected the action.

Debra Brown serves out her sentences in Ohio Reformatory for Women, Alton Coleman in the Mansfield Correctional Institution. His death by capital punishment awaits somewhere down the line, as he left too many corpses on the roads ever to completely escape: if one state dropped a death sentence, another behind it would pick up the baton, making ghosts of the living to appease the dead.

BIBLIOGRAPHY

Indiana Death Row: http://www.clarkprosecutor.org/html/death/rownew.htm

Gribben, Mark, 'Alton Coleman & Debra Brown: Odyssey of Mayhem', http://www.crimelibrary.com

Lohr, David, 'Thrill Killers', www.serialkillerarchive.com

9. LOVE WILL TEAR US APART – DAVID AND CATHERINE BIRNIE

'What a pointless loss of young life.'[1]

> David Birnie to Detective Sergeant Vince Katich,
> after showing the police burial sites of
> four women he had murdered.

The last thing Detective Sergeant Vince Katich expected when questioning the scrawny David Birnie on the evening of 10 November 1986 about an alleged rape was for him to confess to multiple murder. Australian police in the city of Perth had been concerned about the disappearances of young local women for some time, but, if they were going to solve the cases they predicted, it would take a lot of legwork. Birnie's confession, in response to a joke made by Katich about digging up bodies, was instantaneous and complete, and Birnie and his wife even went on immediately to show the police where they'd buried each of their victims.

Maybe the lovers had had enough. Maybe the most recent killing, a botched rape-murder in which the victim had been stabbed repeatedly, following which her head was split open twice with an axe, had proved too messy. Whatever the case, the Birnies now ranked with notorious sex killers such as Fred and Rose West as their country's most infamous killer couple.

YOUNG LOVE

David John Birnie was the oldest of six children born to Margaret and John Birnie. Both parents had a long history of chronic alcoholism and their children were periodically taken away from them and institutionalised;

when David was twelve he was taken away for good to grow up in foster homes in the suburbs of Perth. Much later journalists would track down Birnie's mother, only to find her living in terminal squalor in a filthy flat, having given up hope of seeing her children again; John Birnie died in 1986 following a protracted illness.

Catherine Johnston's childhood was similarly blighted. When she was just ten months old her mother died and she was taken by her father to live with him in South Africa. Two years later she was sent back to Australia to be taken care of by her grandparents. She was a lonely child who had difficulty in forming friendships, and was shunned by her peers. She met David Birnie when they were both still children, their families living next door to each other; as he was the first of her peers to show an interest in her she adored him, and they became lovers at fourteen.

The families moved, and David and Catherine saw nothing more of each other until they were reunited in their late teens. By this time David already had an extensive record of juvenile offences, and was widely suspected to have committed many crimes for which he had not been caught. His one legitimate job had come when he was employed by a horse trainer, Eric Parnham, who recalled picking up the pale, sickly youth at the latter's derelict, dog-ridden home. Birnie showed promise and was recommended as an apprentice prospect, staying in the stables for eleven months and demonstrating a natural flair for racing – he was considered to have potential as a good jockey. But Birnie was finally sacked when he was alleged to have assaulted and robbed the elderly owner of a boarding house.

Catherine and David were to become firm partners upon their reunion – his lover would do anything to stay close to him, as she would amply prove in time. Keen to avoid working so that they could spend more time together, the couple embarked on a spree of petty crime. On 11 June 1969 they pleaded guilty in the Perth police court to eleven charges of breaking, entering and stealing goods worth almost $3,000. They also admitted that they had stolen oxyacetylene equipment, which they'd then used to attempt a safe-cracking at the Waverley drive-in cinema. Catherine – who the court heard was pregnant by another man – was placed on probation, while David was sent to prison for nine months. On 9 July 1969 the couple pleaded guilty to eight further charges of breaking, entering and stealing at a trial brought at the Supreme Court. David's sentence was extended by three years, Catherine's probation period by four.

On 21 June the following year David Birnie escaped from Karnet Prison in Western Australia and again teamed up with Catherine to embark on another spate of robberies. Upon their capture on 10 July they were charged with 53 counts of stealing, receiving, breaking and entering, unlawful entry into premises and unlawful driving and use of motor vehicles. Police found them equipped with wigs and a variety of outfits, a hundred sticks of gelignite, 120 detonators and three fuses. Catherine told police that she knew what she'd done was wrong, but that she loved David so much that she'd do anything for him.

David Birnie received a jail sentence of two and a half years, while Catherine received six months, probation being considered both unworkable – she'd been on probation during her last two crime sprees – and unnecessary, now that she'd given birth. Her baby was taken away by welfare workers but returned to her on her release.

Catherine then went to work for a family in Fremantle as a live-in domestic. Away from David Birnie, her criminal tendencies were less pronounced, and the son of the family, Donald McLaughlan, fell in love with her. The couple married on 31 May 1972, the date of Catherine's 21st birthday. They were to have five children together, the first of whom, 'Little Donny', was born shortly after the marriage. Seven months later, the child was killed, crushed by a car in front of Catherine; psychiatrists later speculated on the emotional impact of the child's death on Catherine in relation to her dependence upon David Birnie.

Catherine eventually left her husband, a development that surprised few who knew her. The family had been living in a squalid State Housing Commission home in Victoria Park, a poor suburb of Perth. Catherine was looking after not only her unemployed husband and five children but also her father and uncle, and the house was a tip, with never enough money to feed every mouth. She called Donald one day and told him she wouldn't be coming back: she'd been seeing David Birnie for the past two years and was going to live with him. After a thirteen-year separation she returned to her first love, and although they never married Catherine changed her surname by deed poll to Birnie, becoming his common-law wife.

David's tastes had grown more esoteric since he'd initially known Catherine, and his interest in the more extreme manifestations of sex – including bondage and rape fantasies – was matched only by the size of his pornographic video collection. James Birnie, one of David's younger brothers, who demonstrated amply that extreme aberrant sexual behaviour ran in the Birnie family, stayed with the couple briefly on his release from prison following a five-month sentence for indecently interfering with his six-year-old niece. He told reporters later:

> [The six-year-old] led me on. You don't know what they can be like. When I left prison, I had nowhere to go. I couldn't go back to my mother's place because I had assaulted her and there was a restraining order out against me. I had a couple of fights with Mum and the police chased me off. Mum has alcohol problems. So David and Catherine let me move in. They weren't real happy about it and David kept saying that he was going to kill me to keep me in line . . . He has to have sex four or five times a day. I saw him use a hypodermic of that stuff you have when they're going to put stitches in your leg. It makes you numb. He put the needle in his penis. Then he had sex. David has had many women. He always has someone.[2]

THE KILLINGS

David and Catherine had discussed kidnapping and rape as part of their pillow talk. It would turn them on to talk about it: about how Catherine would have powerful orgasms if she watched David having sex with another woman who was bound and gagged. About how Catherine wanted to lick David's genitals while he was having sex with another woman – she wanted to pull his penis out of the other woman and suck it as it came. Perhaps she was already wary of David's involvement with these other women, worried that they might replace her, or that he might find them more attractive. If she made sure he treated them as objects, then he couldn't love them; and if she controlled his orgasms she'd keep her hold on him.

Fantasy became reality on 6 October 1986. Mary Frances Neilson was a 22-year-old student of psychology at the University of Western Australia and worked part-time at a delicatessen to make ends meet. She hoped her degree would lead to a job as a counsellor at the Community Welfare Department. Her lecturer parents were away on holiday in the UK at the time of Mary's disappearance. She left the delicatessen to go to a lecture, and that was the last anyone had seen of her. Anyone except the Birnies.

Mary had been looking for some cheap car tyres, and had visited the spare-parts yard where David Birnie worked as a labourer. Birnie recommended that she come to his home for a cheap deal, and she duly drove her Galant sedan to the address he'd supplied. As soon as she'd stepped through the door she was held at knifepoint, gagged and then chained to the Birnies' bed. Catherine watched, excited, as David repeatedly raped her; they talked throughout, Catherine asking David what he liked doing most, keen to learn for the future what really turned her lover on.

Their fantasy hadn't got far enough to discuss what they'd do to a girl once they'd raped her, but it was clear to Catherine that they couldn't just let her go. She'd seen their faces, and knew where they lived. That evening they drove to the nearby Gleneagles National Park with Mary bundled up in the back of the car. In a forest there David raped her again before wrapping a nylon cord around her neck and slowly tightening it with a branch, choking her to death. He dug a shallow grave and stabbed his victim's body once before burying her, telling Catherine that he'd read in a magazine that the puncture would allow gas to escape as the body decomposed. Later David drove his victim's car away from his bungalow, leaving it in a car park near the local police headquarters. It was discovered six days later.

Buoyed by the success of their first foray into rape-murder, the couple decided to try again. Fifteen-year-old Susannah Candy lived in Nedlands with her parents, two brothers and a sister. She had a bright future ahead of her: she was an exceptional student at a good school, and her father was one of the top ophthalmic surgeons in the state of Western Australia. Two weeks after the killing of Mary Neilson, Susannah was hitchhiking on the Stirling Highway in Claremont when she was picked up by the Birnies. The couple had been driving for a couple of hours before they found Susannah, who met their criteria perfectly.

As soon as she'd accepted the ride, her hands were tied and a knife was put to her throat. They drove her back to their home, where she in turn was gagged, chained to the bed and raped. Acting on what David had told her last time they'd raped a girl, Catherine joined the couple in bed as soon as David had finished – she knew this was what turned him on. Kidnapping Susannah was especially risky – she was still young enough for her parents to worry when she didn't come home – so they forced her to write two letters to her family, stalling any search by asking them not to worry about her. One of the letters was posted from Perth and another, a week later, from Fremantle.

When they'd finally tired of Susannah, David attempted to throttle her with a nylon cord, but she began to thrash and scream, so he stopped, worried that the cries would attract unwelcome attention. They sedated her by forcing sleeping pills down her throat, and as soon as she was unconscious David handed the cord to Catherine, asking her to demonstrate her love for him by killing Susannah.

Catherine didn't hesitate in carrying out David's request, and they later took Susannah's body to the

Gleneagles National Park, where it was buried near that of Mary Neilson. Later on, when asked why she'd done it, she replied:

> Because I wanted to see how strong I was within my inner self. I didn't feel a thing. It was like I expected. I was prepared to follow him to the end of the earth and do anything to see that his desires were satisfied. She was a female. Females hurt and destroy males.[3]

This curious defeminisation – Catherine's implicit denial in her statement that she herself was 'female' – demonstrates the depth of her fear of losing David Birnie. She had subsumed herself to him utterly, even to the extent of apparently denying her own humanity. Her complaint that 'females hurt and destroy males' following her part in a sequence of rape-murders of women initiated by a man is faintly ironic until we understand that her sole concern was with David Birnie. Her fear was that another woman would take him from her, and she would do anything to prevent that from happening.

Thirty-one-year-old Noelene Patterson worked as a bar manager at the Nedlands Golf Club. She lived with her mother in the suburb of Bicton and had been working for nine years as a flight attendant with Ansett Airlines, then for two years as a hostess on the tycoon Alan Bond's private jet, before taking the golf-club job, where over the past year she'd grown to be extremely popular. On 1 November her car had run out of petrol on the Canning highway in East Fremantle, and the Birnies, driving past, spotted her standing by the side of the road.

She was running late and only too happy to accept the offer of a lift, but as soon as she was in the car a knife was held to her throat, her hands were tied and she was told not to move or she'd be killed. Back at the Birnies' bungalow she was chained to the bed, gagged and repeatedly raped by David Birnie. David liked Noelene more than their other victims – she was beautiful and elegant, everything Catherine was not, and he ignored their original plan of killing her that evening.

Noelene was kept prisoner in the bungalow for three days before Catherine persuaded David to kill her. It seemed as though Catherine's worst fears were coming true – David was becoming besotted with one of their victims. Catherine threatened to kill herself, holding a knife to her chest, unless David killed Noelene immediately, and David took the threat seriously. He sedated Noelene by forcing sleeping pills down her throat, then strangled her as soon as she was unconscious. They then drove to the forest where they'd buried the first two victims and dug a shallow grave for Noelene nearby. Catherine hated this woman, the one who'd almost taken her David away from her, and threw sand in the body's face. But her fears of the influence of other women on David didn't stop the couple from killing again.

Twenty-one-year-old Denise Karen Brown worked part-time as a computer operator in Perth. She lived with her boyfriend and another couple in Nedlands, and loved going out dancing – she'd gone out the night before and ended up staying at the Coolbellup Hotel with a female friend. The Birnies picked her up outside the Stoned Crow Wine House in Fremantle. Denise was described by a friend later as being the kind of person who 'would do anything to help anyone. She trusted too many people. Perhaps that is why she didn't think twice about taking a lift.'[4]

This time her trust was misplaced, as she realised when a knife was put to her throat as she entered the car. The Birnies took her home, chained her to the bed and raped her, making her phone a friend to let everyone know that she was OK and thereby put off any police investigation.

The following day, they were driving her to the Wanneroo pine plantation, bundled up in the back of the car but still alive, when they almost picked up another hitcher. Following the Birnies' arrest a nineteen-year-old student told police that she'd been walking along Pinjar Road in Wanneroo when a car had pulled up alongside her. She'd seen two people in the front and one slumped in the back; the two in the front she later recognised from police photos as being David and Catherine Birnie, and she realised that the person in the back had probably been Denise Brown. She didn't accept the lift:

> I felt uneasy. I didn't recognise the car. There was a man driving and a woman in the front seat of the car. The man kept looking down, not looking at me, and the woman was drinking a can of UDL rum and coke. I thought the fact that she was drinking at that time of day was strange. He didn't look at me the whole time. It was the woman who did all the talking. She asked me if I wanted a lift anywhere. I said, 'No, I only live up the road.'
>
> They continued to sit there and I looked into the back seat where I saw a small person with short brown hair lying across the seat. I thought it must have been their son or daughter asleep in the back. The person was in a sleeping position and, from the haircut, looked like a boy but for some reason I got the feeling it was a girl. I told them again I didn't want a lift because walking was good exercise. The man looked up for the first time and gazed at me before looking away again. By this

time, more cars had appeared and I started to walk away but they continued to sit in the car. Finally the car started and they did another U-turn and drove up Pinjar Road towards the pine plantation. It wasn't until I saw a really good photo of Catherine Birnie that I realised who they were. Somebody must have been looking after me that day. I don't know what would have happened to me if I had got into that car.[5]

The Birnies wanted to wait until the sun had gone down before killing and burying Denise Brown; while they waited David raped their victim in the back of the car. As soon as it was dark they dragged Denise from the car and David raped her again, stabbing her in the neck while Catherine held a torch, helping him to find his aim. But the girl didn't die immediately. Catherine found a larger knife in the car and told David to stab her again. When the body had finally stopped moving they dug a shallow grave and started to cover their victim with sand; but she still wasn't dead, and sat bolt upright in the grave. David Birnie grabbed an axe from the car and hit her on the head with its blunt end with all his strength. She lay down in the grave, only to rise again moments later, whereupon Birnie hit her with the blade of the axe, splitting her head open, before finishing the job of covering her.

Catherine Birnie had been horrified by the violence of Denise Brown's death. The strangulations had been quiet, bloodless, but this was something else altogether. She didn't want it to happen again.

DISCOVERY

Local police were already concerned by reports of four women who'd gone missing in under a month. They didn't seem like runaways either: they were from good homes where they appeared to be well loved and happy; no drugs seemed to be involved, and there was no connection between the girls. Strangely, though, two of the women had got in touch with friends or relatives after going missing – Susannah Candy had sent two letters to her family and Denise Brown had called a friend the day after her disappearance – but since then nothing had been heard.

Detective Sergeant Paul Ferguson feared the worst, suspecting that a serial killer may be on the loose. Senior policemen in most countries are notoriously reluctant ever to admit that a serial killer could be at work, fearing copycat crimes and a muddying of the investigation, but Ferguson managed to enlist the support of a former Criminal Investigations Bureau chief, Bill Neilson, who'd brought the Perth serial killer Eric Edgar Cooke to justice, for his theory.

On 10 November Ferguson and Detective Sergeant Vince Katich were investigating leads on Denise Brown's whereabouts, five days after her disappearance, when they received a call. A half-naked, disoriented young woman had just wandered into a Willagee shopping complex claiming to have been kidnapped and raped; she'd been taken to the nearby Palmyra police station. Ferguson and Katich strongly suspected that the girl was Brown, and drove to the police station. What they found instead was Thelma Cree, a sixteen-year-old who told them about her experiences at the hands of the Birnies.

She said that she'd been abducted by a couple while walking near her home in Nedlands. The couple had taken her to a bungalow where they stripped her and chained her to a bed before the man raped her. The woman watched, intermittently licking around the man's testicles and anus, and discussing with the man how they should inject cocaine into the head of his penis so that the sex could last for longer.

The next day, after the man had left the bungalow, presumably to go to work, the woman unchained the girl and made her phone her parents to tell them that she was staying with friends and was OK. The girl noted the number while using the phone, and as soon as the woman left the room, possibly to answer the door to their cocaine dealer, the girl found an open window and escaped.

She gave the police a full description of the couple, along with their address and telephone number. She'd also been astute enough to hide a packet of cigarettes in a specific place in the bedroom, to prove that she had been there. When she told Ferguson and Katich of the telephone call she'd been forced to make they were reminded of Denise Brown, who'd made a similar call. Perhaps this couple were responsible for her disappearance – and perhaps for those of the three other missing women as well. They were alarmed, moreover, that the couple had let the girl see their faces clearly, as well as where they lived; this indicated that they probably planned to kill the girl when they'd finished with her. If they were prepared to kill this time, they may well have killed before.

A team of armed detectives drove to the bungalow at 3 Moorhouse Street, directed by the girl. The detectives were struck by the dilapidated state of the bungalow, paint peeling off the walls and the garden overrun with weeds; they rang the doorbell but there was nobody home. Two detectives hid in a panel van in the driveway and took Catherine Birnie in for questioning when she arrived home. She seemed very tense and nervous, and told them where to find David, who was in turn apprehended.

The Birnies denied the girl's allegations, maintaining that they'd invited her back to the bungalow for a marijuana bong, and that she'd had sex with David willingly. A search of the house revealed the girl's bag and the packet of cigarettes she'd hidden, but little else supporting her story or the idea that they'd been involved in the other disappearances; it was her word against theirs.

Ferguson and Katich questioned the Birnies separately at the police station, hoping that under intense interrogation one would crack, admitting at least to the rape of the girl. Just after seven that evening Katich half-jokingly said, in reference to the missing women, 'It's getting dark. Best we take the shovel and dig them up.' Astonishingly, David Birnie agreed. 'OK. There's four of them.'[6]

Confronted with her lover's confession, Catherine also broke. When asked why she'd left the girl who'd led to their arrest unchained and unguarded in the house, she stated that she'd been particularly disturbed by the killing of Denise Brown:

> I think I must have come to a decision that, sooner or later, there had to be an end to the rampage. I had reached the stage when I didn't know what to do. I suppose I came to a decision that I was prepared to give her a chance.
>
> I knew that it was a foregone conclusion that David would kill her, and probably do it that night. I was just fed up with the killings. I thought if something did not happen soon it would simply go on and on and never end.
>
> Deep and dark in the back of my mind was yet another fear. I had a great fear that I would have to look at another killing like that of Denise Brown,

the girl he murdered with the axe. I wanted to avoid that at all costs. In the back of my mind I had come to the position where I really did not care if the girl escaped or not. When I found out that the girl had escaped, I felt a twinge of terror run down my spine. I thought to myself: 'David will be furious. What shall I tell him?'[7]

Once the couple had confessed to the crime they agreed to help detectives locate the bodies, leading a convoy of vehicles out of the city towards the State Forest. David Birnie seemed at ease, relaxed and conversational with the detectives, so much so that he initially missed the turning into the pine plantation, so that they had to turn around and go back. About 400 metres into the Gnangara plantation Birnie told the detectives to stop – he'd spotted a mound of sand he'd left, and instructed them to dig there. They quickly unearthed the corpse of Denise Brown, and a guard remained there as Birnie directed the detectives to the next grave.

They drove to the Gleneagles National Park, where Birnie directed them to the body of Mary Neilson, buried about forty metres from a narrow track in the forest. One kilometre (just over half a mile) further down the track Birnie pointed out the shallow grave of Susannah Candy. Detectives were surprised by the lack of any emotion or remorse shown by the Birnies, who appeared if anything to revel in the attention. Catherine even clamoured that it was now her turn to direct detectives, and duly took them to the site where Noelene Patterson had been buried. She explained to the detectives that she'd hated Noelene ever since they had picked her up. She was glad that Noelene was dead, and spat on her grave as she pointed it out to them.

TRIAL AND PRISON

The couple appeared in Fremantle Magistrates' Court on 12 November 1986, charged with four counts of wilful murder. The brutality of their crimes had outraged the local community, and threats had been made; police searched the bags of everyone entering the court and placed a heavy guard on the holding cell leading to the courtroom. Some called for a reintroduction of the death penalty for the couple.

Neither David nor Catherine had any legal representation, and nor did they enter any plea. Bail was officially refused, and the couple were remanded in custody; when Catherine was asked whether she wanted to be remanded for eight or thirty days before the trial, she answered, looking at David, 'I'll go when he goes.'[8]

On 10 February 1987 the Birnies were escorted in a fortified prison truck to the Perth Supreme Court to face trial. The holding cell was again placed under heavy police guard. As the charges of abduction, rape, torture and murder were being read out to David Birnie, Catherine sat behind him, stroking his hands, which were tied behind his back. A reporter covering the story for the *Perth Daily News* stated that 'there has probably never before been such a declaration of undying love in the Western Australian Supreme Court dock'.[9] David Birnie's demeanour in court was sheepish, as though he were awed by the majesty of the space; but Catherine fought with her guards, kicking and screaming, content only when she was close to her common-law husband.

David Birnie pleaded guilty to four counts of murder and one of abduction and rape, sparing the victims' relatives a long and painful trial. He told detectives, 'That's the least I could do.'[10] The trial was over within thirty minutes. Mr Justice Wallace sentenced David Birnie to the maximum sentence of life imprisonment with strict security for his crimes, noting the 'remarkable violence, and grave cause to look at the power resultant when virtually harmless people join to forge a lethal union – this needs further scrutiny.'[11]

Would the Birnies individually have been capable of what they did together? It seems clear that Catherine had a strong personality dependence on David, a finding upheld by the court's psychiatric report on her; her assertion that 'females hurt and destroy males', probably a verbatim repetition of what David had told her, may well be indicative of how unquestioning her reliance on him had become. For David Birnie the question becomes a little murkier. He had a long history of criminal behaviour outside of his relationship with Catherine, and the spree of rape-murders appears to have been his idea, although it is unlikely that he couched it in these terms to Catherine at first: they would have a sex slave, and the slave's fate would be decided when they'd finished with her. What is likely is that David would not have found it nearly so easy to persuade female hitchhikers to join him had he been working alone – as a couple they would have appeared far more trustworthy than a lone male. It is conceivable also that, because they were working together, any guilt they may have felt individually would be commuted; their sex slave would be a toy, an unreal adjunct to the reality of their partnership.

The judge, when sentencing David Birnie, added, 'The law is not strong enough to express the community's horror at this sadistic killer who tortured, raped and murdered four women. In my opinion, David John Birnie is such a danger to society that he should never be released from prison.'[12] As he was led from the court into a prison van, Birnie blew the enraged crowd a kiss.

Catherine Birnie was not required to plead until a month later, her barrister delaying her trial until the delivery of a psychiatric report to determine her sanity. After she was found sane enough to plead, she admitted her part in the killings. David Birnie was also in court that day, and they held hands and chatted as the court heard in detail of their crimes. Although Catherine had been found sane enough to plead, a psychiatrist in court stated that she was utterly dependent on David Birnie, and would never have committed such crimes had it not been for his malign influence – 'It is the worst case of personality dependence I have seen in my career.'[13]

On 3 March 1987 Mr Justice Wallace sentenced Catherine Birnie exactly as he had her lover, stating, 'In my opinion, you should never be released to be with David Birnie. You should never be allowed to see him again.'[14] As she was escorted from court, she saw David for the last time.

Prison life was not kind to David Birnie, prisoners traditionally reserving a special vitriol for rapists and other sex criminals. He was beaten up repeatedly and tried to kill himself in 1987, finally being moved to Fremantle Prison's former death row cells for his own protection. He kept in touch with Catherine – in their first four years apart they wrote to each other over two thousand times – but they were denied the right to see each other, to marry or to speak together on the phone.

In 1990 David Birnie argued that the criminal justice system had gone too far in denying them the contact they craved, and that a denial of these rights was illegal, 'a punishment over and above that decreed by the law'.[15] He claimed that he and Catherine were close to suicide and mental breakdown through being kept apart. Few had any sympathy for their plight, however, and his argument was dismissed.

The Birnies were suspected to have been involved in other killings as well, and police hoped to clear up four unsolved murders of Perth women by talking to David Birnie. It was also known that the couple were friendly with Barrie Watts, a Queenslander who was convicted for the gruesome torture and murder of a twelve-year-old schoolgirl, Sian King. Crime squad detectives drove David Birnie around Perth and the outlying suburbs for five hours in 1992 in the hope that he'd admit to more murders, but their efforts were unrewarded. In 1993 his PC was removed from his cell in the protection unit at Casuarina Prison when it was discovered that Birnie had been using it to store pornographic material.

In January 2000 Catherine's husband and the father of four of her children, Donald McLaughlan, died suddenly aged 59. Her application to attend his funeral was turned down; commenting on the decision at the time, the West Australian Premier, Richard Court, stated that as far as he was concerned 'the Birnies have forfeited any rights for those types of privileges'.[16] In the same month, the acting West Australian Attorney General, Kevin Prince, said that while the Birnies could be legally considered for parole in 2007, twenty years after their sentencing, it was highly unlikely that they would ever be released unless they became too senile or frail. Mr Justice Wallace's recommendation that they were 'never to be released' looks likely to hold.

NOTES

1. David Birnie, quoted in Kidd, Paul B, *Australia's Serial Killers*, Pan Macmillan, Australia, 2000, p. 219.
2. James Birnie, quoted ibid., p. 222.
3. Catherine Birnie, quoted ibid., p. 224.
4. Ibid., p. 225.
5. Ibid., p. 226.
6. Vince Katich and David Birnie, quoted ibid., p. 218.

7. Catherine Birnie, quoted ibid., p. 227.
8. Catherine Birnie, quoted ibid., p. 227.
9. Bill Power, quoted ibid., p. 228.
10. David Birnie, quoted ibid., p. 229.
11. Mr Justice Wallace, quoted in Sands, Rachel, *Partners in Crime*, University of Austin Press, USA, 2000, p. 78.
12. Mr Justice Wallace, quoted in Kidd, op. cit. p. 229.
13. Ibid., p. 229.
14. Mr Justice Wallace, quoted ibid., p. 229.
15. David Birnie, quoted ibid., p. 230.
16. Richard Court, quoted ibid., p. 230.

10. THE KEN AND BARBIE KILLERS – PAUL BERNARDO AND KARLA HOMOLKA

'Stop foolin' yourself, give up the chase
You got no confession, you got no case
You ever get caught? You ever get caught?
No, why?
'Cause I'm a deadly innocent guy.'

> Rap lyric by Paul Bernardo

'I'm your cuntlicking slut, the keeper of your virgins. Your asslicking bitch. And I love you, I want to marry you.'

> Karla Homolka, after the murder of her sister Tammy, recorded on a videotape recovered by police and played to jurors during Bernardo's trial.

'The Most Powerful Man in the World.'

> Kristen French's placatory words to Paul Bernardo as he raped her

Nicknamed the Ken and Barbie killers owing to their clean-cut good looks, Paul Bernardo and Karla Homolka appeared an unlikely pair to be involved in the kidnapping, rape, torture and murder of young girls. Bernardo's philosophy was a blend of male supremacism and 1980s yuppie aspirational capitalism. His obsession with bettering himself financially led to his seeking a career in accountancy and embarking on a series of self-motivational training courses; when these methods of improving his life became too much effort for him he walked out of his accountancy job and made money smuggling cigarettes across the US–Canada border.

Culturally, Bernardo was a product of the era in which he lived, obsessed with his fantasy of becoming a white rap star. It is also unsurprising that one of the few books that the pair had read was Bret Easton Ellis's *American Psycho*, a novel published in 1991 depicting the sadistic sexual crimes of a young and wealthy Wall Street banker.

PAUL BERNARDO

Paul Bernardo was conceived on 22 November 1963 – the day President Kennedy was shot. On that day his mother Marilyn Bernardo, who had married Ken Bernardo in 1960 and had two children with him, sought refuge from her unhappy marriage and comforted herself in the face of the devastating news of the President's death by having sex with an ex-boyfriend named Bill.

When Paul was born, on 27 August 1964, the name of the father on his birth certificate was given as Ken Bernardo – although Ken knew of his wife's infidelity, it does not seem that he saw it as a problem.

Marilyn Bernardo was born in Ontario in 1940 and had then been given up for adoption by her natural parents, Ross and Elizabeth Hamilton. After some time spent in foster homes she was brought up by Gerald and Elizabeth Eastman. Gerald Eastman was a wealthy lawyer, and Marilyn's childhood appears to have been a happy one. In 1955 she met Kenneth Bernardo, the son of an Italian immigrant, Frank Bernardo, and his English wife Mary. Born in 1935, Ken Bernardo was seen as a good catch for Marilyn, as he was a professional accountant.

Paul's childhood was far from happy. A year after Paul was born, the family moved to 21 Sir Raymond Drive in Scarborough, Toronto. Ken's violence towards Marilyn and the children accelerated, and the atmosphere in the house became increasingly unpleasant. Ken's father

Frank had been a strict disciplinarian who was brutal towards his wife and children. Ken copied his father in this respect, and Marilyn often found herself on the receiving end of his brutal temper. Marilyn suffered from increasing psychiatric problems, including acute hypochondria, for which she sought professional help. She also became increasingly obese owing to a thyroid condition, and paid little attention to her appearance. As her children grew up, Marilyn withdrew to a world of her own, neglecting the upkeep and cleaning of the house and spending most of her time in the darkened basement. She and Ken now slept in separate rooms, and the intimate side of their marriage was over, apart from Ken's occasional forays to the basement for quick sexual relief.

Ken Bernardo became notorious in the neighbourhood for his habit of leaving his house at night wearing his pyjamas and spying on young girls as they undressed in their bedrooms. He also began seriously sexually abusing his daughter Debbie when she was eight years old, fingering her while the family watched television, spying on her from the garden as she undressed at night, and repeatedly raping her while the rest of the family was asleep.

Paul was a good student at school, and was popular because of his blond good looks and friendly demeanour. He managed to charm girls from an early age. When he was sixteen, however, his mother told him something that dealt a severe blow to his self-esteem. During an argument, she told him that Ken was not his real father, and showed him a photograph of her lover Bill.

The effect on Paul was catastrophic – he developed a deep hatred of his mother and began calling her a whore to her face, to which she would respond by calling him a bastard from hell. He also loathed his father for his deviant sexual behaviour and for his weakness in allowing another man to sleep with his wife.

Paul continued to do well at school, being particularly good at science and maths. He dated girls, and became friends with the Smirnis brothers, Steve, Alex and Van, who were next-door neighbours. The Smirnises were a negative influence on Paul – they had a macho attitude, treated women badly and were involved in petty crime. In 1980 Paul became involved in Amway, a motivational programme for aspiring businessmen.This was the first in a series of self-improvement systems that Paul would join and learn from.

In 1983 Paul attended Toronto University, where he studied business and commerce. His continued his pursuit of women, developing a preference for anal sex, and becoming increasingly sadistic and violent towards the girls he dated. Paul had expensive tastes in clothing, hi-fi systems and vehicles and got the money for these by selling stolen goods.

Following his graduation, in September 1987 Paul began working for Price Waterhouse as a trainee accountant. His appearance by now was that of the classic yuppie – impeccably groomed, and wearing ostentatiously expensive suits and shoes.

When he started at Price Waterhouse Paul was going out with Jennifer Galligan, whom he had met during the previous year when on a double date with Steve Smirnis. He had been two-timing Jennifer with Lenore Marcos, who had been at university with him and now worked for the same company. Both women finished with Paul – Jennifer because of his relationship with Lenore, and Lenore because of his infidelity with Jennifer as well as her worries about his increasingly sadistic behaviour and sexual demands.

PAUL'S CAREER OF RAPE

Around the time that Paul started his accountancy job, he embarked on a series of terrifying sexual assaults and rapes. His victims were young girls whom he would approach from behind at night, threaten with a knife and force to have oral sex as well as raping them vaginally and anally. In many of these cases the victims caught sight of their attacker and would have been able to recognise Paul's voice, because during the attacks Paul taunted the victims, calling them obscene names and forcing them to say how much they were enjoying being assaulted. The rapes received much coverage in the local media and police received several tip-offs, including one from Paul's friend Alex Smirnis, that they should investigate him in connection with the rapes.

Paul was questioned by detectives on 19 November 1989. His accountancy qualifications, the fact that he was engaged and his polite and straightforward demeanour impressed the police who were interviewing him. They did not think that this confident and apparently sociable character could possibly be the man they were looking for. Paul co-operated in giving hair, saliva and blood samples. These were kept by a forensic laboratory, but were not prioritised for urgent analysis. A lack of resources prevented all the samples that had been provided being processed.

A composite picture of the 'Scarborough Rapist' was distributed in the area in May 1990. This bore a distinct resemblance to Paul; when he was teased by his workmates about this he would become very angry and defensive.

KARLA HOMOLKA

By the autumn of 1987 Paul Bernardo, having no steady girlfriend, was a free agent, and, by chance, at a restaurant in Toronto, he met the woman he would marry, and whose name would be for ever linked with his, owing to the horrifying crimes they would commit together.

Karla Leanne Homolka was born on 4 May 1970 in Ontario, Canada. She was the first child of Dorothy and Karel Homolka. Karel, who worked as a salesman, had emigrated from Czechoslovakia as a boy and married Dorothy, who was Canadian. During Karla's early childhood the Homolkas lived in St Catherines, near Lake Ontario. Dorothy had two further children, both girls – Lori was born in 1972 and Tammy Lyn in 1975.

As a child, Karla suffered from asthma attacks. An attractive blonde child who was fond of animals and kept pets, Karla performed well academically at school where she enjoyed drama and English studies. Her parents' marriage was not a happy one – Dorothy felt that Karel wanted too much sex from her, and at one point proposed that he bring home one of her female colleagues from the hospital where she worked to join them in bed. Karel was also prone to drinking bouts, and when intoxicated would become increasingly argumentative.

As they grew up, the three daughters openly expressed their dislike of their father, calling him to his face a 'dumb Czech' and an 'asshole'. Karla displayed signs of adolescent rebellion to the extent of wearing black clothing, using unconventional make-up and dying her hair brown. Her schoolfriends recall her behaviour as being sometimes outrageous – she would shout obscene words in public and was always arguing with her parents. She also showed a precocious interest in boys and from the age of thirteen she would wave at men she found attractive as they drove by in their cars. Attending the Sir Winston Churchill Secondary School,

Karla stood out from the other students because of her non-preppy appearance, and gained a reputation as a nonconformist. She also enjoyed drinking, and used a fake ID that she had bought through the mail to buy alcohol for herself and her friends. While in her last years at school she began working in the Pen Center pet store.

When Karla was seventeen, she travelled to Kansas by herself to visit a former classmate named Doug, who had moved to the USA with his family. On her return from the trip Karla boasted to her friends about what she had done with Doug. The pair had experimented with alcohol and taken cocaine together. Not only that, but Karla had sex with Doug, during which he tied her up and hit her violently. Her friends were horrified, but Karla seemed unaffected by the experience.

PAUL AND KARLA MEET

In October 1987, the seventeen-year-old Karla, her co-worker Debbie Purdie and their boss at the pet store, Kristy Maan, attended a pet-industry sales convention in Toronto, which would involve an overnight stay away from home. Eating at the hotel restaurant, Debbie and Karla were approached by Paul Bernardo and Van Smirnis. Paul had noticed Karla across the room and she had smiled back at him. He then went over to the girls' table and asked if he and his friend could join them. Paul and Van went over. The attraction between Paul and Karla was immediate. The four of them went up to Debbie and Karla's hotel room, where, once the lights were turned out, Paul and Karla had sex while Debbie and Van were trying to sleep in the same room. Debbie was not attracted to Van and spent the night on the couch. Paul and Van left early the next morning, after Paul and Karla had got up and showered together.

The following weekend Paul Bernardo visited Karla at her parents' home in St Catherines, where she threw a party for her friends. The couple slipped away from Karla's guests, and went down to the basement, where she presented Paul with a pair of handcuffs and asked him to fasten them on her wrists and then have sex with her from behind. Paul asked her what she would think of him if he was a rapist, and her reply was that she would like that. From that moment on, Paul knew he had found his perfect match. Paul became a regular visitor at Karla's parents' home, and began spending weekends there. In December 1989 Paul and Karla announced their engagement; Paul had proposed to her on a trip to Niagara Falls. In 1990 they became engaged, and Paul handed his bride-to-be not only an engagement ring but a wedding planner. On their return to St Catherines, Karla began eagerly making plans for her wedding. Now all she could do was to talk about how marvellous Paul was and how great the wedding was going to be.

24 DECEMBER 1990 – THE MURDER OF TAMMY LYN HOMOLKA

Since he first met her Paul had fantasised about having sex with Karla's fifteen-year-old sister Tammy. He developed an intense obsession with Tammy, finding her youth, virginity and resemblance to Karla extremely exciting. Tammy seems to have liked Paul, and must have found the attention he paid to her somewhat flattering. Karla would dress in Tammy's clothes and underwear and pretend to be her younger sister while having sex with Paul. The couple discovered Tammy's vibrator, which she kept hidden in her bedroom, and Paul got a thrill out of seeing Karla use this on herself. Paul repeatedly asked Karla to help him have sex with

Tammy by assisting him in drugging her, but Karla kept refusing, which made Paul angry and violent with her.

Eventually Karla gave in, and agreed to dose Tammy's food with valium. After Tammy, who was made drowsy by the drug, went to bed early and fell asleep, Paul went into her bedroom and masturbated inches from her face. When he tried to penetrate her with his erection, Tammy seemed to be waking up, so he had to stop. Karla knew that this must not happen again and that next time Tammy should be thoroughly sedated – Tammy's stirring in her sleep had greatly displeased Paul. Karla had been prescribed Halcion, a powerful sedative, by her doctor, and stole a quantity of halothane from her employers. Halothane is an animal anaesthetic in liquid form whose vapour is inhaled.

Christmas Eve 1990 at the Homolka household presented the perfect opportunity for Paul finally to rape Tammy. He had a new Sony camcorder, with which he filmed the family as they sat around drinking and watching TV. Tammy's cocktails, which Paul and Karla had mixed for her, were laced with Halcion tablets, which they had ground into powder for this purpose a couple of days before. The girl became increasingly drunk and confused, and after the rest of the family had gone upstairs to their bedrooms she insisted on staying in the living room with Karla and Paul, who wanted to watch a videotape they had rented.

As they watched the movie – *Lisa and the Devil*, a horror film starring Elke Sommer and Telly Savalas – Tammy drifted into a deep sleep. Karla went out of the room and came back with the bottle of halothane. After pouring the anaesthetic on to a rag, she held it against Tammy's face. Paul pressed the record button on his camcorder and filmed himself pulling down her trousers and rubbing her vagina. Then he got a close-up of his penis going in and out of Tammy's vagina, while Karla, still holding the rag over her sister's face, kept urging Paul to use a condom. Paul withdrew his penis and filmed Karla sucking on Tammy's breasts and licking her vagina, which she disliked doing because her sister was menstruating. Urged by Paul, Karla put her fingers inside Tammy's vagina and then, on camera, licked them clean of blood. Tammy was then turned over and Paul began raping her anally, proclaiming to Karla, who now held the video camera, 'Up her cunt, up her ass, how's that?' A second later, sensing that something had gone wrong, Paul suddenly pulled his erection out of Tammy, who then began vomiting.

The pair panicked; Karla grabbed Tammy's legs and held her upside down, which is what she had been taught to do to animals who were being sick. This had no positive effect, and Tammy's face had turned blue. Paul and Karla carried the body over to Karla's bedroom, where they put her clothes back on. Paul tried to give her mouth-to-mouth resuscitation while Karla hurriedly hid the halothane bottle and the container of ground-up Halcion and then called 911. Police and ambulance crews arrived on the scene, the sirens and engines waking up the rest of the family, who were shocked and horrified on being told by Karla that Tammy had stopped breathing. Paramedics examined Tammy, noting the grey colour of her skin and an area of inflamed skin around her mouth, before she was taken out of the house on a stretcher and carried to the ambulance. Questioned by police while calming himself down from what seemed like an excessive combination of rage and grief, Paul denied that any drugs had been involved, and said that while Tammy had been watching TV with them she had complained that her vision was blurred, which Paul thought was because of the alcohol she had consumed. He said that he and Karla had fallen asleep in front of the television, and had been woken by the sound of Tammy vomiting.

The mark on Tammy's face, Paul said, had been caused by her being dragged along the carpet as Karla and he had tried to resuscitate her. Paul and Karla were then taken to the police station to make formal statements. Karel Homolka was also questioned about Paul and Karla's relationship and about Tammy's asthma. An autopsy was ordered, but no charges relating to Tammy's death were made at the time, although police were suspicious about the cause of the inflammation around Tammy's mouth.

On their return from the police station, Paul and Karla tried to find the videotape they had made of Tammy's rape, which they thought they had hurriedly hidden in the basement. When it was not at first found, they assumed that police had discovered it, and were considerably relieved to find the tape elsewhere in the basement.

Tammy's funeral was held on Boxing Day. She was in an open casket, and the redness around her mouth was still visible. Paul and Karla both placed notes inside the coffin before she was buried in the Victoria Lawn Cemetery. In Paul's note, he twice asked Tammy, 'Please forgive me', and referred to his 'deep sorrow and regret'. During the wake at the Homolkas' home, Paul took Karla down to the basement and threatened to kill her and her family if she ever told anyone the truth about how Tammy had died.

A few days later the family were informed of the results of the autopsy. The cause of death, it stated, was suffocation due to fluid in the lungs. Tammy had passed out and vomited, inhaling her own vomit and then choking to death. Alcohol was in her bloodstream. The report mentioned no trauma to Tammy's vagina or anus.

Only the red mark around her mouth could not be explained, but the autopsy report suggested that this may have been caused by acid in the vomit. Police interpreted the report as indicating that Tammy's death was a tragic accident; the case was closed. The truth was that Tammy had asphyxiated when her airways had been blocked as her neck was pushed to one side while Paul anally raped her.

After Tammy's death, the Homolka family felt less kindly disposed towards Paul. They felt that he was partly responsible for the loss of Tammy, as it was he who had encouraged her to drink so much alcohol. They also resented that Paul now seemed incapable of leaving Karla, and that he now appeared to be ordering her around. In private, Paul and Karla continued their erotic fixation with Tammy: Karla would pretend to be Tammy while Paul had sex with her, while he looked not at Karla but at photographs of the dead girl.

At the end of January 1991 Karla's parents asked if Paul could stop staying at their home. He reacted with rage towards Karla, and became determined to find them a place to live together. He found a large detatched property for rent on Bayview Drive in Dalhousie. To finance the payments, his cigarette-smuggling trips across the border became more frequent. He told the owners of the property that he had inherited some money, and provided them with forward-dated cheques. They were delighted to have found such an apparently reliable, well-heeled and respectable tenant. Karla moved in with him, and enthused to her friends how great the house was and how much she was in love with Paul. In reality, Paul was now increasingly violent towards Karla. He began to think of himself as a potential rap star, and admired the white rapper Vanilla Ice, whose career he thought he could emulate.

By this time Paul had given up his job at Price Waterhouse, and was making easy money by smuggling cigarettes over from the border with the USA, hiding the contraband in secret panels in his car. He spent some of the profits from this illegal trade on recording equipment and record decks, which he installed in one of the rooms. He spent hours alone, writing and recording rap lyrics filled with misogynic bragging.

15 JUNE 1991 – THE MURDER OF LESLIE MAHAFFY

Leslie Erin Mahaffy, born in July 1976, was the oldest child of Deborah and Dan Mahaffy; her brother Ryan was seven years her junior. The family lived in Burlington, Toronto, where Leslie attended the local MM Robinson High School. An attractive blonde child, Leslie was becoming a difficult and rebellious adolescent – she would stay out late, breaking the terms of a curfew agreement with her parents, and had recently been caught shoplifting. She had absconded from home several times; on the first occasion police found that she was staying in a motel in Burlington with a boy.

On Friday, 14 June 1991, Deborah Mahaffy drove Leslie to a nearby funeral home so the girl could pay her respects to one of her best friends, Chris Evans, who, with three other teenagers, had been killed in a car crash earlier that week. After the funeral service, Chris's friends had arranged to meet at a clearing in some nearby woods, to drink, smoke and remember their classmate in a more informal setting. Leslie was among them, and she drank beers until past her curfew hour of 11 o'clock. Then Leslie got a lift with some friends that took her in the direction of her home; she sat smoking cigarettes in the street with a friend, Martin McSweeney, who then walked her home, having arranged to take her to the funeral the next day. Shortly before 2 a.m., Leslie tried to get into her house, but all the doors were locked, and her parents did not trust her with a key. Not wanting to ring the bell, wake her parents up and have to face their anger, Leslie went to a payphone and called her friend Amanda Carpino, asking if she could stay at her place – but Amanda refused, as Leslie had stayed over before and this had not pleased the Mahaffy parents. Leslie said she would go back and ring the bell.

On her return to her house, Leslie did not wake her parents up. She went and sat on a bench in the back garden. She was surprised to see a man wearing a hooded top walk over to her, and asked him what he was doing. The man was Paul Bernardo; he told Leslie that he was looking for houses to steal from. Leslie asked the man for a cigarette; he said he had some in his car. Leslie went with Paul to the vehicle, which was in a nearby street. She got into the car, but was wary of closing the passenger door. Bernardo gave her a cigarette, and while she was smoking it he held a knife to her face and forced her to get right inside the car. Closing the door, he pushed Leslie's reclining seat back and blindfolded her. He drove her to his house in Dalhousie, the journey taking about half an hour.

Once they were inside Bernardo's living room, the video camera was switched on. Leslie was made to undress, and taken to the bathroom where Bernardo filmed her urinating while he masturbated. He then took Leslie to a spare bedroom and tied her to the bed. Going downstairs, Paul woke Karla and told her that he had brought a girl back to the house, and then let her go back to sleep. Paul then went downstairs and smacked Leslie around and then raped her vaginally and anally before forcing her to suck his penis. He then made her masturbate on camera while telling him that he was her 'favourite guy'. Leslie was then given champagne to drink, laced with Halcion. She then fell asleep. The next morning, Bernardo told Karla to keep out of the way. He then filmed Leslie, still blindfolded, having a shower, after which he raped her again, twice, and forced her to give him oral sex and swallow his ejaculate.

Later that day Paul was joined by Karla; they took off Leslie's clothes, and Paul filmed the two girls kissing. He asked them both to lick and suck his penis and anus, and then forced Leslie to suck Karla's breasts and lick her vagina. Leslie was then filmed urinating and afterwards taken back to the bedroom for further abuse. Having failed to obey Bernardo's command to defecate on camera, Leslie was repeatedly anally raped. Interrogated by Bernardo as to whether she would go to the police if she was freed, Leslie said that she would not tell anyone. Bernardo called her a 'lying cunt' and made his decision: Leslie would have to be killed.

In the early hours of Sunday, Leslie pleaded with Paul and Karla for her life – their response was to sedate her with Halcion. Bernardo then strangled Leslie with electrical cord, watched by Karla Homolka. Leslie's body was taken down to the basement. Karla's parents came for Sunday lunch, where conversation centred on Paul and Karla's wedding. On Monday, Paul went down to the basement and, using an electric saw, cut off Leslie's arms, legs and head. The body was cut into a total of ten pieces. He mixed up several bags of quick-drying cement with water and poured the mixture into boxes, in which he placed the body parts. A total of eight concrete boxes were taken to Lake Gibson late at night and dumped in the water.

Deborah and Dan Mahaffy reported their daughter as missing on the Saturday morning. It appeared that she had vanished into thin air.

29 JUNE 1991 – WEDDING OF PAUL AND KARLA; LESLIE'S BODY IS FOUND

Only two weeks after the abduction, rape and murder of Leslie Mahaffy, Paul Bernardo and Karla Homolka were married at St Mark's Anglican Church at Niagara-On-The-Lake. The wedding celebrations were a vulgar display of ostentation, overshadowed by the grotesque appearance and behaviour of Marilyn Bernardo, who welcomed some of the guests while lying on the floor. Karel Homolka made a speech in which he asked the guests to toast Tammy, whom he described as 'our little angel'. The newlyweds spent the night in a Niagara hotel before jetting off to Hawaii, where during their honeymoon Paul repeatedly beat and hit Karla.

On that Saturday, while Paul and Karla took their vows in church, Michael Doucette took his son, Michael Jr, on a fishing trip to Lake Gibson. He noticed several boxlike objects in the shallow water, and went up to have a closer look. What he saw shocked him: there were human limbs embedded in the concrete. Police were called to the scene and the eight blocks were taken to be examined by pathologists. Examination of dental records proved that the body was that of Leslie Mahaffy.

On their return from honeymoon, Paul and Karla's life continued as before. Karla went back to work; Paul carried on smuggling cigarettes and stayed at home during the day recording and writing his rap music. Paul's moods became darker, and he started hitting Karla more frequently.

18 APRIL 1992 – MURDER OF KRISTEN FRENCH

On this occasion, Karla helped Paul entrap their victim. On the afternoon of 16 April 1992 – the day before the Good Friday holiday – they drove off from their home to find a young girl for Paul to rape. Kristen Dawn

French was fifteen years old and attended the Holy Cross School in St Catherines. She was a popular girl at school, where she was an academic high scorer. She had a steady boyfriend named Elton Wade, of whom her parents, Donna and Doug French, approved. She was walking along the road on her way home when Karla called out from Paul's car and asked for directions. Having lured the girl over, Karla got out of the vehicle and spread out a map on the roof. As Kristen was looking at the map, Paul got out of the car on the other side and rushed over.

Then Paul and Karla forced Kristen into the car, Kristen putting up a struggle, but being no match for the combined strength of Paul and Karla. Kristen was given the same treatment as Leslie Mahaffy – taken into the house, blindfolded, videotaped while urinating, forced to suck Paul's penis and repeatedly raped both vaginally and anally. When Paul wanted to sleep, Kristen was heavily drugged so she could not attempt an escape. Paul forced Kristen to have sex with Karla while he filmed them and masturbated. The assault on Kristen was relentless: for three days she was repeatedly raped, urinated on by Paul and forced to perform sexual acts with Karla; for much of the time the video camera was trained on her.

One of the last humiliations to be filmed by Paul involved Karla forcing the neck of a wine bottle into Kristen's anus. The torment stopped only when she was allowed to eat or was drugged to sleep.

Kristen French was finally strangled to death by Paul Bernardo late on the night of Saturday, 18 April. On the following day, after visiting Karla's parents for an Easter Sunday meal, Paul and Karla washed Kristen's body, in an attempt to eliminate semen stains, and cut off the dead girl's hair. Then they took the body and, in the middle of the night, dumped it on a rubbish tip near Burlington.

KARLA INFORMS POLICE

Following the murder of Kristen French, Paul's behaviour towards Karla became increasingly abusive. She visited hospital on a number of occasions to be treated for minor injuries such as cracked ribs. On New Year's Day 1993, on his return from a trip to Montreal with some male friends, Paul attacked Karla with a torch. There was dark-black bruising around her eyes, which alarmed Karla's parents sufficiently for them to make their daughter stay with a friend of theirs whose husband was a police officer. Karla was persuaded to leave her husband and to press charges against him. Paul was arrested on 6 January and charged with assault on his wife.

On 1 February 1993, the DNA samples Paul had given after his questioning by police about the rapes in Scarborough were analysed, and found to match semen samples taken from three of the victims. From that point on Bernardo was followed by undercover officers wherever he went. He was considered a prime suspect in the Mahaffy and French murders. Karla was interviewed by detectives at length about her relationship with Paul; after this interview she told her aunt and uncle, with whom she was staying, that Paul was not only responsible for the Scarborough rapes but that he had killed the two schoolgirls.

Karla then briefed her lawyer, George Walker. She told him that Paul had killed her sister Tammy as well as Mahaffy and French, and that she had been present when they had been murdered. Karla also said that sex acts with the victims before they had been murdered had been recorded on Paul's video camera. During her recounting of events to Walker, she emphasised how she had been constantly abused by Bernardo.

Walker then met with the St Catherines regional prosecutor, Ray Houlahan, and informed him that Karla would be willing to testify against Paul Bernardo on a condition of being granted immunity from prosecution. In March 1993 Karla was admitted to a psychiatric ward, where she spent her time heavily sedated.

The prosecutor made an offer to Karla – a sentence of twelve years in return for her testimony against Paul – which she accepted. A ruling was made banning all mention in the Canadian media of Karla's involvement in the crimes – which caused uproar because this information was freely available in newspapers in the USA and on the Internet. Having been charged with manslaughter, Karla was released on bail.

THE TRIAL OF KARLA HOMOLKA
Karla appeared in court on 6 July 1993 charged with manslaughter. Canadian journalists were present, but were forbidden to publish any account of the proceedings or the result of the trial until after a verdict had been reached in the trial of Paul Bernardo. During her trial, the videotapes that showed Karla's participation in the abuse of the murder victims were neither spoken of nor presented as evidence. Karla's defence lawyers painted her as a classic battered wife and as yet another victim of Paul Bernardo.

Karla was sentenced to a total of twelve years in prison for her participation in the deaths of her sister Tammy, Kristen French and Leslie Mahaffy.

THE TRIAL OF PAUL BERNARDO
Bernardo's trial commenced on 18 May 1995, when the jury of eight men and four women were sworn in. There

were nine charges against him relating to the deaths of Mahaffy and French: two of first-degree murder, forcible confinement, kidnapping and aggravated sexual assault, and one charge of performing an indignity on a human body. During the trial, key and explicit parts of videos detailing the assaults on Leslie Mahaffy and Kristen French were shown to the court, including sections that showed Karla's full and apparently willing participation; one segment showed close-ups of Karla masturbating for the camera. A number of incriminating and intimate letters sent between Karla and Paul were also presented as evidence.

Karla appeared in the witness box and described how Paul had degraded her and forced her to take part in sadomasochistic sex with him. Paul admitted to the court that he had abducted the two girls but blamed their deaths on Karla. Paul's defence also tried to sway the jury into believing that Karla, far from being a victim, had been willing to take part in these acts and in the homicides.

On 1 September 1995 Paul Bernardo was found guilty of all charges. He was given a life sentence, with an additional condition that he may not be considered for parole until he has served 25 years in prison.

WHY DID THEY COMMIT THESE CRIMES?

During their trials, Karla Homolka and Paul Bernardo appeared to show very little emotion, even when horrific evidence was being presented to the court. This type of reaction is typical of psychopathic personalities – those who lack any moral conscience about how they behave.

There is little doubt that both Paul and Karla were paraphiliacs – compelled to repeat violent sexual acts, in their case culminating in murder, in order to achieve sexual stimulation. Paul Bernardo was a classic sexual sadist – for him, sexual pleasure could be obtained only by acts of power and aggression towards women. Karla Homolka appears to have been willing to submit herself to Paul's every desire. Her defence claimed that she had suffered from battered-women's syndrome, in which a victim of domestic violence supposedly becomes forced into committing crimes due to the influence of a dominant partner. A psychiatric assessment by Dr Angus McDonald – commissioned by the prosecution at Bernardo's trial but not presented in court – claimed that Homolka was 'a diagnostic mystery' and said that no explanation could be found for her apparent 'moral vacuity'.

NO PAROLE FOR KARLA

In March 2001, Karla Homolka's application for parole was turned down by the National Parole Board, which recommended that she be kept in prison until July 2005. The board had made its decision having read psychiatric reports on Homolka that conclude that she had 'a persistent violent character' and demonstrated 'an anti-social personality or psychopathy' and may commit a serious offence if released, and stated that she still demonstrated 'a high degree of indifference to the consequences of [her] acts against everyone'. Karla Homolka is detained in the Joliette Institution, seventy kilometres (43 miles) from Montreal, where the female prisoners live in bungalows, cook their own food and can wear what clothes they like.

PAUL BERNARDO IN PRISON

Bernardo is held in solitary confinement for 23 hours per day in a tiny cell in Kingston Penitentiary. He is kept under constant video surveillance in his room, which contains a bed, a television and a toilet. He has complained that the conditions in which he is held are unsatisfactory. He spends his days watching television and practising martial-arts moves, using his pillow as a punch bag, in training for when he hopes to be released into the general population of the prison. According to the Canadian media, he believes that he will get parole in 2010.

BIBLIOGRAPHY

Burnside, Scott, and Cairns, Alan, *Deadly Innocence*, Warner Books, New York, 1995.

Pron, Nick, *Lethal Marriage*, McClelland-Bantam, Canada, 1995.

Williams, Stephen, *Invisible Darkness*, Little, Brown & Co, Canada, 1996.

11. THE BANALITY OF EVIL* – FRED AND ROSE WEST

INTRODUCTION

The crimes of Fred and Rose West shed light on a number of weaknesses in the social fabric of Britain in the 1970s: the shortage of housing for young people, which led to the large turnover of lodgers who were housed in the upstairs rooms of the 'House of Horrors' at 25 Cromwell Street; the ineffectiveness of social workers; the apparent inability of police to realise that appalling serial crimes were being committed in an inner-city area; and the frequency with which people disappeared without questions being asked or investigations pursued.

It is a measure of those times that the disturbed and incestuous paedophile Fred West and his sadistic partner Rose could capitalise on so-called 'permissive society', misinterpreting the new freedoms enjoyed by women as a green light to exploit them. Both of Fred West's wives were prostitutes and were encouraged by him to continue being paid for sex. A man brought up in rural poverty by parents who saw incest with their children as a natural activity, Fred West viewed women as beasts whose suffering he was to prolong and delight in. Rose was happy to be regarded as his 'cow' and to procure him further women and girls to torture. It is tragic that their activities, directed at any young girl they could ensnare and even involving their own offspring, resulted in so many needless deaths.

---

* Title taken from the Hannah Arendt book on Adolf Eichmann.

FRED WEST

Frederick Walter Stephen West was born in Much Marcle, a village in Herefordshire, on 29 September 1941. He was the first child born to Walter and Daisy West. Daisy was Walter's second wife; they met in 1939 when he was 25 and she was 16. The Wests would have another six children after Fred, and the family lived in a cottage attached to the farm where Walter was a poorly paid labourer. Motherhood turned Daisy into a grotesquely obese woman who disciplined her brood with a leather belt. She was very protective of Fred, who was her favourite. It is believed that Walter and Daisy West subjected their children to sexual abuse: from the age of twelve until he left home Fred had regular sexual intercourse with his mother, which she initiated. Fred also admitted to incestuous involvement with his own sisters. Walter West believed that as a father he had the right to have sex with his own daughters, and told Fred that this was something that all men did.

Anne Marie West, the daughter of Fred and his first wife, Rena Costello, claims in her book *Out of the Shadows* (written after she had changed her name from Anne Marie) that Walter West also abused Fred sexually. Fred was a dirty, unruly and malodorous child who had no interest in school, where he was often beaten for his inability to control his behaviour. Being seduced by his mother ignited Fred's libido and from early adolescence he was obsessed with sex, and would often behave crudely towards girls, occasionally forcing his attentions on them and raping them. When Fred was fifteen he left school and worked alongside his father on the farm. A year later he went to work on a building site in Hereford, where he could earn more money than he could in Much Marcle. He came back to live with his family when he had saved enough money to buy himself a motorcycle, which he proudly rode around the village. In November 1958, while riding the motorbike, he was involved in a road accident that resulted in serious head injuries. Fred remained unconscious in hospital for nearly a week. The accident caused Fred's personality to change and he became depressed, ill-tempered and even more driven by his sexual urges.

Fred returned to Much Marcle where, in 1960, he met and began a sexual relationship with Catherine 'Rena' Costello, a sixteen-year-old blonde prostitute from Glasgow, who had been in trouble with the police and had served time in a detention centre. Later that year Rena returned to Glasgow after her relationship with Fred deteriorated and she found herself unable to find work. After Rena's departure, Fred suffered a further head injury when he was pushed off a fire escape by a girl he was pursuing. He was taken to hospital where he was to remain unconscious for 24 hours. After this second accident, Fred's manner became even more aggressive. West then went to Bristol, where he worked in the docks. On several occasions his work took him abroad, including one trip to the West Indies.

In April 1961 Fred made his first court appearance. He and a friend named Brian Hill were accused of shoplifting and pleaded guilty – they were both fined. In June of that year Fred faced a far more serious charge – that of unlawful sex with his thirteen-year-old sister, whom he had made pregnant. Fred's attitude towards incest with an underage child did not impress social workers, of whom he asked, 'Doesn't everybody do it?' Walter and Daisy reacted to Fred's arrest by refusing to let him stay in the family home. In November 1961, Fred appeared at Herefordshire Assizes, charged with sexual offences against his sister.

Fred's doctor, Brian Hardy, was a defence witness, and he put it to the court that Fred's behaviour may have been caused by the head injuries he had suffered recently. The case came to an unexpected conclusion when his sister told the court she was unwilling to give evidence, and Fred West was released. His unborn child was aborted.

Fred worked as a labourer on a building site, and then returned to live with his family. Then, in the autumn of 1962, Rena Costello reappeared in Hereford, having been made pregnant by a Pakistani bus driver in Glasgow. This didn't bother Fred, who, after making an unsuccessful attempt to abort the baby using home-made instruments, married Rena at Ledbury Register Office. The happy couple then went to live in Glasgow, where Rena continued her career in prostitution and Fred earned a living as an ice-cream seller.

The Mr Whippy van he rented came in useful, as it gave him a place to have sex with young girls who were seduced by his boastful patter. Fred had a disdain for using contraception; at least two illegitimate children resulted from his adulterous liaisons in Scotland during this time.

Rena gave birth to the bus driver's child, whom they named Charmaine. Fred impregnated Rena and she gave birth to their child Anna-Marie in July 1964. The marriage was not a happy one as Fred was hardly at home and Rena started drinking heavily and began a serious affair with a local man named John McLachlan. At the same time Fred began an affair with fifteen-year-old Anne McFall, who was friendly with Rena. Then Fred, out in his ice-cream van, accidentally ran over a young boy, who died of his injuries; though no criminal charges ensued, Fred thought it best to leave Scotland.

He took Charmaine and Anna-Marie to Much Marcle in December 1965; Rena, accompanied by Anne McFall and another friend, Isa McNeill, joined them in

February 1966. They then moved to a caravan site, and Fred began working in an abattoir, where he became fascinated by the physiology of dead animals. Then he got a job in a corn mill in nearby Bishop's Cleve.

The affair with Anne continued, and she became pregnant in November 1966. One month before she was due to give birth, Anne McFall decided to move back to Scotland. Fred murdered Anne, and dismembered her body, removing the foetus and cutting off toes, fingers and kneecaps, which were never recovered. Her remains were buried in a field near Much Marcle.

In January 1968 Fred murdered Mary Bastholme, a waitress at the Pop-In café in Gloucester with whom he had been having an affair. He buried her body in a field, but her remains have never been found. By this time he had yet another job, this time driving a van for a bakery firm.

In February 1968 Daisy West died; Fred expressed his grief by committing a series of petty thefts.

In the summer of 1969 Fred West was waiting for a bus in Cheltenham when he noticed a teenage girl on her own. He approached her and attempted to chat her up, asking her if she would go out for a drink with him. Her name was Rosemary Letts, she was fifteen years old and worked at a bread shop in Cheltenham High Street.

ROSEMARY WEST

Rosemary Pauline Letts was born in Northam, Devon on 29 November 1953. Rose was the fourth child born to her parents, who both suffered from severe mental illness. Bill Letts, who had been in the Royal Navy and now worked as an electrician, was a paranoid schizophrenic and a brutal disciplinarian who was prone to episodes of extreme violence towards his family. A cruel bully, Bill would force the children to clean their home, and beat them mercilessly if his instructions were not obeyed.

Her mother Daisy suffered from depression, for which she had received electroconvulsive therapy, which had been administered to her during the time she was pregnant with Rose. This treatment, which involves the sedation of the patient and a number of high-voltage shocks delivered to the head via electrodes, causing bodily convulsions, may well have had a detrimental effect on the unborn child. Daisy had also suffered a number of mental breakdowns.

As an infant, Rose would rock backwards and forwards in her cot repeatedly, not showing any interest in the world around her, which was seen as an indication of some kind of mental retardation. Her intelligence was low and she did not do well at school, where the other children named her 'Dozy Rosie'. From an early age, Bill Letts was having sex with his daughter Rose; for this reason he seems to have been more lenient with her than with his other children. His abuse of her seems to have been accompanied by an outwardly puritanical attitude towards sex. He would never discuss sexual matters and would go into a rage if anyone in the house spoke about sex. Sex scenes appearing on television would cause Bill to rush over and switch the set off. On reaching puberty, Rose became keen to flaunt her new-found sexuality, and after she had a bath would habitually walk around naked. She also seduced her younger brother Graham by masturbating him after she got into his bed. When Rose was fifteen, her mother left Bill and, taking Rose with her, went to live with Glenys, her oldest daughter, who had left home to get married. After a while, she moved back with Bill Letts and started working in Cheltenham. At this point in her life, she had the fateful meeting with Fred West.

FRED AND ROSE MEET

Rose's first impression of Fred was not a good one – she thought he looked 'like a tramp, a real mess', having noticed his filthy teeth, unwashed curly hair and soiled clothes. Fred's attention towards her was persistent. They got on the same bus and Fred sat next to her, and began to charm Rose with his outlandish stories. She also felt flattered that an older man was interested in her. Having found out where Rose worked, he kept turning up and asking her to go out with him. Eventually she gave in, and agreed to go out with Fred for a drink. On their first date together Fred told Rose that he was married, but that his wife, who was a prostitute, had left him to go to live in Scotland, leaving their two children in his care. This was only partly true: he had separated from Rena after an argument, but she was living in Gloucester.

Rose was happy to visit Fred in his disgustingly filthy caravan and enjoyed looking after Charmaine and Anna-Marie, who were now aged five and six. The attraction between Fred and Rose was very strong – Fred had found someone whose sex drive and interest in sex were as high as his, and who shared his tastes in sexual aggression, bondage and sadomasochism. Fred encouraged Rose to engage in prostitution, and she took men to the caravan to have sex with them for money. When word of this reached Daisy and Bill Letts, Rose was taken into care and sent to a home for teenagers. She lied to the authorities about where she was going at weekends: instead of visiting her parents, she went off to the caravan site to see Fred.

Rose left the home on her sixteenth birthday, to find that Fred was in prison in Gloucester, serving a 30-day sentence for non-payment of fines. When Fred was released, Rose joined him in the caravan with the two children – who were briefly sent to foster parents. Then Rena arrived in Gloucester and met with Fred and Rose, apparently showing some concern about her children, but not minding that the man who was legally her husband was now living with a sixteen-year-old girl.

In the summer of 1970 Fred and Rose moved into 25 Midland Road, Gloucester. On 17 October of that year Rose gave birth to their daughter Heather. In December, Fred was sent to prison for nine months, having been found guilty of theft and motoring offences. Left in Midland Road with her new baby as well as Anna-Marie and Charmaine to look after, Rose found her frustration revealing itself in violence towards the children. During Fred's time in prison, he and Rose exchanged a series of badly spelled but affectionate and romantic letters. A correspondence ensued between them on whether Rose should discipline her eldest child, including a reference by her to 'treating Charmaine rough'.

1971 – CHARMAINE WEST AND RENA COSTELLO MURDERED

Sometime during the summer of 1971, with Fred away in prison, Rose West killed Charmaine in Midland Road. Rose told Anna-Marie and anyone who asked that Charmaine had been taken away by Rena and had gone to live in Bristol. On Fred's release on 24 June 1971, it is likely that Rose told him what had happened to Charmaine, and that Fred cut the body in half, removed the fingers and kneecaps, which were never found, and buried the remains in a hole in the garden.

In August 1971, Rena was back in the area, and was asking to see her children. The precise circumstances of how Fred murdered her are not known. Rena was buried in Letterbox Field in Much Marcle, near where Fred had hidden the remains of Anne McFall in 1967.

Rena had been decapitated and her limbs sawn off; as with McFall, her fingers and toes had been cut off.

THE WESTS' LIFESTYLE

With Rena now eliminated from their lives, Fred and Rose felt able to marry – despite the fact that, as far as officialdom was concerned, Rena was still alive. Fred and Rose married in 1971. The certificate signed in the register office stated that Fred had never been married before. Their life together was unusual: they had sex frequently with each other, but Fred was incapable of foreplay and always ejaculated quickly inside her. Rose needed more sex than Fred was able to give her, and with her husband's approval Rose would sleep with other men and women. Often she would be paid by punters she had picked up through advertising in contact magazines. Sometimes her services would come free of charge, especially for the middle-aged West Indian men to whom Rose felt especially attracted. Fred would watch this activity through a hole in the wall, or listen to the sounds of lovemaking through an intercom system. Pictures were taken of Rose, both alone and with her clients and lovers, in pornographic poses. The Wests kept these photographs in albums in their bedroom alongside a growing collection of explicit and sadomasochistic magazines. In the 1980s Fred got hold of a video camera and habitually filmed his wife having sex with other men.

From an early age, Anna-Marie, Heather and Mae were sexually abused by both parents. Anna-Marie was repeatedly raped from the age of eight. Fred's attitude was that his daughters were his own property, whom he had the right to abuse whenever he liked.

In 1971, Fred and Rose's neighbour in Midland Road, Liz Agius, who was then aged nineteen, was drugged and raped by the Wests after she refused to have sex with them. In September 1972 the Wests moved from Midland Road to their new home: 25 Cromwell Street. They rented out rooms to young lodgers in order to help pay the rent. For some young men, included in the board and lodging was free sex with the landlady.

Fred was popular with his neighbours, because he could be relied on to do building and plumbing jobs at short notice. He did this work using stolen building materials, for which he would cruise the streets of Gloucester in his van. Fred's main passion, apart from his obsession with sex and young girls, was building and DIY work. Once he had bought Cromwell Street from the landlord, he began knocking down walls and adding extensions. He spent a lot of time refurbishing the cellar area, which was to be the scene of many crimes of rape, torture and murder.

In December 1972 Fred and Rose raped Caroline Owens, who had been employed as a live-in childminder to look after their Anna-Marie, Heather and new baby Mae – who was born in June of that year. Caroline had left Cromwell Street due to the Wests' incessant pressure on her to have sex with them. In January 1973 they were fined £25 each for sexual assault on Caroline.

1973 – LYNDA GOUGH, CAROL ANN COOPER AND LUCY PARTINGTON MURDERED

Bespectacled Lynda Gough worked as a seamstress in Gloucester. In early 1973 one of the Wests' lodgers named Ben Stanniland took her to Cromwell Street where she had sex with him and his friend David Evans. She became a regular visitor to 25 Cromwell Street and got to know Fred and Rose, becoming involved in sadomasochistic sex sessions with them. In April 1973 the Wests asked her to stay in Cromwell Street and look after their children; Lynda agreed. Within two weeks of

Lynda Gough's moving into the Wests' home she had been murdered. Her body was found in 1994 in an inspection pit under what had formerly been a garage at 25 Cromwell Street, tied up and with masking tape wrapped tightly around her head.

In November 1973 a fifteen-year-old girl named Carol Ann Cooper, who lived in a children's home in Worcester, was brought to Cromwell Street by Fred and Rose specifically to be raped and murdered. When her body was found in a pit Fred had built under the cellar floor, the legs and head had been severed. The remains of an elasticated gag were found around her face.

Middle-class 21-year-old Lucy Partington was studying medieval English and history at Exeter University. On the evening of 27 December 1973 she was on her way to her mother's house, having visited a disabled friend in Cheltenham. It is believed that, having missed the last bus, she was offered a lift by Fred and Rose. She was then taken to Cromwell Street, where the torture and abuse began. Masking tape was wound around her head and rope attached to her neck. Records kept at the Gloucestershire Royal Hospital show that Fred went to the casualty department on 3 January 1974 with a serious cut to his hand. If this injury had been the result of an accident while dismembering the body, Lucy Partington may have been alive for a week before finally either dying of her injuries or being killed by the Wests. When the body was discovered buried under the cellar floor, alongside it was the sharp knife used to dismember Lucy, which it may be presumed Fred abandoned after cutting himself and then forgot to retrieve.

Ever the fantasist, Fred later told police that he had been having an affair with Lucy Partington, and that he had to kill her because she was becoming a threat to his marriage after she told Fred that she had fallen in love with him.

All evidence points to the fact that these three women were taken down to the cellar at 25 Cromwell Street – which was a large soundproof area accessible only to the Wests – tied up and kept alive only to be tormented and sexually abused. Fred had left his signature on all the bodies – the removal of the fingers, toes and kneecaps of the victims. It is not known whether this butchery occurred before or after the girls were killed.

Fred and Rose's son Stephen was born in 1973.

1974 – THERESE SIEGENTHALER AND SHIRLEY ANN HUBBARD MURDERED

Twenty-one-year-old Therese Siegenthaler was brought up in Switzerland and was a sociology student in London. On 15 April 1974 she set off on a trip to Ireland to visit a friend who was a Catholic priest. Therese hoped to hitch a lift as far as Holyhead in Wales, where she intended to catch the ferry. She was lured into a car by Fred and Rose and then driven to Cromwell Street, where she was raped and murdered. Her decapitated body was buried under the cellar floor after Fred had removed her fingers, toes and collarbone.

Shirley Ann Hubbard was fifteen years old, had been in care and now lived in a foster home in Droitwich. On the evening of 14 November 1974 she disappeared, having been last seen alive by her boyfriend Daniel. It may be assumed that she was offered a lift by the Wests and then driven to 25 Cromwell Street to be abused and killed. Her body was found buried in the cellar; as well as body parts being missing and her being decapitated, Shirley's head had been completely bound with tape, with a plastic tube inserted through the mask and into one nostril, allowing her to breathe.

1975 – JUANITA MOTT MURDERED

Juanita Mott, the next known victim of the Wests, had been a lodger at Cromwell Street but had moved out and was now living with a friend of her mother's in a bungalow in Newent, Gloucestershire. On 11 April 1975 she went back to Cromwell Street – either to visit someone there or having been picked up by Fred and Rose – and was subjected to rape and torture. Her dismembered body was found in the cellar, tied up with a plastic clothes line and with a pair of tights around her severed head.

1978 – SHIRLEY ROBINSON MURDERED

Shirley Robinson was yet another lodger at 25 Cromwell Street who was murdered by the Wests. Shirley was a bisexual prostitute who became involved in a relationship with both Fred and Rose. Shirley became pregnant with Fred West's baby. Rose, who was pregnant at the time by one of her West Indian clients – the child, Tara, was born in December 1977 – felt threatened by Shirley's closeness to her husband. Shirley was killed in May 1978. The space in the cellar was now full of bodies, so her remains were buried in the Wests' back garden. The girl was dismembered and the eight-month-old foetus torn from her body and interred alongside her.

Fred and Rose's daughter Louise was born in November 1978. During that year Anna-Marie had an abortion after becoming pregnant by her father.

1979 – ALISON CHAMBERS MURDERED

Sixteen-year-old Alison Chambers was a resident of Jordan's Brook House, a children's home in Gloucester. She absconded and moved into Cromwell Street, having met Fred and Rose, who enticed the vulnerable child with promises that they would let her stay on a farm they said they owned in the nearby countryside. She became involved in sadomasochistic threesomes with Fred and Rose. In September 1979 she was killed by them and buried in the garden, in an area Fred would later cover with a patio. Around this time Fred caused Rose to become pregnant, and she gave birth in June 1980 to a son whom they named Barry. Rose had two further children by her West Indian lovers – Rosemary was born in 1982 and Lucyanna in 1983.

It is likely that the Wests continued to abduct and murder further young women during the 1980s. In a conversation with his son Stephen, Fred indicated that he was responsible for many more murders than those for which he was facing charges.

1987 – THE MURDER OF HEATHER WEST

At the age of fifteen, Anna-Marie West left home to live with her boyfriend. The violence and sexual abuse she had suffered at the hands of her parents had become too much to bear. Heather West then began to bear the brunt of Fred and Rose's anger. Fred started to make increased sexual demands on her. Heather spoke to one of her classmates at her secondary school about the violence at home and her parents' sexual proclivities. News of this reached her parents, who subjected her to a sadistic beating.

During an argument with Fred and Rose, Heather was assaulted and strangled to death. Her body was buried in the garden. Unlike the other victims, she had not been gagged, although she had been stripped naked and tied up with rope, which suggests that she had been raped before being killed. Fred then cut the body into pieces and removed Heather's head. Heather's fingernails were pulled out and buried with the body, which indicates she may have been tortured before being killed.

When the other children asked about Heather's whereabouts, they were told that she had gone off to live with a lesbian lover, and warned they were never to mention her name in the house again.

1992 – POLICE INVESTIGATE THE WESTS

In early 1992 a thirteen-year-old girl was brought to 25 Cromwell Street by Fred, who raped and sodomised her, capturing these acts on videotape. The girl informed one of her friends at school of what had happened, and this friend went to the police and reported what she had been told, adding that she was also aware of abuse of the children within the West family. In August 1992 police went to Cromwell Street and searched for evidence of the rape and of child abuse. They took away whips, sex toys and 99 videotapes. Rose was arrested for her part in the rape of the thirteen-year-old, obstructing the police and neglect of her children. Fred was arrested for rape and buggery of the girl. The investigation broadened and other members of the family were interviewed, including Anna-Marie, who told police the full details of how she had been abused and also of her suspicions about what had happened to Charmaine.

The case against Fred and Rose West did not come to trial, because the thirteen-year-old girl withdrew her testimony at the last minute, frightened of what the consequences might be if she were to proceed. On 7 June 1993 Fred, who had been remanded in custody in Gloucester Prison and then sent to live in a bail hostel, was able to walk free from the courtroom and return home with Rose.

Following the arrest of their parents, the five youngest children had been taken into care, where they were overheard by staff repeating the 'joke' that Fred had often made in front of them: that Heather was buried under the patio. This information was passed on to police, who added it to the considerable files they now held on suspicious disappearances connected with 25 Cromwell Street and the Wests.

1994 – FRED AND ROSE CHARGED WITH MURDER; BODIES DISCOVERED

At 1.25 p.m. on 24 February 1994 police arrived at 25 Cromwell Street with a warrant to search for the body of Heather West. Fred was not at home; Stephen West told him on the phone that the house and garden were about to be searched, but his father did not appear at Cromwell Street until around 6 p.m. When he arrived, he saw the garden roped off and lit by arc lamps. Fred told police that they were wasting their time searching his property for bodies. On the following day, Heather's body was discovered, together with the femur from another corpse. Fred was arrested and charged with the murder of Heather West. He admitted to police that he had killed her in the course of an argument and that Rose had nothing to do with the crime. Meanwhile, Rose was being questioned about the disappearances of Heather, Charmaine and Rena West, and then released. During the next month the bodies of all ten victims plus Shirley Robinson's unborn child were painstakingly recovered from the cellar and patio areas. Then the old flat in Midland Road was searched, and Charmaine's remains were found. The field near Much Marcle was searched and the bodies of Rena West and Anne McFall were discovered.

In June 1994 Fred West was charged with 12 counts of murder. In April Rose had been charged with the murder of Lynda Gough; to this charge were added another eight counts of murder. Once Rose had been charged, bizarrely, Fred now told police that he was completely innocent and had not killed any of the girls, and that he had been lying to protect Rose, who had confessed to him that she was responsible for all the murders.

1995 – FRED COMMITS SUICIDE; ROSE TRIED AND FOUND GUILTY OF TEN MURDERS

On 1 January 1995, Fred West hanged himself in his cell in Winson Green Prison with a rope he had painstakingly and secretly made from strips of torn-off blanket. He left a note for Rose wishing her a happy New Year.

On 3 October 1995 Rose West's trial began at Winchester Crown Court. She was found guilty of the murders of Heather and Charmaine West, Lynda Gough, Carol Ann Cooper, Lucy Partington, Therese Siegenthaler, Shirley Hubbard, Juanita Mott, Shirley Robinson and Alison Chambers. Witnesses for the Crown included Caroline Owens, Anna-Marie West and Kathryn Halliday, who had had an affair with Rose during which she was subjected to increasingly sadistic treatment. The prosecution sought to prove that Rose West was a sexual sadist, which would imply that she must have not only known of the murders but had fully taken part in them. The defence team focused on the lack of direct forensic evidence linking Rose to the murders.

On 20 November the jury delivered guilty verdicts for the murders of Heather and Charmaine West and Shirley Robinson; the following day the court reconvened and the jury found Rose guilty of the seven other murder charges. On 22 November the presiding judge, Mr Justice Mantell, sentenced Rose

West to life imprisonment, telling her, 'If attention is paid to what I think, you will never be released.'

WHY?

The writer Colin Wilson calls the Wests' crimes 'arguably the worst case of serial murder in British criminal history'. Despite the conviction of Rose West, there remain some puzzling and possibly unanswerable questions. What was the motivation for torturing young women in this particular way, obstructing their breathing and binding their faces with tape? What made Fred and Rose West kill again and again? What was the reason for the removal of bones, fingers and toes from the majority of the victims, and where were these body parts taken? How many more murders did Fred and Rose commit? Why and how were they able to conceal their murderous activities for so long?

The details of Fred's childhood and the malign influence of his parents certainly hold a key to his behaviour: the incest with his mother that may have led him to despise women; Walter West's view that sex with his daughters was both natural and a father's right. The exposure of Fred at a young age to the behaviour of farm animals – which is amoral, openly sexual and sometimes violent – and man's treatment of them, which involves cruelty and death, may also have had an effect on him.

Rose's upbringing, too, was abnormal and involved her being both a victim of incest when her father forced his attentions on her and the instigator of it when she seduced her younger brother Graham.

In the Wests' relationship, Rose appears to have been the dominant partner, while Fred's behaviour towards her was submissive, placatory and even chivalrous. Both were obsessed with sex, but in different ways – Rose as participant, Fred as voyeur – and their tastes complemented each other. Once the taboo of murder had been breached, they were compelled to repeat the act. Killing had become, for Fred and Rose, the ultimate fetish.

BIBLIOGRAPHY

Burn, Gordon, *Happy Like Murderers*, Faber & Faber, London, 1998.

Gekoski, Anna, *Murder By Numbers – British Serial Killers Since 1950*, André Deutsch, London, 1998.

Masters, Brian, *She Must Have Known*, Doubleday, London, 1996.

Sounes, Howard, *Fred And Rose*, Warner Books, London, 1995.

Wansel, Geoffrey, *An Evil Love*, Headline, London, 1996.

West, Anne Marie (with Virginia Hill) *Out of the Shadows*, Simon & Schuster, London, 1995.

West, Stephen and West, Mae, *Inside 25 Cromwell St*, News Group, London, 1995.

Wilson, Colin, *The Corpse Garden*, True Crime Library, London, 1998.

12. TRAILER PARK TERROR – DAVID PARKER RAY AND CYNTHIA HENDY

Elephant Butte Lake State Park in New Mexico is a popular tourist destination all year round. The main attraction is the lake itself. No village pond, it stretches 43 miles long and five miles wide. Its surface covers 38,000 acres and it boasts 200 miles of shoreline. It is New Mexico's premier water recreation facility and the largest lake in the state. The mild climate of the area and numerous recreational facilities on offer attract upwards of 100,000 visitors at holiday weekends. Located five miles south of the small town of Truth or Consequences, the lake – or reservoir – and its dam were originally constructed in 1916 to provide irrigation to an arid location. The area it serves stretches from the environment of the Elephant Butte Reservoir itself, in Socorro County, right down to the city of El Paso, Texas, forty miles away.

In the 1950s the reservoir began to operate as a holiday destination. The post-war years saw a boom in recreational pursuits, and this swiftly established the lake's secondary function. Its popularity provides a healthy revenue stream for local businesses. There are numerous places to hire boating and fishing hardware and there's plenty of space for every imaginable pursuit. If you want to enjoy a spot of tranquil fishing – for catfish, pike, black bass or crappie – you don't have to worry that a jet-ski will frighten off the fish, as they are loaned out twenty miles up the shoreline. If you are camping in the park, you can be self-contained in near wilderness or enjoy a home from home in the RV (recreation vehicle) park. Yes, there's something for everyone who enjoys healthy outdoor pursuits at Elephant Butte Lake State Park.

This wholesome environment had provided 59-year-old David Parker Ray with employment for over five years before he was charged on 23 March 1999 on 25 counts including kidnapping, aggravated battery and criminal sexual penetration. He was a State Parks maintenance worker, and his duties included fixing vehicles and heavy machinery in a garage on the grounds by the lake. Fastidious in everything, the heavily moustached Ray was known for doing excellent work, for being really competent with tools and enjoying renovating his two boats. In the locale he was known as an excellent welder.

But handy Ray had been devoting his spare time to more deviant interests than restoring boats – and he hadn't been acting alone. Arrested along with him on charges of kidnapping and accessory to criminal sexual penetration was his live-in girlfriend, Cynthia 'Cindy' Lea Hendy, aged 39. As the State Parks Department began looking for a replacement maintenance man, a series of bizarre allegations came to light, prompted by events that had begun the previous day.

HORROR AT THE LAKESIDE

Late in the afternoon of 22 March 1999, a 22-year-old woman staggered along the narrow sandy road outside Ray and Hendy's trailer-park home. She was naked but for a padlocked metal collar attached to a chain. The woman, Cynthia Vigil, described as looking 'wild and scared' by an El Paso resident into whose car she tried to climb, finally found refuge in the nearby house of Darlene Breech, who immediately threw a robe around the dishevelled woman and dialled 911.

Two sheriff's deputies, David Elston and Lucas Alvarez, based in the nearby town of Truth or Consequences, had earlier been dispatched by their radio controller to the scene of a 911 hangup call at 513 Bass Road, down by the lake. There was noise in the background – some kind of commotion was occurring. While en route to the scene, the officers received a further call saying a naked woman was running along an adjacent street. Then, finally, the third call, from Darlene Breech, put an end to the emergency trail. A traumatised woman was finally in safe hands. Leaving Alvarez with Vigil at Breech's address, Deputy Elston proceeded to 513 Bass Road, where he found the rear sliding glass doors of the property unlocked. With assistance from one of the State Park rangers, Elston checked the residence for signs of life. In so doing, the officer noticed the bedroom contained a number of sexual devices and restraints. The ranger identified the residence as belonging to David Parker Ray. This wasn't difficult to verify. There, on the entrance gate to the property, was the name David P Ray, 513 Bass, K8. On finding the premises deserted, the State Parks ranger mentioned that the occupants had been spotted driving their camper van a short while earlier, with Ray's girlfriend bleeding from the back of her head. It was only minutes before the couple were apprehended in their RV by armed officers a few blocks away, headed back towards their trailer. Ray and Hendy were told to walk backwards away from their RV and get down on the ground. Officers then handcuffed them.

CHAINED UP LIKE AN ANIMAL

I'm alive! I'm alive! I broke free! I broke free!' Vigil told Alvarez and Elston, who interviewed her that evening at the Sierra Vista Hospital in Truth or Consequences, after she had the brutal collar removed with bolt cutters. Vigil was still in extreme distress, and claimed to have undergone three days of aggravated molestation at the hands of Ray and Hendy, including rapes with sexual devices, beatings and torture by electric shocks. Vigil's wounds included bruising, abrasions on her wrists and welts on her back. Most disturbing were the small puncture wounds and bruising around her nipples.

Vigil told authorities she had been introduced to the couple by an acquaintance on 20 March at around 11 a.m. outside a bar in Albuquerque. She discussed the price of a sex act with Ray and went to the couple's RV, where Ray then produced a badge and said she was under arrest for prostitution. While Vigil was trying to make sense of what was happening, Hendy emerged from the RV's restroom and handcuffed her. They then drove her 150 miles south to Elephant Butte.

It soon dawned on Vigil that her 'arrest' was really a kidnapping, and her captors were not police but sadistic sexual deviants. Once Vigil was ensconced in Ray and Hendy's trailer, the couple set about subjecting her to terrifying humiliations. She was restrained to a bed as Ray proceeded to insert dildos into her vagina and rectum while Hendy waved a revolver around, threatening to shoot her if she tried to escape. On at least two occasions over the next 72 hours, Vigil had electrical devices attached to her nipples and received electric shocks through her whole body. On the Sunday, the 21st, the couple whipped her on her back and she was restrained and hung from the ceiling. After the whipping Ray inserted a metal dildo into her vagina. At some point during the course of the three-day torture spree, the loose-lipped blonde Hendy mentioned to Vigil that she had 'only been kidnapping, raping and murdering for the last year', but that Ray had been 'doing it much longer'. Cynthia Vigil took advantage of Hendy's inexperience at kidnapping the following day when Ray was out of the house at work. The chained woman used her legs to drag a coffee table towards herself, on which lay the key to the padlocked collar. Hendy realised what was happening and a vicious struggle ensued. Using an ice pick, Vigil bravely fought off Hendy's attack and snapped her leash in the scuffle, but not before being bashed on the head with a lamp by an angry Hendy.

After the couple's arrest, police swiftly descended on Ray's double-wide trailer home and the soundproofed annexe outside it that had been converted into the couple's torture chamber. The trailer contained a shocking collection of unpleasant devices: a cattle prod, a stun gun, leather restraints, medical instruments and even a gynaecological examination chair, complete with stirrups, its own securing straps and electrical wiring. Above the chair were lights reminiscent of those in an operating theatre. As if this weren't enough, police soon uncovered photographs and videotapes of bound women being subjected to sexual humiliations. The tapes had a man's (presumably Ray's) voice on them, informing the women he would use drugs on them that made them susceptible to hypnosis and were able to erase memory. 'You're going to be kept naked and chained up like an animal and used and abused in any way we want to,' the man's voice says. Books on human anatomy, serial killing and sketches of women being tortured were also found.

Deputy District Attorney Jim Yontz describes his first impressions of Ray and Hendy's DIY torture chamber: 'I went down there and went through the trailer, and just came out shaking my head,' he said. [1]

FBI profilers who went to investigate the scene said it

was one of only five or six cases they could name in all their days for the Bureau that had similar circumstances. Even then, the effort that had gone into the construction of their home-made torture chamber was staggering. One long-serving officer said, 'This is in the realm of the truly unique. I've been an agent 23 years and I haven't seen anything quite like this.'[2]

MEDIA FRENZY

Thirty FBI agents and state police searched the dusty half-acre property during the week after the arrests and had to ask for backup because they didn't have the resources to process the amount of material their search uncovered. All in all, the investigators recovered more than 1,500 pieces of evidence from the property. The investigation wasn't managed under any veil of secrecy. The arrests and the salacious nature of the charges brought a lot of unwelcome attention for Elephant Butte's 3,000 inhabitants.

Many residents agreed the media descended on an area only when something gruesome was afoot. The month prior to the arrests had been the fiftieth anniversary of the renaming of neighbouring town Truth or Consequences, and a big family fiesta had not attracted any outside reporters. Elephant Butte's mayor, Bob Barnes, was also disappointed with the huge influx of curiosity seekers since the arrests. No longer able to take his afternoon nap because of the news helicopters circling the area, he told reporters that his town was a close-knit community where there had never been any trouble other than minor incidents of vandalism. 'To get your picture in the paper around here, usually, you catch a very big fish,' he said.[3] Ray's attorney, Jeff Rein, was also concerned, saying the media frenzy would mean his client would not get a fair trial.

VICTIMS COME FORWARD

Despite the protests by upstanding members of the community that their town was being violated by prurient media, worse was to come. A preliminary hearing scheduled for the following week was postponed because Ray's attorney had sought a continuance (extension), as he anticipated that further charges would be brought against the couple in the very near future. Police put out a request for people who had suffered at the hands of the couple, or who could supply further information, to come forward.

Come forward they did. The charges Ray and Hendy faced were grave enough, then a 'friend' of Hendy piped up. John Branaugh told the local station, KOB-TV, that Hendy, while drunk in a bar, had told him that Ray had thrown four to six bodies in Elephant Butte Lake, while others had been buried in the desert. The reason the bodies in the lake had never surfaced was, according to Branaugh's memory of what Hendy had told him, that Ray split them down the middle with his surgical tools, preventing any buoyancy. She also told Branaugh about the 'toy box' (the trailer annexe) and said she participated in the crimes for the 'adrenaline rush'.

Then a female acquaintance of the couple, Angie Montano, contacted the authorities, saying she had popped round to borrow some cake mix from Cindy Hendy in February 1999 and had ended up being held captive for the couple's sick sex games. Better known for her alcohol abuse and bad temper than her baking, Hendy seized the woman, who was then told she was being kidnapped and held against her will. Ray held her at knifepoint and Hendy brandished what looked like a gun. Over the next three days she was kept prisoner in a room at the couple's home but also taken on several occasions to the 'toy box', where she was tied to a table, molested with a 'sexual device', jolted with electrodes attached to her breasts and vagina and made to perform oral sex on Ray. It was also alleged that Ray had set up a pulley system with weights to stretch victims' breasts. Despite undergoing this horror, Montano persuaded the couple to release her on a highway on 21 February, promising to keep quiet about what had happened.

Worse was yet to come. On 9 April 1999, a fourth party, Dennis Roy Yancy, aged 27, a friend of the couple, was arrested on the even graver charge of the murder of a 22-year-old Truth or Consequences woman. Yancy's wife told reporters that David Parker Ray had forced Yancy to strangle the woman, Marie Parker, while Ray took photographs of the act. Parker had not been seen since disappearing from Elephant Butte's Blue Waters Saloon on 5 July 1997. The District Attorney felt there was sufficient evidence to bring a conviction against Yancy even without a body, and Yancy was moved to Dona Ana County Detention Center in Las Cruces, where he was held without bail. Despite his pleading not guilty at his original arrest, Yancy allegedly told police in his post-arrest interview that he had indeed strangled Marie Parker.

And yet even more sordid allegations followed. When Ray's own daughter, Glenda Jean 'Jesse' Ray, aged 31, was arrested on 26 April and charged as an accomplice to her father in the sex-torture case of a 25-year-old Colorado woman – Kelly van Cleave – dating back to 1996, the town was shocked into disbelief. Van Cleave had been out drinking with Ray's daughter one Thursday night and had accepted a lift on Jesse's motorcycle back to her place to sober up. Instead, she was taken to the elder Ray's trailer, where father and daughter held a knife to her throat, bound her with duct tape and put a dog collar around her neck. She was then held captive and repeatedly assaulted with dildos and other items until David Ray drove her home on the Sunday. Van Cleave alleged David Ray had told her she was wanted as some kind of sex toy and that he was part of a satanic group. Of Glenda Jean, Deputy District Attorney Yontz said, 'She procured the victim for Daddy.'[4]

Thomas Pastak, a New Mexico magistrate, ordered that Glenda Jean be held in jail on a bond of $1 million until her trial. This ruling came after a day of sensational testimony in which prosecutors played some of the audio-visual evidence they had uncovered at Ray's home. A videotape – allegedly shown to Ray's victims before they were tortured – had a man's voice (again presumably Ray's) saying, 'We snatch anything young, clean and well built. Most of them is very easy to get . . . I've been raping bitches ever since I was old enough to [masturbate].' And, 'If we killed every bitch we kidnapped, there'd be bodies strewn across the country.'[5]

THE UNDERBELLY OF SMALL-TOWN AMERICA

What unbelievable acts of horror had been going on in Elephant Butte? A dark underbelly of unspeakable behaviour, like something out of a David Lynch movie, seemed to be unfolding. The claustrophobic circumstances of the crimes and their darkly bizarre nature were a complete contrast to the outdoor family pursuits enjoyed not a stone's throw from the trailer of horrors. How could David Parker Ray have carried out his heinous antics for so long without anyone blowing the whistle? A murder had possibly occurred. What deterrent had prevented Yancy's wife from coming forward earlier? Her young husband had not only strangled someone to death, but also allowed a much older acquaintance to photograph the crime for sexual thrills.

Yontz again: 'The guys who act crazy and are nuts get stopped real quick. The ones that are successful are the John Wayne Gacys, the Ted Bundys. These people that carry on, carry on, because they fit. Not because they stand out.'[6]

The veneer of the hard-working, pleasant-natured handyman seems to be a useful cover. Like Fred West, Ray managed to fool his neighbours into thinking he was just a regular guy. Jo McClean, the manager of the Earl's Shamrock gas station, where Ray stopped by each morning to buy coffee, doughnuts or a burrito, had been on small-talk terms with Ray since he moved to the town in 1984. She had never suspected her regular customer was anything but an intelligent, clean-cut man who talked about his boat and complained about work – like everyone else. David Parker Ray not only held down a job, he was seen as a model employee. Ray's co-workers were flabbergasted at his arrest, describing him as the 'neatest, cleanest, politest person you could ever want to meet'.

Hendy, conversely, had a reputation for drunkenness. A former Seattle resident, she had previous convictions for forgery, possession of stolen goods, heroin, and drink-driving. A former boyfriend said she drank far too much, and she continued to abuse alcohol even when taking the drugs she had been prescribed for manic depression. What Ray's colleagues and neighbours thought of his girlfriend is unknown, but one can assume he was seen as the 'respectable' half of the couple. It would be reasonable to assume that Hendy's inebriated ramblings in the drinking holes of Elephant Butte were ignored as drunken fantasies. The exaggerated yarn-spinning one hears among small-town America's barfly culture often stretches the bounds of credibility. There was no reason for anyone to take

seriously the outlandish claims of this slightly dishevelled, often drunk, but still attractive blonde.

HUMAN REMAINS IN A BURLAP SACK

After Yancy's arrest for the murder of Marie Parker,
crime-scene specialists began an extensive and pains-
taking search of Ray's property, but failed to turn up any
human remains. Bones found at the end of March 1999
caused a flurry of media activity but these turned out to
be animal remains. Still they did not rule out the
possibility of other homicides, and began checking
hundreds of leads in up to ten states, including Tucson
and Phoenix in Arizona and El Paso, Texas, and
anywhere Ray had lived, worked or had contacts. FBI
agent David Kitchen said investigators were looking at
possible connections with a series of more than a
hundred sex murders of women around the Mexican
city of Juarez. Then rumours began flying around
Elephant Butte that David Parker Ray had made and
sold 'snuff' movies but no evidence of this was found.

In May 1999, Ray's 'toy box' was taken to a storage
facility in Santa Fe, and it was decided that police were
not about to dredge the lake, despite Hendy's drunken
claims of sliced-up bodies being cast into it. Then, in
late June, a fisherman, Ralph Tutor, found four small
pieces of flesh floating in a burlap sack on the east side
of the lake. Tests concluded in September determined
that the remains were human. However, the bad state of
decomposition meant that the police crime lab were
unable to make a DNA profile as to whether they were
male, female, young or old.

Before this kind of evidence had literally floated to the
surface, Cindy Lea Hendy began trying to find a way out
of her predicament. On 6 April 1999 – not two weeks
since her arrest – she put the wheels in motion for a plea

bargain with her prosecutors when she pleaded guilty to five of the 25 counts in exchange for a reduced prison sentence. A successful plea bargain would see a sentence of up to 198 years being reduced to 12 to 54 years. Someone was going to go down for a long time for these crimes and it seems Cindy was determined it wouldn't be her. District Judge Neil Mertz – who was to preside over Hendy's preliminary hearing on 15 April 1999 – signed an order sealing the 'plea and disposition agreement'.

TRIALS AND SENTENCING

In December 1999 Dennis Roy Yancy changed his plea to one of guilty to second-degree murder and conspiracy to commit murder in the Marie Parker case. Yancy said he and Glenda Jean had lured Marie Parker into captivity on the pretext of a drug transaction. Yancy was sentenced to twenty years in jail. Marie Parker's body was never found despite the FBI taking Yancy down to the lake, where he'd said she had ended up.

Cynthia Lea Hendy was held on remand until 11 May 2000, when Judge Neil Mertz sentenced her to 36 years in prison. Her defence brought up a past history of abuse from men to get the sentence reduced, but it was overruled. Jim Yontz said that Hendy was not shy, and seemed to have no problems in whipping, chaining and sexually torturing her victims. Hendy – who did not speak during her sentencing – was transferred to a female correctional facility in New Mexico.

David Parker Ray faced three separate trials – one for each of his accusers. The initial trial in Tierra Amarilla – the van Cleave case – collapsed in summer 2000 when the jury could not reach a majority verdict. The November retrial in Estancia was then halted when Judge Neil Mertz died of a heart attack. In the meantime,

Ray's second victim, Angie Montano, died of pneumonia and heart failure – causes unrelated to the Ray case.

A new judge – Kevin Sweazea – was sworn in and, after only one week, David Parker Ray was found guilty in April 2001 on twelve counts in the case of Kelly van Cleave. The prosecution had brought up new evidence – an audiotape on which Ray talks about his 'method, plan and preparation'. He was ordered to return for sentencing later in 2001.

GLENDA JEAN GOES FREE

David and Glenda Jean Ray had stuck to their pleas of innocence since their initial arrests, and had each been held on a $1 million bond. But a deal was to be struck that would allow Jesse to walk free while her father would have to spend the rest of his life incarcerated. Facing twelve counts involving the kidnapping and torture of one woman – and a possible eighty years in jail – Jesse, like Cynthia Hendy, was to benefit from a plea bargain. David Ray was told charges against Jesse would be dropped if he pleaded guilty. In early July 2001 he complied, magnanimously remarking, 'Freedom is the ultimate gift a father can give to his daughter.' Friends of Jesse are reported to have said they thought the authorities may be more lenient with her because she had gone to the FBI thirteen years previously with claims that her father kidnapped, tortured and sold women in Mexico. The FBI was, however, unable to substantiate these claims, having closed the investigation in 1987 owing to insufficient evidence and an absence of victims. Glenda Jean ended up being handed a nine-year prison sentence, suspended for six years and seven months. Seeing that she had spent two years and five months in jail before the case came to trial, she was allowed to walk free with a suspended sentence of five years. No charges of conspiracy to murder in the Marie Parker case were ever brought against her. She now lives in Albuquerque.

PARKER RAY IS SENTENCED

Ray's sentencing in September 2001 gave the victims and their families an opportunity to vent their anger and disgust at the crimes that had shocked New Mexico. Everyone who had something to say said it with as much vitriol as they could muster. Despite this, Ray's attorney, Lee McMillian, did the best he could for his client. McMillian claimed Ray's plea of guilty should be ignored because of impaired mental faculties while Ray was on medication. This was overturned, as Jim Yontz and Judge Sweazea both agreed that the defendant had appeared completely cogent, alert and responsive during his previous trials and other proceedings.

In the case of Kelly Garret (née van Cleave) – who held hands with Cynthia Vigil during the sentencing – McMillian implied the victim was a troubled person who took part willingly in the Rays' rough sex games. His suggestion fell on deaf ears.

Angie Montano's mother was in court and said she was there for Angie and her two small sons, whose lives Ray had ruined. In a surprise outburst, she said that, while she could never forget what Ray had done, she did forgive him and Angie would forgive him too.

As a contrast to this, Cynthia Vigil and her family had nothing but loathing for Ray. Vigil claimed she still bore the scars inside and out, and they would never heal, and she now suffers terrors, is afraid of the dark and cannot go out alone. Cynthia's grandmother, Bertha Vigil, was also in court. She said she would pray for Ray to suffer every day for the rest of his life. 'Satan has a place for you,' she said. 'I hope you burn in hell for ever.'

It seems that anyone who wielded any clout went full throttle for the maximum sentencing. Mary Ellen O'Toole – the FBI's foremost expert in crimes of sexual sadism – declared, to no one's surprise, that Ray was in her opinion a 'criminal sexual sadist'. She said his 'toy box' and custom-made equipment were impressive for the time, money and effort it took to keep them a secret. O'Toole finished by saying that psychosexual disorders such as Ray's are not treatable.

Attorney General Patricia Madrid announced she was happy to be at Ray's sentencing, declaring his behaviour worse than that of any animal. She pleaded with the court to impose the maximum penalty. Madrid said evidence such as his illustrated manual of anatomy made it clear he would soon torture other victims if allowed any freedom. Yontz backed up her warnings, adding that Ray would probably offend before arriving home if he were released that day.

McMillian – in a last-ditch attempt to have Ray's sentence reduced to a suspended one – remarked that the term 'paraphilia' did not adequately explain the 'disease' his client had 'successfully' fought against for fifty years, and that he had made good efforts to reform himself while in protective custody. Ray himself declared that the two and a half years of confinement prior to the trial had given him the chance to reflect, read the Bible and 'get right with God'. He claimed that his life was now in God's hands and, although he couldn't change the past, he was sorry for what he had done.

This cut no ice with prosecutor Yontz, whose language in his summing up against Ray seems redolent of that used in 1940s and 50s pulp fiction: 'This monster should never be allowed to walk the streets again. There should be no light at the end of the tunnel and he should realize that a cell will be his home for the rest of his life and that he will leave only in a box.'[7]

Judge Sweazea – who in his spare time enters rope and steer rallies and is listed on the Booger Barter website's 'Who's Who of Local Cowboys' – handed out sentences totalling a staggering 224 years, despite no charge or conviction of murder. The primary purpose of the sentencing was, according to Sweazea, to ensure that no one else would ever suffer at Ray's hands again. For Ray's crimes against Kelly van Cleave, Sweazea laid down nine years for kidnapping, three years for conspiracy to commit kidnapping, eighteen years for each of six counts of criminal sexual penetration, eighteen months for criminal sexual contact and eighteen months for conspiracy to commit criminal sexual contact. For the crimes against Cynthia Vigil, Ray was handed eighteen years for kidnapping, nine years for conspiracy to kidnap and nine years for criminal sexual penetration. On top of this he added an additional third of the total sentences for the aggravated nature of the crimes – the premeditation, planning and preparation. Ray was remanded in the custody of the New Mexico Department of Corrections.

Despite receiving the maximum sentence, Ray appeared sanguine and, at times during his sentencing, even appeared to be in good spirits. He told the court that no one bar his attorney had listened to his side of the story and said many lies and distortions of the facts had been heard. Ray said he had lost everything following his arrest, including his home, possessions and health. He commended the late Judge Neil Mertz, who had said that Ray would never have the chance of a fair trial if it were held in Sierra County. Ray then went on to criticise Judge Sweazea for moving the second trial to a location near to the judge's home. With nothing to lose, he then put the boot into Patricia Madrid, saying that she was trying to take all the credit after another prosecutor, Claire Harwell, had done all the work.

FACTS REMAIN UNCLEAR

A number of questions arise from the Elephant Butte crimes. The curious fact, for instance, that although David Parker Ray was guilty of criminal sexual penetration, he was not charged with actual rape. At no point did he perform sexual intercourse with his victims and one has to wonder whether he was impotent and, moreover, whether the claims made on the video and audiotapes – that he had been 'raping for years' – were nothing more than sordid fantasies. And what of the bodies in the lake and the desert? Despite Hendy's drunken claims, no bodies were ever recovered and the fleshy remains found in the lake proved too insubstantial for identification. It seems also that some of the evidence was questionable: owning an illustrated encyclopedia of anatomy is not a criminal offence but the sensationalism surrounding the case was bound to prejudice opinion and read sinister motives into possibly unrelated materials.

It is also possible to purchase in sex shops small electrical devices that issue mild currents. The voltage in them is well within the safety zone. Could it be that Ray and Hendy were using equipment of this type and not the 'Frankenstein's laboratory' conductors that one would imagine from reading newspaper reports about the evidence? And why – while being charged with everything the authorities could throw at him – was Ray not charged with conspiracy to murder the woman for whom Yancy is now serving twenty years? Could Yancy have indicted Ray, thinking the bondage freak was an easy target?

There is no question that David Parker Ray and his cohorts committed acts of sexual penetration with threatening behaviour and held at least three women against their will at his trailer by the lake – which were terrifying ordeals for the victims. It is also hard fact that he had an obsessive interest in rough sex and bondage.

But it is not inconceivable that both Ray and Hendy got carried away acting a part. They were no Bernardo and Homolka, for sure, and they do not fit into the profile of the other sadistic serial-killer couples covered in this book. The maintenance man and his drunken petty criminal accomplice were never going to set the world on fire with glittering careers or tales of achievement; maybe turning Ray's hardcore fantasies into reality seemed a way to claw some power out of their downbeat lives. In their endeavours to be Elephant Butte's king and queen of depravity, did the line between fantasy and reality get horribly blurred?

One must remember there is no actual evidence that Ray murdered anybody; he had let both Angie Montano and Kelly van Cleave go free after their ordeals and it is possible that Vigil too would have been allowed to walk away had she not escaped first. Whether or not defence attorney Lee McMillian's comment when Ray was found guilty of the crimes against van Cleave – that 'Nobody who engages in alternative sexual practices is going to be safe'[8] – has been borne out is open to question. However, one thing is for certain: it would have been better for all involved if Ray and Hendy had kept their fantasies to themselves and opened their toy box only in each other's company.

Jo McLean of the Earl's Shamrock gas station summed up the only good thing that seems to have come out of the whole sorry business. She said it had taken the Ray and Hendy case to get outsiders to pronounce the name of their town correctly. At least everyone now says 'Bute' instead of 'Butt'.

NOTES
1. Zitrin, Richard, 'Echoes of Evil at Elephant Butte' www.apbnews.com 17 May, 1999.

2. Ibid.
3. Ibid.
4. 'Trial Ordered for Daughter of Sex-Torture Suspect', www.afgen.com
5. Ibid.
6. Richard Zitrin, 'Echoes of Evil at Elephant Butte'.
7. Mramor, Fred, 'David Ray gets 224 Years', www.desertjournalonline.com, 21 September 2001.
8. Simons, Jeff, *The Round Up – The Student Voice of New Mexico*, 19 April 2001, http://roundup.nmsu.edu/public

BIBLIOGRAPHY

Mramor, Fred, www.desertjournalonline.com
Roswell Daily Record, News www.roswellrecord.com/archives/070301/news05.html
www.thesmokinggun.com/archive/nmtorture3.shtml
Amarillo Globe News www.amarillonet.com/stories
www.cnn.com/US/9903/30/torture.probe.02

AUTHOR BIOGS

Patrick Blackden is the author of the forthcoming *Danger Down Under – The Dark Side of the Australian Dream*. The well-travelled, mountain-climbing Blackden is an expert on the world's most dangerous places, although he is often to be found relaxing in pubs in the Cotswolds.

Antonio Mendoza is one of the world's leading true crime aficionados. He is the author of *Killers on the Loose* (Virgin Books, 2000) and forthcoming *Teenage Rampage* (Virgin Books, 2002). He is responsible for one of the most interesting websites in existence – www.mayhem.net

Russell Gould is the author of *Unsolved Murders* (Virgin Books, 2000). He lives in London.

Simon Whitechapel was born in Madagascar, where he had an agnostic upbringing. Since contributing to early issues of *Headpress* magazine he has appeared in *The Mammoth Book of Jack the Ripper*, *Fortean Studies*, *Chaotic Order*, *Chronicles of the Cthulhu Codex*, and *Right NOW!*. *Crossing to Kill*, his study of serial killing in the Mexican border-city of Ciudad Juárez, was published by Virgin Books in 2000 and has now been re-issued in a revised edition. By mid-2002 he should have finished *Kamp Sex: A History of Nazi exploitation for Creation Books. He lives in the north of England.

Martin Jones is the author of *Psychedelic Decadence: Sex Drugs Low-Art in 60's & 70's Britain* (Critical Vision). With Oliver Tomlinson, he is the co-editor of *Careful*, a comic so sinister one would normally shun it – http://www.altarimage.co.uk/careful

erri Sharp is a film-school graduate and the editor of
ne Black Lace series of women's erotica. Her book,
*appropriate Behaviour – Prada Sucks! and other De-
ented Descants*, co-edited with Jessica Berens, was
ublished by Serpent's Tail, London, May 2002. For
1ore information go to www.squidsex.co.uk

Look out for other compelling True Crime titles
from Virgin Books in 2002

August 2002

Death Cults – Murder, Mayhem and Mind Control

Edited by Jack Sargeant

The deadly belief systems of cults worldwide hold an immense fascination for those desperate to look for 'ultimate truths'. Throughout history thousands of people have joined cults and even committed acts of atrocity in the belief they would attain power and everlasting life. From Charles Manson's 'family' of the late 1960s to the horrific Ten Commandments of God killings in Uganda in March 2000, deluded and brainwashed followers of cults and their charismatic megalomaniac leaders have been responsible for history's most shocking and bizarre killings. The book takes an in-depth look at cults about which very little has previously been written, such as the Russian castration sect and the bizarre Japanese Aum doomsday cult that leaked sarin gas into Tokyo's subways.

£7.99 ISBN: 0 7535 0644 0

September 2002

Danger Down Under

By Patrick Blackden

Australia is one of the most popular long-haul tourist destinations for Britons, but its image of a carefree, 'no worries' BBQ, beach and beers culture set in a landscape of stunning natural beauty tells only one side of the story. *Danger Down Under* lets you know what the tourist board won't – the dark side of the Australian dream. The mysterious vanishing of Briton Peter Falconio in summer 2001 is just one of many puzzling unsolved cases of tourist disappearances. With a landscape that can be extremely hostile to those unfamiliar to its size and extremes, and an undying macho culture – not to mention the occasional psychotic who murders backpackers, or crazed gangs of bikers and cultists – there is much to be cautious of when venturing down under.

£7.99 ISBN: 0 7535 0649 1

October 2002

Dirty Cash – Organised Crime in the 21st Century

By David Southwell

Once there was only one Mafia. Now, every country seems to have its own. Until fairly recently gangsters kept to their territories, but crime – like every other business – has been quick to take advantage of the new global economy. Business, it seems, is good, with over $150 billion laundered each year in Europe alone. London crime firms sell Lebanese heroin provided by Turkish gangs, Colombian cocaine obtained from Nigerian groups, and crack produced by Jamaican Yardies. Arrangements with the Mafia, the Triads, the Yakuza, the Russian Mafiya and the South Amercan cartels allow a tide of misery to enter the UK through the back door. The book will look in detail at the specific groups involved, the horrifying crimes they commit, and the everyday lives of their members. The vicious war between crime and law enforcement is raging all around us, and it's a war we can't afford to lose.

£7.99 ISBN: 0 7535 0702 1

November 2002

Teenage Rampage – The Worldwide Youth Crime Explosion

By Antonio Mendoza

A spring morning at Columbine High School, Colorado, 1999. By the afternoon, 12 of its schoolchildren and one teacher lay dead, gunned down by two of its pupils. Two boys have gone on a killing spree, venting their anger at those in their immediate environment before turning their guns on themselves. Cases such as Columbine are occurring with increasing regularity. And guns are not always involved. In Japan, in 1998, a 13-year-old schoolboy murdered his teacher in a frenzied knife attack – one of many similar crimes that has shocked that country. What is happening in society that young people are running amok, fuelled by hatred and nihilism, with little regard for their own lives and the lives of those around them? Antonio Mendoza investigates this worldwide problem and comes up with some shocking findings that call for a global rethink on how we bring up – and punish – those responsible for the worldwide teenage crimewave.

£7.99 ISBN: 0 7535 0715 3

December 2002

Female Terror – Scary Women, Modern Crimes

By Ann Magma

Statistics show that female crime and female violence is on the rise, particularly in America where, in 1999, over two million female offenders were recorded and the rise was cited as 137%. Women are becoming increasingly prominent in traditionally male-oriented work environments, but their ever-growing presence in crime is also on the increase. They are now a major force in both organised crime and terrorism. In the last ten years they have also come to the fore as homicidal leaders of religious sects and gun-toting leaders of Los Angeles street gangs, whose members are every bit as tough and violent as their male 'gangsta' counterparts. From Ulrike Meinhof to Rose West; from IRA terrorists to Mafia godmothers, this book will look at the rise and rise of female terror.

£7.99 ISBN: 0 7535 0718 8